Cooking Healthy

with Splenda®

ALSO BY JOANNA M. LUND

The Healthy Exchanges Cookbook
HELP: The Healthy Exchanges Lifetime Plan
Cooking Healthy with a Man in Mind
Cooking Healthy with the Kids in Mind
Dessert Every Night!
Diabetic Desserts
Make a Joyful Table
Cooking Healthy Across America
A Potful of Recipes
Another Potful of Recipes
The Open Road Cookbook
Sensational Smoothies
Hot Off the Grill: The Healthy Exchanges Electric Grilling Cookbook
The Diabetic's Healthy Exchanges Cookbook
The Strong Bones Healthy Exchanges Cookbook
The Arthritis Healthy Exchanges Cookbook
The Heart Smart Healthy Exchanges Cookbook
The Cancer Recovery Healthy Exchanges Cookbook
The Best of Healthy Exchanges Food Newsletter '92 Cookbook
String of Pearls

Cooking Healthy with Splenda®

A Healthy Exchanges® Cookbook

JoAnna M. Lund
with Barbara Alpert

A Perigee Book

A Perigee Book
Published by The Berkley Publishing Group
A division of Penguin Group (USA) Inc.
375 Hudson Street
New York, New York 10014

Copyright © 2004 by Healthy Exchanges, Inc.
Diabetic exchanges calculated by Rose Hoenig, R.D., L.D.
Cover design by Ben Gibson

Perigee trade paperback edition: June 2004

ISBN: 0-399-53025-8

For more information about Healthy Exchanges products, contact:
Healthy Exchanges, Inc.
P.O. Box 80
DeWitt, Iowa 52742-0080
(563) 659-8234
www.HealthyExchanges.com

Visit our website at www.penguin.com

This book has been catalogued by the Library of Congress

Printed in the United States of America
10   9   8   7

This cookbook is dedicated in loving memory to my parents, Jerome and Agnes McAndrews.

I think I enjoy creating recipes every bit as much as Mom enjoyed writing poetry. In looking through my mother's vast collection of poems, I came upon this special one in which she wrote about her private thinking place in our backyard—the secret to her success in sharing such inspiring words. I thought it the perfect poem to share with you in this cookbook. I hope you enjoy both Mom's thoughtful words and my tasty recipes!

My Secret

I found a private secluded corner, a place
just made for me.
It's underneath the maples, not too far
from a peach and apple tree.
Here, in quiet solitude, I can spend many
leisure hours
While gleaning inspiration, nestled among
the trees and flowers.
There is so much I could write about, if
only I did it well,
So many wonderful things to see and hear,
far too much to tell.
Like watching the mother birds build their nests,
then feed their babies wee.
Or, listening to the rhythm orchestra of the
busy honey bee.
But time is far too short and I have so
many tasks yet to do.
Still, it's nice to know I have a special place
where I can play hookie. Do you?

Agnes Carrington McAndrews

Acknowledgments

How Sweet It Is! That's just how I feel toward everyone who helped me write yet another cookbook. Not only did we work hard, we had fun. Yes, we had fun taste testing all the wonderful recipes in this collection, but just plain fun while working on this project, too! For making my life that much sweeter, I want to thank:

Shirley Morrow, Rita Ahlers, Phyllis Bickford, Gina Griep, and Jean Martens. Some typed, others cooked or washed dishes, but all enjoyed our luncheon dates every noon. Each would sample the dishes stirred up that morning, then write down their comments. Thank goodness, most everything passed the "this is good" test the first time. For those few recipes that I had to go back to the mixing bowl for, their comments were invaluable!

Cliff Lund. He had a great time trying the various recipes, especially the desserts. But I think he had an even greater time sitting around our kitchen table with six women every day!

Barbara Alpert. Even though she had many other "pans in the fire" while I was working on this project, Barbara still managed to give me quality time and help me make my cookbook that much better!

Coleen O'Shea. I shared with her over the phone that I was creating so many new recipes with SPLENDA® as the sweetener that I just had to write a cookbook on the subject. Hearing the excitement in my voice, she quickly agreed!

John Duff. He thought that a cookbook featuring SPLENDA® was a perfect fit with all my other books on the bookshelf and promptly asked me to start working on the project!

God. One of my daily prayers is that He help me share the earthly talents He blessed me with—with others for the honor and glory of God. This cookbook is another answer to my prayers!

Contents

How I Came to Find SPLENDA® — and How SPLENDA® Came to Be

Years before I shared a single Healthy Exchanges recipe, I began wishing for a sugar substitute that would taste as good as sugar and wouldn't leave a bitter aftertaste. I also wanted to find a product that would bake beautifully and not lose its sweetness. For the next decade, I tried everything that came on the market and decided that several brands did a pretty good job—not spectacular, but good enough. I never stopped hoping that someone could do it even better.

Then one day I was skimming through reader comments on my Healthy Exchanges website. That's where I first "heard" about a remarkable sweetener called SPLENDA®. It had been available in Canada for years, and in many other places around the world, but it hadn't yet been approved in the United States. (Yes, these ladies had been "importing" it for their own use from north of the border!)

What I read in those letters was irresistible—my readers made

SPLENDA® sound like a true treasure. I had to try it for myself. But did I need to go to Canada to get some? I corresponded with a couple of readers who told me that SPLENDA® now had a website, and that I could order this "miracle" product directly from them. Though I was still "finding my way" around the Internet, I bravely did as they suggested: I found the SPLENDA® site, I ordered some of the product, and like an explorer dreaming of undiscovered countries, I set out to learn just how yummy a sugar substitute could be! I tested up a storm—using SPLENDA® in everything from baked sweets to hearty entrées, and the difference was so clear I could taste it! After all those years, the dream had become a reality, and I knew that SPLENDA® was going to change the world of food and recipe creation as I knew it.

I've had such a great time inventing recipes that showcase this spectacular new product. Take it from me—SPLENDA® will simply change the way you feel about what we always called "artificial sweeteners." It tastes delicious, it cooks perfectly, and we've already seen how it's changing the food industry, with many tasty products on grocery shelves that are sweetened with SPLENDA®. I'm sure there will be many more in the months and years to come. It's just *that good.*

We've tested and retested every recipe in my Healthy Exchanges kitchen to make sure each will produce a dish you and your family will love. Even Cliff, my truck drivin' husband (who, like many men, has never been a fan of sugar substitutes), says that SPLENDA® is as good tasting as the real thing. When you learn that SPLENDA® is the only sugar substitute that is actually made from sugar, it all makes sense.

Want to know more about this amazing product (which you can now purchase everywhere from your local grocery to Super Wal-Mart) and how it came to be? I'm sure you do! Read on, and you'll soon be cooking up a storm with SPLENDA®!

In April 1998 the U.S. Food and Drug Administration (FDA) gave its approval to McNeil Specialty Products Company (a member of the Johnson & Johnson Family of Companies) to market sucralose, "the only no-calorie sweetener that is made from sugar, tastes like sugar, and can be used virtually anywhere sugar is used, including cooking and baking." They were granted initial approval to use sucralose in food and beverage categories that included baked goods and baking mixes, beverages, dairy products, processed fruits, and fruit juices. (To give you a sense of how positive their reaction to this product was, the FDA approval for sucralose was the broadest initial approval ever granted to a food additive!)

The United States took its time to approve the use of sucralose. By the time the FDA's approval came, millions of people worldwide had been using sucralose since 1991. It was used in dozens of reduced-calorie and reduced-sugar products such as soft drinks, shelf-stable food drinks, jams, processed fruit products like applesauce, yogurt, and baked goods. The public responded warmly to the product, which seemed revolutionary: it had no unpleasant aftertaste, and it kept its sweet taste over time and when exposed to high temperatures. Best of all, sucralose had no calories and didn't promote tooth decay.

Manufacturers liked sucralose because it kept its sugarlike taste longer than other no-calorie sweeteners, extending the shelf life of many products. It was sure to make a big difference when used in baked goods, canned goods, and carbonated soft drinks.

In August 1999, just 16 months after its initial approval, the FDA approved sucralose for use in *all* food and beverage products, which now included nutritional products, medical foods, and vitamin and mineral supplements. SPLENDA®, as this revolutionary new product had been named, was already available in soft drinks, juices, syrup, and pie filling. It took a while longer to become available in stores, but clever consumers learned they could visit the website and purchase SPLENDA® in boxes of convenient single-serve packets and in a granular form that measured and poured just like sugar.

What Is SPLENDA®?

Originally discovered in 1976, SPLENDA® is the brand name for sucralose, which is made from sucrose, a form of sugar. What makes it different—and calorie free—is a patented, multistep manufacturing process that substitutes three chlorine atoms for three hydrogen-oxygen groups in the sugar molecule. The new structure creates a product that is approximately 600 times sweeter than sugar. Unlike sugar, sucralose is not broken down and utilized by the body for energy. It's highly soluble in water and passes through the digestive system. SPLENDA®-sweetened products are shelf stable and retain their sweetness when heated. In fact, foods baked at temperatures up to 450 degrees keep their flavor.

People were enthusiastic about the possibilities, but they wanted to know, was SPLENDA® really safe? The news was good. More than one hundred scientific studies were conducted on sucralose over two decades, and the tests proved that SPLENDA® can safely be consumed by everyone. It's been approved in more than 40 countries since 1991, it's consumed by millions of people worldwide, and it's available in hundreds of food and beverage products! Also, it doesn't affect how the body produces insulin, doesn't affect carbohydrate metabolism, and doesn't promote cavities!

What does it all mean? Simply that SPLENDA® has been extensively tested and found to be safe, so we can all use it with confidence. If you want to reduce your sugar intake and/or calorie intake, it's for you. If you have diabetes, it's for you. Even if you're pregnant or nursing, it's for you. It's even okay as part of your children's healthy eating plan. What I like about SPLENDA® is that it can help you follow a healthy diet. Because it provides the sweet taste of sugar without the calories and is ideal for cooking and baking, it can help all of us satisfy that desire for good-tasting low-calorie foods and beverages.

SPLENDA® is also great news for anyone with diabetes. Because the body doesn't respond to SPLENDA® as sugar or carbohydrates, it will pass through your body quickly after you eat it. That means you can enjoy foods prepared with SPLENDA® that you might have skipped because they were high in sugar and carbohydrates.

Here's why: SPLENDA® or sucralose, doesn't affect blood sugar or blood insulin levels because the body doesn't recognize it as a carbohydrate. (This has been shown in people with and without diabetes.) The granular and packet forms of SPLENDA® do contain a small amount of calories from maltodextrin and dextrose, but the number of calories is so small that your blood sugar levels should not be affected.

What does the American Diabetes Association say about all this? The ADA has stated that "these products [non-nutritive sweeteners] undergo rigorous scrutiny by the FDA and are not allowed on the market unless they are safe for the public, including people with diabetes, to consume." Similarly, the American Dietetic Association states, "non-nutritive sweeteners are safe to use and widely advocated and used by persons with diabetes."

So there you are. Whatever your reasons for limiting or eliminating sugar from your daily menus, you can use the granular and packet forms of SPLENDA® as you would use any sugar substitute. Foods sweetened with SPLENDA® can fit easily into your healthy meal plan. They'll help lower the amount of calories, carbohydrates, and sugar you consume.

Ready to go? If you've never used SPLENDA® before, it's time to try it in these scrumptious recipes—from soups to baked goods, from side dishes to my most delectable desserts. I'm sure you'll agree that SPLENDA® can replace sugar, spoon for spoon and cup for cup, in lots of your family's favorite foods!

Enjoy!

Living the

Sweet Life

What does it mean to you to live a life that you would call "sweet"? I'm sure the definition is different for every person, yet I think there are certain beliefs that affect and influence our feelings about the lives we are leading.

For me, a sweet life once meant marrying and having a family, but I discovered that the quality of the marriage was more important than just the act of being married.

For me, a sweet life meant working at a job that gave me a chance to develop as a person and earn money to support my kids. But then I discovered I could live a sweeter life that was shaped by my own creativity, and Healthy Exchanges was born.

A sweet life for most (if not all) of us is a life lived in health, and yet an enormous percentage of Americans are described as overweight or obese. Diabetes and high blood pressure are epidemic, and too many of us don't take good care of ourselves. So perhaps it's a good idea to examine the elements of what could and perhaps should make it possible for you to begin living the sweet life.

Family

I believe it's true that for most people, feeling part of a family is important to feeling good about themselves. Yet I have many readers who are single or widowed and live alone. Some have children but many do not. Some are close to their brothers and sisters in their middle and later years, and some are not, while others never had siblings.

But we all have the potential to experience the special sweetness that a family can provide. I had a letter not long ago from a woman in New Jersey who said, "We can choose not to be alone or lonely. My friends are my family. We celebrate important occasions together, we call each other with good news and with terrible news, and we know that our family of friends is as strong and vital as any family related by blood or upbringing."

Are you tasting the sweetness of a close family relationship, or if you lack that, are you making sure that someone in your life fills the role of a sister or an aunt? I hope you are, and I hope that you make the time in your life to cherish that person or those people who are so dear to you.

Friends

I know that I mentioned friends as family just a moment ago, but I wanted to revisit the sweet possibilities of friendship. I have learned through personal experience that while there can be a real sweetness in the friendships we carry from childhood, sometimes the sweetest and most enduring friendships are those we make as adults. Why? Perhaps because we know ourselves better and we bring more complete selves to join as friends with people who demonstrate the capacity to love and care for us.

Take a moment and think about some sweet moments in friendships that you treasure. Who was your maid or matron of honor at your wedding, and have you stayed in touch with her? I'm not far from my 25th wedding anniversary, and I recently found myself thinking back to the woman I was when I married Cliff. Who were her friends? Would I, could I still be friends with those women now? I hope so.

Who is your gym buddy, your walking partner, your favorite movie pal? Does she know how much sweeter she makes your life? If you haven't told her lately, tell her now. Time is precious, and friendship is sweet.

Fidelity

No, my computer keyboard isn't stuck on the letter F, but I like this word, which I will use here to talk about being true to yourself. There's no sweeter satisfaction than knowing you are doing what you are meant to do in this life.

For many people, it takes years, even a lifetime to know with confidence that they've chosen the right path, the "true" path for themselves. I think that navigating along that route requires you to pay attention to those times when you feel good about your choices, when you feel a sensation of sweet satisfaction in what you have accomplished or said.

In Shakespeare's play *Hamlet,* a character says to his child, "This above all: to thine own self be true. And it must follow as the night the day, Thou canst not then be false to any man." It's good advice, and a sentiment that, if followed honestly and always, has the power to help you create a sweet life.

Fantasies

Ever have a moment during the day when you close your eyes or let your mind drift just a bit to a fantasy that seems so delicious, so sweet? Maybe it's a dream of what your life might be like if you had more money or a slimmer figure, if you lived somewhere else or had more passion and love in your life. These glimpses of "a world that could be" aren't just daydreams that waste time and teach us nothing. Often, they allow us to dare to express a wish that we've never given voice to, a hope that seems almost impossible.

Pay attention to those fantastic images. They come from deep inside our brains and may hold the key to taking a step toward what might be from the land of what is. I've learned so much during such times—envisioned books that I didn't know I wanted to write, figured out what to say in a speech, even discovered the solution to a recipe that wasn't working.

How sweet it is to know that even when we're heading in one

direction, we may still be imagining a sweeter life that is not necessarily beyond our reach!

Feeding the Soul

This book is jam-packed with recipes that will let your lips, teeth, tongue, and tummy taste the sweet life, but those aren't the only appetites you need to nourish. There is astonishing sweetness in many things that have nothing to do with food, that pack not a single calorie or carbohydrate, and that will add only joy to the life you lead.

For me, the place I seek sweetness for my soul is in my garden. I take the time to smell the flowers, sure, but I also yank the weeds, inhale the scent of the fresh-turned dirt of a new flower bed, and let my eyes feast on the colors of nature that continue to surprise me with their beauty.

What feeds your soul? Is it music, and should you think about not just singing in the shower but lending the sweetness of your voice to a church choir or school benefit concert? Is it teaching others a skill you enjoy, and do you need to carve out a little time to give back to your community by offering instruction in crochet or English as a second language?

Whatever nourishes your spirit has the power to increase the sweetness in your everyday life. Seek it out, and you will increase the sweetness in the world.

Faith

I speak for myself when I say that my faith is one of the sweetest gifts I have been given in this lifetime, but I hope you feel the same, in considering what place faith has in your life. It's not just a religious faith that I'm talking about, although mine draws much comfort and sustenance from the Bible. I've been inspired by religious leaders like Dr. Dobson and Billy Graham, and I've been moved by the beautiful concerts that are broadcast from the Crystal Cathedral and most recently by Bill Gaither's Homecoming Gospel music that we listen to every week on television. What is that feeling that washes over me when I listen to a song sung by those remarkable voices?

I think it might be a moment of recognition, a sense of life's tender sweetness and faith's power to heal. I believe that a major part of my journey through life has been my daily affirmation of faith and my constant appreciation of the sweetest gift, that of life itself.

Please note:

In many of my cookbooks, I've included my Healthy Exchanges eating plan, which explains how to use my version of the "exchange" system for planning what to eat and how much to eat for optimum health and weight loss (or maintenance). Because this is a "special interest" cookbook, I've chosen to focus just on the recipes in this volume. If this is your first Healthy Exchanges cookbook, please check one of my other books for an explanation of the exchange system.

Baking and Cooking for Success with SPLENDA®

Even if you're an expert cook and baker with years of kitchen experience, there are things you need to know to get the best results from the healthy, delicious, and easy-to-fix recipes in this book. And if you've never spent much time in the kitchen, you'll want to consult these "insider" tips to make the most of your time and effort. Low-fat, low-sugar cooking and baking require some special knowledge and finesse to produce truly tasty treats, but when you follow these simple and effective rules, you'll get the dishes you dream about—and they'll fulfill most (if not all) of your food fantasies!

First, here are my six basic tips for success with SPLENDA®:

1. SPLENDA® in granular form can be used with confidence in cooking and baking. You can measure and pour it just as you do sugar—one cup of SPLENDA® equals one cup of sugar, and one tablespoon of SPLENDA® is the equivalent of a tablespoon of sugar. What could be easier?

   Note: You can use SPLENDA® Granular in any of my

older recipes that call for other sweeteners—spoon for spoon and cup for cup. It tastes so good, some of my best "classic" desserts are likely to taste better than ever!

2. When you cook or bake with SPLENDA® Granular, you're likely to notice that your yield is smaller than when you prepare similar foods with sugar. Why? Because SPLENDA® Granular doesn't add volume to your recipes in the same way that sugar does. In my recipes, I've adjusted the proportions of other ingredients and fine-tuned them to make them work. In some cases, I'll add a couple of teaspoons of other dry ingredients.

3. I don't sift my ingredients very often. But in other people's recipes, you may choose to adapt by substituting SPLENDA® Granular for sugar. If sifting is called for, add your SPLENDA® Granular after you've sifted the other ingredients together. Why? Because the granules of sugar are larger than those of SPLENDA® Granular.

4. If a recipe asks you to "cream" or "beat" the ingredients together (usually butter or margarine, eggs, and sugar) and you're replacing the sugar with SPLENDA® Granular, it's likely to take extra time to produce a fluffy texture. Why? Because when you cream or beat your ingredients, you're adding air to your mixture, and SPLENDA® Granular blends just a bit differently than sugar does.

5. Have you tried substituting SPLENDA® Granular for sugar in family recipes and discovered that your batter didn't brown quite the same way? It's true that baked goods made with SPLENDA® don't turn brown the way foods made with sugar do. The solution: add a little "darkening" ingredient to your mixture, such as molasses or cocoa, and your cookies and cakes will look just as you wish. (I've already taken care of this in my recipes, and you should be pleased with the results!)

6. When I bake using SPLENDA® Granular, I always remember that my baked goods will bake more quickly than

those made with sugar. I've suggested cooking and baking times that worked for me and in my oven, but the first time you prepare a new recipe with SPLENDA® Granular instead of sugar, check your dish for doneness a little early— 1 to 2 minutes for cookies, and 7 to 10 minutes for cakes. (For more on baking, see below.)

Some Common Questions and Answers

I'm confused when a recipe specifies a range of baking times like 22 to 28 minutes. I'm not sure what to do when!
When I suggest a range of baking times, it's because every kitchen, every stove, and every chef's cooking technique is slightly different. On a hot and humid day in Iowa, the optimum cooking time won't be the same as on a cold, dry day. Some stoves bake hotter than the temperature setting indicates; other stoves bake cooler. Electric ovens usually are more temperamental than gas ovens. If you place your baking pan on a lower shelf, the temperature is different than if you place it on a higher shelf. If you stir the mixture more vigorously than I do, you could affect the required baking time by a minute or more.

The best way to gauge the heat of your particular oven is to purchase an oven temperature gauge that hangs in the oven. These can be found in any discount store or kitchen equipment store, and if you're going to be cooking and baking regularly, it's a good idea to own one. Set the oven to 350 degrees, and when the oven indicates that it has reached that temperature, check the reading on the gauge. If it's less than 350 degrees, you know your oven cooks cooler, and you need to add a few minutes to the cooking time *or* set your oven at a higher temperature. If it's more than 350 degrees, then your oven is warmer, and you need to subtract a few minutes from the cooking time and maybe lower the temperature.

In any event, always treat the suggested baking time as approximate. Check on your baked product at the earliest suggested time. You can always continue baking a few minutes more if needed, but you can't unbake it once you've cooked it too long.

Why do you put so many of your baked dishes on a wire rack to set for 5 minutes or so before serving? I've never heard of this before.

There's a simple reason behind my advice to put baked dishes on a wire rack before you cut and serve them. It's called "air movement." By placing the pan or dish on a rack, you are elevating the bottom of the pan just enough—less than an inch—thus allowing air to move freely away from the underside of the pan. This keeps your piecrust, bread, or other baked goods from becoming soggy on the bottom.

It also allows your casserole contents to "come together" for a few minutes, which makes for easier serving and tastier eating. If you doubt the validity of this physics "application," I suggest you bake two identical casseroles. Put one baking dish on a rack to rest for 5 minutes before serving it; scoop up and serve the other one just as soon as it comes out of the oven. You'll be amazed at the difference!

A wire rack also works well if you want to set the hot dish on your kitchen or dining table, keeping it from damaging the table's finish—again, because it allows the heat to escape from the bottom of the pan without penetrating the wood of your table.

I haven't got much cabinet space. If I don't have a 9-by-9-inch baking dish, can I use an 8-inch square pan instead?

One of the reasons I often use an 8-by-8-inch baking dish in my recipes is for portion control. If the recipe says it serves 4, just cut down the center, turn the dish, and cut again. Like magic, there's your serving. Also, if this is the only recipe you are preparing requiring an oven, the square dish fits into a tabletop toaster oven easily, and energy can be conserved.

But while many of my recipes call for an 8-by-8-inch baking dish, others ask for a 9-by-9-inch cake pan. If you don't have a 9-inch square pan, is it all right to use your 8-inch dish instead? In most cases, the small difference in the size of these two pans won't significantly affect the finished product, so until you can get your hands on the right size pan, go ahead and use your baking dish.

However, since the 8-inch dish is usually made of glass, and the 9-inch cake pan made of metal, you will want to adjust the baking temperature. If you're using a glass baking dish in a recipe that calls for a 9-inch pan, be sure to lower your baking temperature by 15 degrees *or* check your finished product at least 6 to 8 minutes before the specified baking time is over.

But it really is worthwhile to add a 9-by-9-inch pan to your collection, and if you're going to be baking lots of my Healthy Exchanges cakes, you'll definitely use it a lot. A cake baked in this pan will have a better texture, and the servings will be a little larger. Just think of it—an 8-by-8-inch pan produces 64 square inches of dessert, while a 9-by-9-inch pan delivers 81 square inches. Those 17 extra inches will make your serving appear larger, and you're likely to be more satisfied.

When I make a pie that serves 8, I find myself nibbling at the leftovers in the fridge. What can I do to develop healthier dessert habits?
Most of the recipes are for 4 to 8 servings. If you don't have that many to feed, do what I do: freeze individual portions. Then all you have to do is choose something from the freezer and take it to work for lunch or have your evening meals prepared in advance for the week. In this way, I always have something on hand that is both good to eat and good for me.

I've marked recipes that freeze well with the symbol of a snowflake ❄. This includes most of the cream pies. Divide any recipe up into individual servings and freeze for later. I recommend cutting leftover pie into individual pieces and freezing each one separately in a small Ziploc freezer bag. Here's the best way: Once you've cut the pie into portions, place the pieces on a cookie sheet and put them in the freezer for 15 minutes to "sharp-freeze" them. Then, put each piece in its own freezer bag. That way, the creamy topping won't get smashed, and your pie will keep its shape.

When you want to thaw a piece of pie for yourself, you don't have to thaw the whole pie. You can practice portion control at the same time, and it works really well for brown-bag lunches. Just pull a piece out of the freezer on your way to work, and by lunchtime you will have a wonderful dessert waiting for you.

I read somewhere that I could replace oil or butter in some dessert recipes with applesauce. Does this really work? How much should I use?
Many people have inquired about substituting applesauce for the

butter in treasured family recipes. One woman shared a recipe for her grandmother's cookies that called for 1 cup of butter and 1½ cups of sugar. I told her that any recipe that depends on as much butter and sugar as this one does is probably not a good candidate for a "healthy exchange." It takes a large quantity of fat to produce a crisp cookie just like Grandma used to make.

Applesauce generally doesn't work as well as a replacement for butter, margarine, or lard. But it can often be used instead of vegetable oil. If a recipe calls for ½ cup of vegetable oil or less and your recipe is for a bar cookie, quick bread, muffin, or cake mix, you can try substituting an equal amount of unsweetened applesauce. If the recipe calls for more, try using ½ cup applesauce and the rest in oil. You're cutting down on the fat but shouldn't end up with a taste disaster! This "applesauce shortening" works great in many recipes, but so far I haven't been able to figure out a way to deep fat fry with it!

Here's another trick to try: If you have a recipe that calls for an egg and oil, replace them with ⅓ cup plain yogurt and ¼ cup fat-free mayo. Blend these two ingredients with your liquids in a separate bowl, then add the yogurt mixture to the flour mixture and mix gently just to combine. (Don't overmix or your cake will be tough!)

I've always baked with eggs, but my husband needs to watch his cholesterol. Is a commercially produced egg substitute my only option?
I use eggs in moderation. I enjoy the real thing on an average of three to four times a week. So my recipes are calculated using whole eggs. However, if you choose to use an egg substitute in place of the egg, the finished product will turn out just fine, and the fat grams per serving will be even lower than those listed.

In most recipes calling for egg substitutes, you can use 2 egg whites in place of the equivalent of 1 egg substitute. Just break the eggs open and toss the yolks away. I can hear some of you already saying, "But that's wasteful!" Well, take a look at the price on the egg substitute package (which usually has the equivalent of 4 eggs in it), then look at the price of a dozen eggs, from which you'd get the equivalent of 3 packages of egg substitutes. Now, what's wasteful about that?

(One of my readers suggested that if you need to use egg

whites but like the look of "the real thing," don't use egg substitutes (which are 98 to 99 percent egg whites with added yellow food coloring and a touch of oil). Instead, buy a dozen eggs and use 10 egg whites along with 2 whole eggs. Whip them up and you have your own "yellow" egg substitute that contains less fat and is much cheaper than the commercial brands.

I live alone and prefer to make muffins instead of quick breads because they're easier for me to freeze and reheat. What changes in temperature and baking time need to be made?
I always like to say that my recipes are designed to meet your needs, so you should feel free to adjust them to please yourself! If you'd like to use a quick bread recipe to make muffins, go for it, but do keep these hints in mind:

- Make 8 muffins from a bread recipe that serves 8, so that the nutrient information remains the same.

- Be sure to spray the muffin pan(s) with butter-flavored cooking spray, or line them with paper liners and then spray the inside of the liners before spooning the muffin batter into them. The first makes for easier removal from the pan; the second makes it easier to remove the paper from your fresh-baked muffins.

- Fill any unused muffin wells with water to help ensure more even baking and protect the muffin pan from warping.

- Increase the cooking temperature to 375 or 400 degrees. Muffins need a higher oven temperature to bake properly. Why? Because the total mass of the muffin is much less than that of a loaf of bread. A lower temperature might produce an overdone outside while the inside remains raw or undercooked.

- Shorten the baking time to 15 to 25 minutes. (Why the range? Keep in mind that the thicker the batter, the longer the baking time.) Test the muffins with a wooden toothpick, and remove them from the oven when it comes out clean.

- Once the muffins are completely cooled, use individual Ziploc bags to freeze muffins for future use. Label them clearly with a permanent marker, noting what kind they are and when they were made. Then the next time you want a "fresh from the oven" treat, just put your frozen muffin into the microwave and cook on HIGH for 15 to 30 seconds. Or simply place the freezer bag into your lunch box when you leave for work in the morning, and it will be thawed by lunchtime.

- If you're looking for something a little different for breakfast, why not make a "breakfast sundae"? Crumble the warmed muffin into a cereal bowl. Sprinkle a serving of fresh fruit over it, and top with a couple of tablespoons of nonfat plain yogurt sweetened with SPLENDA® and your choice of extract. The thought of it just might make you jump out of bed with a smile on your face!

- Speaking of sundaes, while we were traveling around Ireland, Cliff and I discovered a delicious way to enjoy muffins for dessert—make a muffin sundae! Just place any leftover muffin in a microwave-safe dessert dish and reheat on HIGH (100%) for about 30 seconds, then immediately spoon a scoop of sugar- and fat-free ice cream over the top and enjoy!

My family likes some flavors better than others. Is it okay to change ingredients in your recipes?
Yes, *some* things can easily be changed to suit your family's tastes, but others should not be tampered with. **What not to change**: the amount of flour, bread crumbs, reduced-fat biscuit baking mix, baking soda, baking powder, liquid, or dry milk powder. And if I include a small amount of salt, it's necessary for the recipe to turn out correctly. **What you can change**: an extract flavor (if you don't like coconut, for example, choose vanilla or almond instead); a spreadable fruit flavor; the type of fruit in a pie filling (but be careful about substituting fresh for frozen and vice versa—sometimes it works but it may not); or the flavor of pudding or gelatin. As long as package sizes and amounts are the same, go for it. It will never

hurt my feelings if you change a recipe, so please your family—and don't worry about me!

(One quick note: Some of my "island inspired" recipes call for **rum or brandy extracts,** which provide the "essence" of liquor without the real thing. I'm a teetotaler by choice, so I choose not to include real liquor in any of my recipes. Extracts are cheaper than liquor, and you won't feel the need to shoo your kids away from the goodies. If you prefer not to use liquor extracts in your cooking, you can always substitute vanilla extract.)

I've tried making your cheesecakes with the fat-free cream cheese you suggested, but mine just don't get firm. What am I doing wrong?

I was in a hurry to use my container of frozen reduced-fat whipped topping, so I popped it into the microwave, and ended up with a runny mess. Help!

I decided to answer these two questions together because the answers are related. I love the chemistry of foods, and so I've gotten great pleasure from analyzing what makes fat-free products tick. By dissecting these "miracle" products, I've learned how to make them work best. They require different handling than the high-fat products we're used to, but if treated properly, these slimmed-down versions can produce delicious results!

Fat-free cream cheese: In the old days, when cream cheese came only in a hard brick, we had to let it sit on the counter for a while to soften, and then mix it on high with an electric mixer to get it soft enough to do anything with it. All the fat in it allowed us to "manhandle" it without it breaking down.

But when the fat was removed from this product, water replaced it. So don't *ever* use an electric mixer on the fat-free version, or you risk releasing the water and having your finished product look more like dip or lumpy soup than cheesecake! (I often wish they'd put a warning about this on the package!)

Instead, place your fat-free cream cheese in a mixing bowl, using a spatula to remove it from the tub it was purchased in. Follow my instructions for stirring it gently with a sturdy plastic or wooden spoon until it softens just as much as it needs to be. And don't be alarmed if the cream cheese gets caught in your wire whisk when you start combining it with other ingredients. Just keep knocking it back down into the bowl by hitting the whisk against the rim of the bowl. As you continue blending, it will soften even more and drop off the whisk. When it's time to pour the filling into your crust, your whisk shouldn't have anything much clinging to it.

Fat-free whipped topping: When the fat went out of the formula, air was stirred in to fill the void. So, if you heat it quickly or stir it too vigorously, you release the air and *decrease* the volume. Handle it with kid gloves—gently. Since the manufacturer forgot to ask for my input, I'll share with you how to make it taste almost the same as it used to. Let the container thaw in the refrigerator for about two hours before you need it; then ever so gently stir in one teaspoon vanilla extract. Now, put the lid back on and enjoy it a tablespoon at a time, the same way you did regular whipped topping.

(Another suggestion: Keep a thawed container of fat-free whipped topping in your refrigerator, as it keeps well for up to two weeks. It actually freezes and thaws and freezes and thaws again quite well, so if you won't be using it soon, you could refreeze your leftovers. Just remember to take it out a few hours before you need it, so it'll be creamy and soft and ready to use.)

Fat-free sour cream: This product is wonderful on a hot baked potato, but have you noticed that it tends to be much gummier than regular sour cream? If you want to use it in a baked product, it helps to stir a tablespoon or two of skim milk into the fat-free sour cream before adding it to other ingredients.

Reduced-fat margarine: Again, the fat was replaced by water. If you try to use the reduced-fat kind in your cookie recipe spoon for spoon, you will end up with a cakelike cookie instead of the crisp kind most of us enjoy. You have to take into consideration that some water will be released as the product bakes. Use less liquid than the recipe calls for (when re-creating your family recipes *only*—I've figured that into Healthy Exchanges recipes). And never, never, never use fat-*free* margarine and expect anyone to ask for seconds!

I was making one of your recipes that uses plain graham crackers for the "crust." When I combined the dry ingredients with the water, the filling seemed very watery, and when I poured the filling over the graham crackers in the bottom of the pan, they got soggy and floated to the top. What advice can you give me?

This is a very common problem with a very "common sense" answer. For most cooks, it comes down to how the liquid is being measured. If you are pouring your liquid into a measuring cup and "eyeballing" it with the cup held in the air, you may be adding as much as ¼ to ⅓ cup of extra liquid without realizing it. The best way to measure liquid is to pour it, set the cup on the counter, and bend down to read it. I think you may be surprised to find more liquid in the cup than you expect!

(What if you forget and measure in the air? Do you have to throw out what you've mixed? Probably not. Just let the pudding mix sit for a few moments and begin to thicken before you pour it over the crackers.)

Also, remember that when we make a "crust" with graham crackers, we must have a little more liquid than we would if we were using a purchased piecrust. Be sure to pour the liquid *very slowly* over the crackers so they can absorb the liquid and won't have a chance to float upward before they are anchored. I also recommend covering the pan with plastic wrap or tinfoil to force the extra liquid down among the crackers so they can soften and form that magic crust.

My cakes and breads look done on the outside, but they are sometimes runny or tough on the inside. What's the problem?

I've gotten many letters over the years about baked goods that just don't live up to expectations. When I've visited on the phone or by mail with these frustrated cooks, I've discovered that one or more of the following suggestions made a so-so result turn out much, much better!

- ***Are you using an oven thermometer?*** Even if you think your oven temperature is exactly what's called for in the recipe, it may not be. By investing just a few dollars in a thermometer that you hang inside your oven, you can be certain—and adjust the oven setting if necessary. Whether you're baking a casserole or a cake, if your oven is hotter than it's supposed to be, the outside may burn while the inside remains doughy. (You can also set your timer for 5 minutes less than the minimum suggested time called for in the recipe. Test for doneness, and only continue baking if the toothpick comes out sticky with batter. You can always continue baking, but there's no going back once you've baked a cake too long.)

- *Are you using fresh baking powder and baking soda?* If not, you won't be pleased with your finished product. If you can't remember the last time you replaced either of these ingredients, then it's time for a change! I replace mine every six months. The discarded baking soda goes into the refrigerator as a fridge freshener, so I don't feel I'm wasting the unused portion.

- *Are you measuring exactly?* If you are using too little flour and a little too much liquid, you may be throwing off the balance of dry to wet ingredients. And yes, even a tablespoon either way can make a huge difference.

- *Are you very gently mixing by hand just to combine?* Or are you beating with an electric mixer? If you are mixing by hand, you may still be stirring too hard or too long. (It's really better almost to undermix than mix too long or too vigorously.) We must be exceedingly gentle when mixing the ingredients in baked goods that don't use butter and sugar. Excessive stirring will cause the gluten to be released from the flour, making the finished product rubbery and tough. Keep Grandma JO's advice in mind: "Remember to use a soft hand, and your baked goods will turn out grand!"

The Delights of Dairy— What You Must Know

Take it from me—nonfat dry milk powder is great! I *do not* use it for drinking, but I *do* use it for cooking. Three good reasons why:

1. It is very **inexpensive**.

2. It does not **sour** because you use it only as needed. Store the box in your refrigerator or freezer, and it will keep almost forever.

3. You can easily **add extra calcium** to just about any recipe without added liquid.

I consider nonfat dry milk powder one of Mother Nature's modern-day miracles of convenience. But do purchase a good national name brand (I like Carnation), and keep it fresh by proper storage.

I've said many times, "Give me my mixing bowl, my wire whisk, and a box of nonfat dry milk powder, and I can conquer the world!" Here are some of my favorite ways to use dry milk powder:

1. Want to make **your own vanilla cook-and-serve pudding mix?** Here's my recipe: 2 tablespoons cornstarch, ½ cup SPLENDA®, ⅔ cup nonfat dry milk powder, 1½ cups water, 2 teaspoons vanilla extract, and 4 to 5 drops yellow food coloring. Combine all this in a medium saucepan and cook over medium heat, stirring constantly, until the mixture comes to a full boil and thickens. This is for basic cooked vanilla sugar-free pudding. For a **chocolate version**, the recipe is 2 tablespoons cornstarch, ¼ cup SPLENDA®, 2 tablespoons sugar-free chocolate drink mix, 1½ cups water, and 1 teaspoon vanilla extract. Follow the same cooking instructions as above.

2. You can **make your own "sour cream"** by combining ¾ cup plain fat-free yogurt with ⅓ cup nonfat dry milk powder. Here's why it works: (1) The dry milk stabilizes the yogurt and keeps the whey from separating. (2) The dry milk slightly helps to cut the tartness of the yogurt. (3) It's still virtually fat free. (4) The calcium has been increased by 100 percent. Isn't it great how we can make that distant relative of sour cream a first kissin' cousin by adding the nonfat dry milk powder? Or if you place 1 cup plain fat-

free yogurt in a sieve lined with a coffee filter, and place the sieve over a small bowl and refrigerate for about 6 hours, you will end up with a very good alternative for sour cream. To **stabilize yogurt** when cooking or baking with it, just add 1 teaspoon cornstarch to every ¾ cup yogurt.

3. You can make **evaporated fat-free milk** by using ⅓ cup nonfat dry milk powder and ½ cup water for every ½ cup evaporated fat-free milk you need. This is handy to know when you want to prepare a recipe calling for evaporated fat-free milk, and you don't have any in the cupboard. And if you are using a recipe that requires only 1 cup evaporated fat-free milk, you don't have to worry about what to do with the leftover milk in the can.

4. You can make **sugar-free and fat-free sweetened condensed milk** by using 1⅓ cups nonfat dry milk powder mixed with ½ cup cold water, microwaved on HIGH until the mixture is hot but not boiling. Then stir in ½ cup SPLENDA® Granular. Cover and chill at least 2 hours.

5. For any recipe that calls for **buttermilk**, you might want to try **JO's Buttermilk**: Blend 1 cup water and ⅔ cup nonfat dry milk powder (the nutrients of 2 cups of fat-free milk). It'll be thicker than this mixed-up milk usually is because it's doubled. Add 1 tablespoon white vinegar and stir, then let it sit for at least 10 minutes.

What else? Nonfat dry milk powder adds calcium without fuss to many recipes, and it can be stored for months in your refrigerator or freezer.

Dazzling Dessert Ideas

Here are a few tips dealing with my all-time favorite dessert—**strawberry shortcake**! If you want the richest, sweetest strawberry shortcakes in the whole wide world, all you need to do is use the recipe on the box of reduced-fat biscuit baking mix. But instead of milk, use fat-free half & half; instead of margarine use fat-free sour cream; and instead of sugar, use SPLENDA® Granular. Use the same amounts of my suggested ingredients as the recipe calls for of the originals, and I promise that the world will be singing your praises! It's a perfect way to showcase these wonderful fruit gems.

Now, here are two glorious sauces to celebrate those "rubies"!

To make **Fresh From The Patch Strawberry Sauce**, finely chop up 4 cups of fresh strawberries. Place ½ cup of the strawberries in a blender container, add 1 teaspoon lemon juice, 2 tablespoons water, and ½ cup SPLENDA® Granular. Cover and process on BLEND for 20 to 30 seconds or until the mixture is smooth. Spoon into a large bowl. Add remaining 3½ cups strawberries. Mix well to combine. Cover and refrigerate for at least 15 minutes.

When fresh strawberries are not available or too highly priced, you can always make **Winter Strawberry Sauce**. Place an unopened 16-ounce bag of unsweetened frozen strawberries in a medium bowl. Put in the refrigerator to thaw overnight. Open the package, place in the bowl, and stir in ½ cup SPLENDA® Granular. Serve at once or cover and refrigerate until ready to serve.

To make a delicious **chocolate glaze for brownies, bars, or a cake** prepared in a 9-by-9-inch pan, all you have to do is melt 4 teaspoons reduced-calorie margarine and 1 (1-ounce) square of unsweetened chocolate in a medium-sized saucepan that has been sprayed with butter-flavored cooking spray, stirring constantly. Remove from heat. Stir in 2 tablespoons fat-free sour cream and 1 teaspoon vanilla extract. Add 1¼ cups SPLENDA® Granular. Mix well to combine. Drizzle warm mixture evenly over top of brownies, bars, or cake.

For a special treat that tastes anything but "diet," try placing **spreadable fruit** in a container and microwaving for about 15 seconds. Then pour the melted fruit spread over a serving of nonfat ice cream or frozen yogurt. One and one-half tablespoons of spreadable fruit is equal to 1 Fruit choice or exchange. Some combinations to get you started are apricot over chocolate ice cream, strawberry over strawberry ice cream, or any flavor over vanilla.

Another way I use spreadable fruit is to make a delicious **topping for a cheesecake or angel food cake**. I take ½ cup fruit and ½ cup lite or fat-free whipped topping and blend the two together with a teaspoon of coconut extract.

Here's a really **good topping** for the fall of the year. Place 1½ cups unsweetened applesauce in a medium saucepan or 4-cup glass measure. Stir in 2 tablespoons raisins, 1 teaspoon apple pie spice, and 2 tablespoons sugar-free maple syrup. Cook over medium heat on the stovetop or microwave on HIGH until warm. Then spoon about ½ cup of the warm mixture over pancakes, French toast, or sugar- and fat-free vanilla ice cream. It's as close as you will get to guilt-free apple pie!

Do you love hot fudge sundaes as much as I do? Here's my secret for making **Almost Sinless Hot Fudge Sauce.** Start with my recipe for homemade sugar-free chocolate cook-and-serve pudding (see **The Delights of Dairy** above). Cook over medium heat, stirring constantly with a wire whisk, until the mixture thickens and starts to boil. Remove from heat and stir in 1 teaspoon vanilla extract, 2 teaspoons reduced-calorie margarine, and ½ cup miniature marshmallows. This makes six ¼ cup servings. Any leftovers can be refrigerated and reheated later in the microwave. Yes, you can buy fat-free chocolate syrup nowadays, but have you checked the sugar content? For a ¼ cup serving of store-bought syrup (and you show me any true hot fudge sundae lover who would settle for less than ¼ cup), it clocks in at over 150 calories with 39 grams of sugar! A commercial light chocolate syrup, while better, still has 100 calories and 10 grams of sugar. But my "homemade" version costs you only 60 calories, less than ½ gram of fat, and just 6 grams of sugar for the same ¼ cup serving. So when I crave a hot fudge sundae, I scoop out some sugar- and fat-free ice cream, then spoon my **Almost Sinless Hot Fudge Sauce** over the top and smile with pleasure.

Here's my vote for the easiest **crumb topping** ever! Simply combine 3 tablespoons of purchased graham cracker crumbs (or three 2½-inch squares made into fine crumbs) with 1 tablespoon SPLENDA® Granular, 2 teaspoons reduced-calorie margarine, and 1 tablespoon (if desired) chopped nuts. Mix this well and sprinkle evenly over the top of your fruit pie and bake as you normally would. You can use either a purchased graham cracker piecrust or an unbaked refrigerated regular piecrust. Another almost effortless crumb topping can be made by combining 6 tablespoons reduced-fat biscuit baking mix and 2 tablespoons SPLENDA® Granular with

2 teaspoons of reduced-calorie margarine until the mixture becomes crumbly. Again, you can stir in 1 tablespoon of chopped nuts if you wish. Evenly sprinkle this mixture over your fruit filling and bake as usual. This works best with a purchased unbaked refrigerated piecrust.

More of Grandma JO's "Wisdom"

When a recipe calls for **chopped nuts** (and you only have whole ones), who wants to dirty the food processor just for a couple of tablespoonsful? You could try to chop them using your cutting board, but be prepared for bits and pieces to fly all over the kitchen. I use "Grandma's food processor." I take the biggest nuts I can find, put them in a small glass bowl, and chop them into chunks just the right size using a metal biscuit cutter.

To quickly **toast nuts** without any fuss, spread about ½ cup of nuts (any kind) in a glass pie plate and microwave on HIGH (100% power) for 6 to 7 minutes or until golden. Stir after the first 3 minutes, then after each minute until done. Store them in an airtight container in your refrigerator. Toasting nuts really brings out their flavor, so it seems as if you used a whole treeful instead of tiny amounts.

A quick hint about **reduced-fat peanut butter:** Don't store it in the refrigerator. Because the fat has been reduced, it won't spread as easily when it's cold. Keep it in your cupboard, and a little will spread a lot further.

Crushing **graham crackers** for topping? A self-seal sandwich bag works great!

An eleven-year-old fan e-mailed me with a great tip recently: If you can't find the **mini chocolate chips** I use in many recipes, simply purchase the regular size and put them in a nut grinder to coarsely chop them.

Try **storing your reduced-fat biscuit baking mix** in the freezer. It won't freeze, and it *will* stay fresh much longer. (It works for coffee, doesn't it?)

To check if your **baking powder** is fresh, put 1 teaspoonful in a bowl and pour 2 tablespoons of very hot tap water over it. If it's fresh, it will bubble very actively. If it doesn't bubble, then it's time to replace your old can with a new one.

In an emergency, you can make **a traditional piecrust using reduced-fat biscuit baking mix.** I mix ¾ cup of the mix with 2 tablespoons SPLENDA® and ½ cup water, then stir and spread this batter in the bottom of a pie plate I've sprayed with butter-flavored cooking spray. If the pie recipe calls for the "crust" to be baked first, then bake this at 400 degrees for 12 to 14 minutes, cool on a wire rack, and then fill as the recipe states. If the "crust" is to be baked with the filling, after the "crust" is in the plate, simply add the filling. The filling will "push" the crust up around the rim. Bake as listed in the recipe instructions. Light and flaky it's not, but fast and easy it is!

Here are two great pie-making tips I discovered at a pie-making contest: First, whenever you are making one of my **meringue pies**, gently slice the meringue into 8 pieces with a sharp knife BEFORE baking. It makes for easier cutting after the pie has cooled.

Second, when you're making custard or pumpkin pies, gently prick the bottom of the crust and bake at 425 degrees for about 8 minutes. Then gently pour the filling into the partially baked crust, lower the heat to 350 degrees, and continue baking as you normally would. This **eliminates soggy crusts**.

Enjoy!

JoAnna's Ten Commandments of Successful Cooking

A very important part of any journey is knowing where you are going and the best way to get there. If you plan and prepare before you start to cook, you should reach mealtime with foods to write home about!

1. **Read the entire recipe from start to finish** and be sure you understand the process involved. Check that you have all the equipment you will need *before* you begin.

2. **Check the ingredient list** and be sure you have *everything* and in the amounts required. Keep cooking sprays handy—while they're not listed as ingredients, I use them all the time (just a quick squirt!).

3. **Set out *all* the ingredients and equipment needed** to prepare the recipe on the counter near you *before* you start. Remember that old saying, *A stitch in time saves nine?* It applies in the kitchen, too.

4. **Do as much advance preparation as possible** before actually cooking. Chop, cut, grate, or do whatever is needed to prepare the ingredients and have them ready before you start to mix. Turn the oven on at least 10 minutes be-

fore putting food in to bake, to allow the oven to preheat to the proper temperature.

5. **Use a kitchen timer** to tell you when the cooking or baking time is up. Because stove temperatures vary slightly by manufacturer, you may want to set your timer for 5 minutes less than the suggested time just to prevent overcooking. Check the progress of your dish at that time, then decide if you need the additional minutes or not.

6. **Measure carefully.** Use glass measures for liquids and metal or plastic cups for dry ingredients. My recipes are based on standard measurements. Unless I tell you it's a scant or full cup, measure the cup level.

7. **For best results, follow the recipe instructions exactly.** Feel free to substitute ingredients that *don't tamper* with the basic chemistry of the recipe, but be sure to leave key ingredients alone. For example, you could substitute sugar-free instant chocolate pudding for sugar-free instant butterscotch pudding, but if you used a 6-serving package when a 4-serving package is listed in the ingredients, or you used instant when cook-and-serve is required, you won't get the right result.

8. **Clean up as you go.** It is much easier to wash a few items at a time than to face a whole counter of dirty dishes later. The same is true for spills on the counter or floor.

9. **Be careful about doubling or halving a recipe.** Though many recipes can be altered successfully to serve more or fewer people, *many cannot.* This is especially true when it comes to spices and liquids. If you try to double a recipe that calls for 1 teaspoon pumpkin pie spice, for example, and you double the spice, you may end up with a too-spicy taste. I usually suggest increasing spices or liquid by 1½ times when doubling a recipe. If it tastes a little bland to you, you can increase the spice to 1¾ times the original amount the next time you prepare the dish. Remember: You can always add more, but you can't take it out after it's stirred in.

The same is true with liquid ingredients. If you wanted to **triple** a main dish recipe because you were planning to serve a crowd, you might think you should use three times as much of every ingredient. Don't, or you could end up with soup instead! If the original recipe calls for 1¾ cup tomato sauce, I'd suggest using 3½ cups when you **triple** the recipe (or 2¾ cups if you **double** it). You'll still have a good-tasting dish that won't run all over the plate.

10. **Write your reactions next to each recipe once you've served it.** Yes, that's right, I'm giving you permission to write in this book. It's yours, after all. Ask yourself: Did everyone like it? Did you have to add another ½ teaspoon of chili seasoning to please your family, who like to live on the spicier side of the street? You may even want to rate the recipe on a scale of 1☆ to 4 ☆, depending on what you thought of it. (Four stars would be the top rating—and I hope you'll feel that way about many of my recipes.) Jotting down your comments while they are fresh in your mind will help you personalize the recipe to your own taste the next time you prepare it.

A Few of My
Favorite Brands

People often ask me what foods I keep on hand and what brands I use. There are lots of good products on the grocery shelves today—many more than we dreamed about even a year or two ago. And I can't wait to see what's out there 12 months from now.

Here are the products I consider my staples and have used to test these recipes. I strongly suggest that you use them to ensure the very best results. I can't tell you what the results will be if you choose to use other brands or off-brands. While they may work out just fine, it's more likely that their properties will be different than the ones I use—making it less likely that you will get a satisfactory result. I feel these products are healthier, tastier, easy to get—and deliver the most flavor for the least amount of fat, sugar, or calories.

Fat-free plain yogurt (*Dannon*)
Nonfat dry milk powder (*Carnation*)
Evaporated fat-free milk (*Carnation*)
Fat-free cream cheese (*Philadelphia*)
Fat-free mayonnaise (*Kraft*)
Fat-free salad dressing (*Kraft*)
No-fat sour cream (*Land O Lakes*)
Reduced-calorie margarine (*I Can't Believe It's Not Butter Light*)
Reduced-calorie whipped topping (*Cool Whip Lite or Cool Whip Free*)
Biscuit baking mix (*Bisquick Reduced Fat*)
Sugar-free pancake syrup (*Log Cabin*)
Parmesan cheese (*Kraft Reduced Fat Parmesan Style Grated Topping*)

Reduced-fat cheese (shredded and sliced) *(Kraft 2% Reduced Fat)*

Shredded frozen potatoes *(Mr. Dell's or Ore-Ida)*

Purchased piecrust
  unbaked *(Pillsbury—in dairy case)*
  graham cracker, shortbread, and chocolate *(Keebler)*

Crescent rolls *(Pillsbury Reduced Fat)*

Pastrami and corned beef *(Carl Buddig Lean)*

Luncheon meats *(Healthy Choice or Oscar Mayer)*

Ham *(Dubuque 97% fat-free and reduced-sodium or Healthy Choice)*

Bacon bits *(Oscar Mayer or Hormel)*

Kielbasa sausage and frankfurters *(Oscar Mayer Light or Healthy Choice)*

Unsweetened applesauce *(Musselman's)*

Pie filling *(Lucky Leaf No Sugar Added Cherry and Apple)*

Sugar-free and fat-free ice cream *(Wells' Blue Bunny)*

The Recipes

How to Read a Healthy Exchanges Recipe

The Healthy Exchanges Nutritional Analysis

Before using these recipes, you may wish to consult your physician or health-care provider to be sure they are appropriate for you. The information in this book is not intended to take the place of any medical advice. It reflects my experiences, studies, research, and opinions regarding healthy eating.

Each recipe includes nutritional information calculated in three ways:

> Healthy Exchanges Weight Loss Choices™ or Exchanges
> Calories; Fat, Protein, Carbohydrates, and Fiber in grams;
> Sodium and Calcium in milligrams
> Diabetic Exchanges

In every Healthy Exchanges recipe, the Diabetic Exchanges have been calculated by a registered dietitian. All the other calculations were done by computer, using the Food Processor II software. When the ingredient listing gives more than one choice, the first ingredient listed is the one used in the recipe analysis. Due to inevitable variations in the ingredients you choose to use, the nutritional values should be considered approximate.

The annotation "(limited)" following Protein counts in some recipes indicates that consumption of whole eggs should be limited to four per week.

Please note the following symbols:

☆ This star means read the recipe's directions carefully for special instructions about **division** of ingredients.

❋ This symbol indicates **FREEZES WELL.**

Savory Soups and
Splendid Salads

One of the more fascinating culinary mysteries is that we add salt to sweet recipes to make them turn out just right; another is that we add sweeteners to dishes that we think of as savory. Why do we do it? Because the ingredients we use—the vegetables and fruits—become more flavorful with these additions. A little sweetness transforms an ordinary bowl of soup into a meal that reminds us of good times; a dash of SPLENDA® gives a plain old salad a touch of magic.

In this section, you'll discover soups hearty enough for an entrée—like **Cliff's East Brunswick Soup**, which satisfies a long-distance trucker's appetite. You'll taste soups too rich to be low in fat, but they are—like my **Iowa Tomato Corn Soup**. You'll savor the kind of dishes that once sat all day on the stove but now can hurry from burner to table in an hour or less, like **Grandma's Beefy-Rice Stew**. You'll also find refreshing salads that sparkle (like **Classic Cranberry Salad**) and those that surprise (**Pennsylvania Hot Slaw**). Some feature fruits and nuts; some are served hot instead of cold. Just think of the wonderful menus you can prepare using these recipes!

Sweet and Sour Veggie Soup

Think you know everything there is to know about vegetable soup? I bet you've never tasted one quite like this tasty combo. It's high in fiber, sweet, *and* tangy. ☻ Serves 4 (1¼ cups)

> 1 (15-ounce) can diced tomatoes, undrained
> 1½ cups water
> ¼ cup apple cider vinegar
> ¼ cup SPLENDA® Granular
> 2 cups shredded cabbage
> ½ cup chopped onion
> 1 (8-ounce) can cut green beans, rinsed and drained
> 2 teaspoons dried parsley flakes

In a large saucepan, combine undrained tomatoes, water, vinegar, and SPLENDA®. Stir in cabbage, onion, green beans, and parsley flakes. Bring mixture to a boil. Lower heat, cover, and simmer for 20 minutes or until cabbage is tender, stirring occasionally.

Each serving equals:

HE: 2¼ Vegetable • 6 Optional Calories

---

60 Calories • 0 gm Fat • 2 gm Protein • 13 gm Carbohydrate • 307 mg Sodium • 53 mg Calcium • 4 gm Fiber

---

DIABETIC EXCHANGES: 2 Vegetable

Vegetable Beet Borscht

Just about every scientific study recommends eating more vegetables for better health. Here's a definitely untraditional beet soup that just brims with all the best stuff!

● Serves 6 (full 1½ cups)

1 (14-ounce) can lower-sodium fat-free beef broth

2¾ cups water

1 cup reduced-sodium tomato juice

1 cup sliced carrots

1 cup diced raw potatoes

2 cups shredded cabbage

½ cup chopped onion

1 (15-ounce) can navy beans, rinsed and drained

1 (15-ounce) can diced beets, drained

2 tablespoons SPLENDA® Granular

1 teaspoon dried dill weed

¼ cup no-fat sour cream

In a large saucepan, combine beef broth, water, and tomato juice. Add carrots, potatoes, cabbage, and onion. Mix well to combine. Stir in navy beans, beets, SPLENDA®, and dill weed. Bring mixture to a boil. Lower heat, cover, and simmer for 30 minutes or until vegetables are tender, stirring occasionally. When serving, garnish each bowl with 1 tablespoon sour cream.

Each serving equals:

HE: 2 Vegetable • ¾ Protein • ¼ Bread •
10 Optional Calories

---

137 Calories • 1 gm Fat • 7 gm Protein •
25 gm Carbohydrate • 570 mg Sodium •
75 mg Calcium • 5 gm Fiber

DIABETIC EXCHANGES: 2 Vegetable • ½ Meat •
½ Starch

Cabbage & White Bean Soup

Here's a truly hearty soup that will make you feel oh-so-satisfied in your tummy and your soul! The caraway seeds work wonderful magic in this dish.   ☻   Serves 4 (1 cup)

> 3 cups chopped cabbage
> 1 (15-ounce) can tomato sauce
> 2 cups water
> 2 tablespoons SPLENDA® Granular
> ½ teaspoon caraway seeds
> 1 (15-ounce) can navy beans, rinsed and drained

In a large saucepan, combine cabbage, tomato sauce, water, SPLENDA®, and caraway seeds. Bring mixture to a boil. Stir in navy beans. Lower heat, cover, and simmer for 20 to 25 minutes or until cabbage is tender, stirring occasionally.

Each serving equals:

HE: 2½ Vegetable • ¾ Protein • ½ Starch •
1 Optional Calorie

132 Calories • 0 gm Fat • 7 gm Protein •
26 gm Carbohydrate • 773 mg Sodium •
81 mg Calcium • 6 gm Fiber

DIABETIC EXCHANGES: 2½ Vegetable • 1 Meat •
1 Starch

Salsa Corn Soup

Corn might be the sweetest veggie there is, which is why it's a wonderful contrast to the spicy flavor of your favorite salsa! It's also fiber rich and creamy, too. ☉ Serves 4 (1⅓ cups)

½ cup chopped onion
1 (14-ounce) can lower-sodium
    fat-free chicken broth
2 tablespoons water
1½ cups chunky salsa (mild,
    medium, or hot)
2 cups frozen whole-kernel corn
1 tablespoon SPLENDA®
    Granular

1 (2-ounce) jar chopped
    pimiento, drained
1 (8-ounce) package fat-free
    cream cheese
¼ cup no-fat sour cream
2 tablespoons chopped fresh
    parsley or 2 teaspoons
    dried parsley flakes

In a large saucepan sprayed with butter-flavored cooking spray, sauté onion for 5 minutes or until tender. Stir in chicken broth, water, salsa, corn, SPLENDA®, and pimiento. Bring mixture to a boil. Remove from heat. In a medium bowl, stir cream cheese with a sturdy spoon until soft. Add ⅓ cup hot soup mixture to cream cheese. Mix well to combine. Stir cream cheese mixture into remaining soup, stirring until well blended. Continue cooking over medium-low heat until mixture is heated through, but not boiling, stirring often. When serving, top each bowl with 1 tablespoon sour cream and ½ tablespoon chopped parsley.

Each serving equals:

HE: 1 Bread • 1 Protein • 1 Vegetable • ¼ Slider •
5 Optional Calories

213 Calories • 1 gm Fat • 16 gm Protein •
35 gm Carbohydrate • 974 mg Sodium •
191 mg Calcium • 5 gm Fiber

DIABETIC EXCHANGES: 1½ Starch/Carbohydrate •
1 Meat • 1 Vegetable

Iowa Tomato Corn Soup

I can remember when there was no such thing as fat-free half & half—can you? In those days, creamy soups like this dazzler were impossible to enjoy when choosing to eat a healthy diet. Now, the sky's the limit—or maybe there isn't one. Enjoy!

◐ Serves 4 (1 cup)

> ½ cup finely chopped onion
> 1 (15-ounce) can diced tomatoes, undrained
> ½ cup water
> 1½ cups frozen whole-kernel corn, thawed
> 1 (12-fluid-ounce) can evaporated fat-free milk
> 1 teaspoon dried basil
> 2 tablespoons SPLENDA® Granular
> ⅛ teaspoon black pepper

In a medium saucepan sprayed with butter-flavored cooking spray, sauté onion for 5 minutes or until tender. Stir in undrained tomatoes, water, and corn. Add evaporated milk, basil, SPLENDA®, and black pepper. Mix well to combine. Lower heat and simmer for 5 to 6 minutes or until mixture is heated through, stirring often.

HINT: Thaw corn by placing in a colander and rinsing under hot water for 1 minute.

Each serving equals:

HE: 1¼ Vegetable • ¾ Fat-Free Milk • ¾ Bread • 3 Optional Calories

---

164 Calories • 0 gm Fat • 9 gm Protein •
32 gm Carbohydrate • 257 mg Sodium •
276 mg Calcium • 4 gm Fiber

DIABETIC EXCHANGES: 1 Vegetable • 1 Fat-Free Milk • 1 Starch

Italian Cream of Tomato Soup

If you've never made your own tomato sauce, you may be surprised to learn one of the secrets good cooks know: Some added sweetener (sugar or, in this case, SPLENDA®) brings out the best in your tomato! ☻ Serves 4 (1 full cup)

½ cup finely chopped onion
1 (15-ounce) can diced tomatoes, undrained
1 (8-ounce) can tomato sauce
½ cup water
1 (2½-ounce) jar sliced mushrooms, chopped and drained
1 (12-fluid-ounce) can evaporated fat-free milk
3 tablespoons all-purpose flour
1 tablespoon SPLENDA® Granular
1 teaspoon Italian seasoning
⅛ teaspoon black pepper

In a medium saucepan sprayed with olive oil-flavored cooking spray, sauté onion for 5 minutes or until tender. Stir in undrained tomatoes, tomato sauce, water, and mushrooms. In a covered jar, combine evaporated milk and flour. Shake well to blend. Stir milk mixture into tomato mixture. Add SPLENDA®, Italian seasoning, and black pepper. Mix well to combine. Continue cooking over medium heat for 5 to 6 minutes or until mixture thickens and is heated through, stirring often.

Each serving equals:

HE: 2½ Vegetable • ¾ Fat-Free Milk • ¼ Bread •
2 Optional Calories

152 Calories • 0 gm Fat • 9 gm Protein •
29 gm Carbohydrate • 631 mg Sodium •
272 mg Calcium • 3 gm Fiber

DIABETIC EXCHANGES: 2 Vegetable • 1 Fat-Free Milk

Garden Veggie Soup

Always remember that those handy boxes and bags of frozen veggies will taste garden-fresh when they're stirred into a rich soup. Instead of traveling long hours to market, they are flash-frozen moments after they're picked—and saved for you.

Serves 6 (1½ cups)

> 8 ounces extra-lean ground sirloin beef or
> turkey breast
> ¾ cup chopped onion
> ¾ cup finely chopped celery
> 1 cup frozen cut carrots, thawed
> 1 cup frozen cut green beans, thawed
> 1 (14-ounce) can lower-sodium fat-free beef broth
> ½ cup water
> 1 (15-ounce) can diced tomatoes, undrained
> ¾ cup frozen peas, thawed
> ¾ cup frozen whole-kernel corn, thawed
> 2 cups chopped cabbage
> 2 tablespoons SPLENDA® Granular
> 1 tablespoon chopped fresh parsley or 1 teaspoon
> dried parsley flakes

In a large saucepan sprayed with butter-flavored cooking spray, brown meat and onion. Stir in celery, carrots, green beans, beef broth, and water. Bring mixture to a boil. Add undrained tomatoes, peas, corn, and cabbage. Mix well to combine. Stir in SPLENDA® and parsley. Lower heat, cover, and simmer for 20 minutes or until vegetables are tender, stirring occasionally.

HINT: Thaw vegetables by placing in a colander and rinsing under hot water for 1 minute.

Each serving equals:

HE: 2 Vegetable • 1 Protein • ½ Bread •
8 Optional Calories

134 Calories • 2 gm Fat • 11 gm Protein •
18 gm Carbohydrate • 398 mg Sodium •
56 mg Calcium • 5 gm Fiber

DIABETIC EXCHANGES: 2 Vegetable • 1 Meat •
½ Starch

Cliff's Easy Brunswick Soup

This New England-style soup is a kitchen-sink kind of recipe, with all sorts of delicious bits and pieces tumbled together. When the wind blows hard outside, this will warm your insides really well.

Serves 4 (2 cups)

8 ounces skinned and boned uncooked chicken breast, cut into 16 pieces

1 (14-ounce) can lower-sodium fat-free chicken broth

1 cup water

½ cup chopped onion

2 cups diced raw potatoes

1 cup frozen cut green beans

1 (15-ounce) can diced tomatoes, undrained

1 (8-ounce) can tomato sauce

1 tablespoon SPLENDA® Granular

1 cup frozen whole-kernel corn, thawed

2 tablespoons purchased real bacon bits

1 teaspoon dried parsley flakes

In a large saucepan, combine chicken, chicken broth, water, onion, potatoes, and green beans. Bring mixture to a boil. Stir in undrained tomatoes, tomato sauce, SPLENDA®, corn, bacon bits, and parsley flakes. Lower heat, cover, and simmer for 15 to 20 minutes or until chicken and vegetables are tender, stirring occasionally.

HINT: Thaw corn by placing in a colander and rinsing under hot water for 1 minute.

Each serving equals:

HE: 2¾ Vegetable • 1½ Protein • 1 Bread • ¼ Slider • 4 Optional Calories

238 Calories • 2 gm Fat • 19 gm Protein • 36 gm Carbohydrate • 806 mg Sodium • 55 mg Calcium • 6 gm Fiber

DIABETIC EXCHANGES: 2½ Vegetable • 1½ Starch • 1½ Meat

Beef and Noodle Soup with Tomatoes

Check your grocer's shelves for different brands of fat-free beef broth and taste test a couple. Once you find the one you like best, you're ready to make delectable soups like this one with very little fuss. ☺ Serves 4 (1¼ cups)

> 8 ounces extra-lean sirloin beef or turkey breast
> ½ cup chopped onion
> 1 (14-ounce) can lower-sodium fat-free beef broth
> 1 (15-ounce) can diced tomatoes, undrained
> 2 cups water
> 1 tablespoon SPLENDA® Granular
> 1 teaspoon dried parsley flakes
> ⅛ teaspoon black pepper
> 1¾ cups uncooked fine egg noodles

In a large saucepan sprayed with butter-flavored cooking spray, brown meat and onion. Stir in beef broth, undrained tomatoes, and water. Add SPLENDA®, parsley flakes, and black pepper. Mix well to combine. Bring mixture to a boil. Stir in uncooked noodles. Lower heat, cover, and simmer for 20 minutes or until noodles are tender, stirring occasionally.

Each serving equals:

HE: 1½ Protein • 1¼ Vegetable • 1 Bread • 10 Optional Calories

---

176 Calories • 4 gm Fat • 15 gm Protein • 20 gm Carbohydrate • 530 mg Sodium • 28 mg Calcium • 2 gm Fiber

---

DIABETIC EXCHANGES: 1½ Meat • 1 Vegetable • 1 Starch

Quick Vegetable Beef Soup

Calling all working parents who need to get a family meal on the table in minutes! This pantry pleaser can be ready in minutes as long as you've stocked your shelves and freezer with handy basics.

● Serves 4 (2 cups)

> 8 ounces extra-lean ground sirloin beef or turkey breast
> 1 (15-ounce) can diced tomatoes, undrained
> 1 (8-ounce) can tomato sauce
> 1 tablespoon SPLENDA® Granular
> 1 (15-ounce) can green beans, undrained
> 1 (15-ounce) can carrots, undrained
> ½ cup frozen whole-kernel corn
> ½ cup frozen peas
> 1 teaspoon Italian seasoning

In a large saucepan sprayed with olive oil-flavored cooking spray, brown meat. Add undrained tomatoes, tomato sauce, SPLENDA®, undrained green beans, undrained carrots, corn, peas, and Italian seasoning. Mix well to combine. Cook over medium heat for 10 minutes or until mixture is heated through, stirring occasionally.

Each serving equals:

HE: 4 Vegetable • 1½ Protein • ½ Bread

195 Calories • 3 gm Fat • 16 gm Protein • 26 gm Carbohydrate • 948 mg Sodium • 70 mg Calcium • 8 gm Fiber

DIABETIC EXCHANGES: 4 Vegetable • 1½ Meat • ½ Starch

James's Cabbage Chili Stew

This savory combo offers tons of texture and flavor for very few calories and lots of fiber. It's perfect for lunch on a winter weekend and leftovers reheat beautifully. ☺ Serves 4 (1 cup)

> 8 ounces extra-lean ground sirloin beef or turkey breast
> ½ cup chopped onion
> ½ teaspoon dried minced garlic
> 1 (15-ounce) can diced tomatoes, undrained
> 1 (8-ounce) can tomato sauce
> 2 tablespoons SPLENDA® Granular
> 2 teaspoons dried parsley flakes
> 2 teaspoons chili seasoning
> 2 cups purchased coleslaw mix
> 1 (8-ounce) can red kidney beans, rinsed and drained

In a large saucepan sprayed with olive oil-flavored cooking spray, brown meat and onion. Stir in garlic, undrained tomatoes, tomato sauce, SPLENDA®, parsley flakes, and chili seasoning. Add coleslaw mix and kidney beans. Mix well to combine. Bring mixture to a boil. Lower heat, cover, and simmer for 30 minutes, stirring occasionally.

HINT: 1½ cups shredded cabbage and ½ cup shredded carrots may be used in place of purchased coleslaw mix.

Each serving equals:

HE: 2¾ Vegetable • 2 Protein • ½ Bread

---

179 Calories • 3 gm Fat • 16 gm Protein •
22 gm Carbohydrate • 580 mg Sodium •
64 mg Calcium • 7 gm Fiber

DIABETIC EXCHANGES: 2½ Vegetable • 2 Meat •
½ Starch

Grandma's Beefy-Rice Stew

I like to think of this as old-fashioned cooking made for today's busy families. You can get that "grandma-made" flavor in much less time!   ◐   Serves 4 (1½ cups)

> 8 ounces extra-lean ground sirloin beef or turkey breast
> 1 cup chopped onion
> 1 (8-ounce) can tomato sauce
> 1 (15-ounce) can diced tomatoes, undrained
> 1½ cups reduced-sodium tomato juice
> 1½ tablespoons Worcestershire sauce
> 2 cups shredded cabbage
> ⅔ cup uncooked instant rice
> 2 tablespoons SPLENDA® Granular
> 1½ teaspoons dried parsley flakes
> ⅛ teaspoon black pepper

In a large saucepan sprayed with butter-flavored cooking spray, brown meat and onion. Stir in tomato sauce, undrained tomatoes, tomato juice, and Worcestershire sauce. Add cabbage, uncooked instant rice, SPLENDA®, parsley flakes, and black pepper. Mix well to combine. Lower heat, cover, and simmer for 15 to 20 minutes or until cabbage and rice are tender, stirring occasionally.

Each serving equals:

HE: 3 Vegetable • 1½ Protein • ½ Bread •
3 Optional Calories

---

207 Calories • 3 gm Fat • 15 gm Protein •
30 gm Carbohydrate • 670 mg Sodium •
74 mg Calcium • 4 gm Fiber

DIABETIC EXCHANGES: 3 Vegetable • 1½ Meat •
1 Starch

Puerto Rican Bean Soup

You don't need a doctor's recommendation to add this healthy, hearty stew-of-a-soup to your menu—high fiber is good for all of us! If you have leftovers from a holiday ham, this dish is ideal for making another marvelous meal of them.   ☻   Serves 4 (1 cup)

> 1 full cup extra-lean diced ham
> ½ cup chopped onion
> ½ cup chopped green bell pepper
> 1 (8-ounce) can tomato sauce
> 2 tablespoons SPLENDA® Granular
> 2 cups water
> ½ teaspoon dried minced garlic
> 1½ teaspoons chili seasoning
> 1 teaspoon Italian seasoning
> 1 (15-ounce) can red kidney or black beans, rinsed and drained
> 1 cup cooked spaghetti, rinsed and drained

In a large saucepan sprayed with butter-flavored cooking spray, sauté ham, onion, and green pepper for 5 minutes. Stir in tomato sauce, SPLENDA®, water, garlic, chili seasoning, and Italian seasoning. Add kidney beans and spaghetti. Mix well to combine. Lower heat, cover, and simmer for 15 minutes, stirring occasionally.

HINT: Usually ¾ cup broken uncooked spaghetti cooks to about 1 cup.

Each serving equals:

HE: 2 Protein • 1½ Vegetable • 1 Bread

194 Calories • 2 gm Fat • 14 gm Protein •
30 gm Carbohydrate • 830 mg Sodium •
36 mg Calcium • 7 gm Fiber

DIABETIC EXCHANGES: 2 Meat • 1½ Starch •
1 Vegetable

Frankfurter Bean Soup

Homemade baked beans are an American classic, but even when you don't have time to slow-cook a big kettle of those, you can enjoy their festive sweet-and-tangy flavor in this tasty soup.

○ Serves 4 (1½ cups)

  ½ cup chopped onion
  ½ cup chopped green bell pepper
  1 (15-ounce) can great northern beans, rinsed and drained
  1 (15-ounce) can diced tomatoes, undrained
  1 cup reduced-sodium tomato juice
  1 (8-ounce) can tomato sauce
  ½ cup water
  2 tablespoons SPLENDA® Granular
  8 ounces reduced-fat frankfurters, diced
  1 teaspoon prepared yellow mustard
  1 teaspoon dried basil flakes

In a large saucepan sprayed with butter-flavored cooking spray, sauté onion and green pepper for 5 minutes or until tender. Stir in great northern beans, undrained tomatoes, tomato juice, tomato sauce, water, and SPLENDA®. Add frankfurters, mustard, and basil flakes. Mix well to combine. Lower heat, cover, and simmer for 15 minutes, stirring occasionally.

Each serving equals:

HE: 2 Protein • 2 Vegetable • ½ Bread •
3 Optional Calories

219 Calories • 3 gm Fat • 15 gm Protein •
33 gm Carbohydrate • 971 mg Sodium •
85 mg Calcium • 6 gm Fiber

DIABETIC EXCHANGES: 2 Meat • 2 Vegetable • 1 Starch

Classic Cranberry Salad

It's a great way to adorn your holiday buffet table, but this spectacular molded salad is too good to enjoy only on special occasions. Just think how pretty this rosy-red delight will look on your dinner plates! ☻ Serves 6

2 envelopes unflavored gelatin
3/4 cup cold water
1 cup reduced-calorie cranberry juice cocktail
1/2 cup SPLENDA® Granular
1 (8-ounce) can crushed pineapple, packed in fruit juice, drained
1 cup chopped fresh or frozen cranberries
1 cup (2 small) cored, unpeeled, and chopped Red Delicious
    apples
1 1/2 cups finely diced celery

In a small saucepan, sprinkle dry gelatin over water and let soften for a few minutes. Cook over low heat until gelatin is completely dissolved, stirring often. Remove from heat. Stir in cranberry juice cocktail. Pour mixture into a large bowl. Add SPLENDA® and pineapple. Mix well to combine. Stir in cranberries, apples, and celery. Pour mixture into an 8-by-8-inch dish. Refrigerate until firm, about 3 hours. Cut into 6 servings.

Each serving equals:

HE: 1 Fruit • 1/2 Vegetable • 8 Optional Calories

64 Calories • 0 gm Fat • 0 gm Protein •
16 gm Carbohydrate • 28 mg Sodium •
23 mg Calcium • 2 gm Fiber

DIABETIC EXCHANGES: 1 Fruit • 1/2 Vegetable

Sunshine Salad

Tangy, crunchy, sweet, and all-around sensational—this dish delivers the joy of a sunny afternoon in every bite.　　❤　Serves 4

> 6 cups torn mixed salad greens
> 1 (11-ounce) can mandarin oranges, rinsed and drained
> ¼ cup apricot spreadable fruit
> 2 tablespoons white distilled vinegar
> 2 tablespoons SPLENDA® Granular
> ¼ cup chopped walnuts

In a large bowl, combine salad greens and mandarin oranges. In a small bowl, combine spreadable fruit, vinegar, and SPLENDA®. Drizzle dressing mixture evenly over salad mixture. Toss gently to coat. For each salad, place 1½ cups salad mixture on a plate and sprinkle 1 tablespoon walnuts over top. Serve at once.

Each serving equals:

HE: 1½ Fruit • 1½ Vegetable • ½ Fat • ¼ Protein • 3 Optional Calories

---

149 Calories • 5 gm Fat • 2 gm Protein • 24 gm Carbohydrate • 26 mg Sodium • 52 mg Calcium • 2 gm Fiber

---

DIABETIC EXCHANGES: 1½ Fruit • 1½ Vegetable • 1 Fat

Layered Party Pea Salad

Peas have their own special sweetness before anything is added to serve them. Maybe that's why I chose to combine them with piquant bits of tangy Swiss cheese and bacon, to make what's already good glorious! ☻ Serves 6

> 2½ cups finely shredded lettuce
> ¼ cup finely chopped onion
> 1½ cups frozen peas, thawed
> ¼ cup purchased real bacon bits
> ½ cup fat-free mayonnaise
> 2 tablespoons fat-free sour cream
> 2 tablespoons SPLENDA® Granular
> 6 tablespoons shredded reduced-fat Cheddar cheese
> 6 tablespoons shredded reduced-fat mozzarella cheese

Evenly arrange lettuce in an 8-by-8-inch glass dish. Layer onion, peas, and bacon bits evenly over lettuce. In a medium bowl, combine mayonnaise, sour cream, and SPLENDA®. Carefully spread dressing mixture over top. Evenly sprinkle shredded Cheddar and mozzarella cheese over dressing mixture. Cover and refrigerate for at least 2 hours or overnight. Divide into 6 servings.

Each serving equals:

HE: ½ Protein • ½ Vegetable • ½ Bread • ¼ Slider • 17 Optional Calories

108 Calories • 4 gm Fat • 8 gm Protein • 10 gm Carbohydrate • 464 mg Sodium • 115 mg Calcium • 2 gm Fiber

DIABETIC EXCHANGES: 1 Starch • ½ Meat • ½ Vegetable

Sour Cream Cucumbers

Luscious is the only word for this creamy delight, which takes crunchy cucumbers and envelops them in a silken sauce. As the saying goes, "Rich is better!"   ☉   Serves 6 (¾ cup)

½ cup no-fat sour cream
2 tablespoons SPLENDA® Granular
1 tablespoon white distilled vinegar
½ teaspoon dried dill weed
4 cups sliced unpeeled cucumbers
½ cup finely chopped onion

In a large bowl, combine sour cream, SPLENDA®, vinegar, and dill weed. Stir in cucumbers and onion. Cover and refrigerate for at least 30 minutes. Gently stir again just before serving.

Each serving equals:

HE: 1½ Vegetable • ¼ Slider • 2 Optional Calories

32 Calories • 0 gm Fat • 1 gm Protein •
7 gm Carbohydrate • 28 mg Sodium •
40 mg Calcium • 1 gm Fiber

DIABETIC EXCHANGES: 1 Vegetable

Apple Orchard Slaw

Too many cooks-in-a-hurry forget just how delightful a festive side salad can be, especially one like this that takes a few minutes to stir up and is good all year round.   ☻   Serves 4 (1 cup)

> ½ cup fat-free mayonnaise
> 1 tablespoon apple cider vinegar
> 2 tablespoons SPLENDA® Granular
> 3 cups purchased coleslaw mix
> 1½ cups (3 small) cored, unpeeled, and finely chopped
>   Red Delicious apples
> 2 tablespoons chopped pecans

In a medium bowl, combine mayonnaise, vinegar, and SPLENDA®. Add coleslaw mix, apples, and pecans. Mix well to combine. Cover and refrigerate for at least 30 minutes. Gently stir again just before serving.

HINT: 2½ cups shredded cabbage and ½ cup shredded carrots may be used in place of purchased coleslaw mix.

Each serving equals:

HE: ¾ Fruit • ¾ Vegetable • ½ Fat • ¼ Slider •
3 Optional Calories

---

95 Calories • 3 gm Fat • 1 gm Protein •
16 gm Carbohydrate • 255 mg Sodium •
37 mg Calcium • 4 gm Fiber

DIABETIC EXCHANGES: 1 Fruit • 1 Vegetable • ½ Fat

Classic Creamy Slaw

Here's a true one-bowl wonder that is sure to become a regular on your patio this summer! It's also a gift for busy chefs who choose to use the packaged coleslaw mix.   ☺   Serves 6 (½ cup)

> ½ cup fat-free mayonnaise
> 2 tablespoons white distilled vinegar
> 2 tablespoons SPLENDA® Granular
> 1 tablespoon chopped fresh parsley or 1 teaspoon dried parsley
>   flakes
> 3 cups purchased coleslaw mix

In a large bowl, combine mayonnaise, vinegar, SPLENDA®, and parsley. Add coleslaw mix. Mix well to combine. Cover and refrigerate for at least 30 minutes. Gently stir again just before serving.

HINT: 2½ cups shredded cabbage and ½ cup shredded carrots may be used in place of purchased coleslaw mix.

Each serving equals:

HE: ½ Vegetable • 15 Optional Calories

28 Calories • 0 gm Fat • 1 gm Protein •
6 gm Carbohydrate • 170 mg Sodium •
22 mg Calcium • 1 gm Fiber

DIABETIC EXCHANGES: ½ Vegetable

South Seas Carrot and Raisin Salad

A taste of this, and you'll start to feel those tropical breezes wafting through your hair! It's amazing how just the right mix of flavors can carry you off to paradise.　　●　Serves 6 (⅔ cup)

> 2 (8-ounce) cans pineapple tidbits, packed in fruit juice, drained
>   and 2 tablespoons liquid reserved
> ½ cup fat-free mayonnaise
> 2 tablespoons SPLENDA® Granular
> 3 cups grated carrots
> ¼ cup seedless raisins

In a medium bowl, combine reserved pineapple liquid, mayonnaise, and SPLENDA®. Add carrots, pineapple, and raisins. Mix well to combine. Cover and refrigerate for at least 30 minutes. Gently stir again just before serving.

Each serving equals:

HE: 1 Fruit • 1 Vegetable • 15 Optional Calories

104 Calories • 0 gm Fat • 1 gm Protein •
25 gm Carbohydrate • 180 mg Sodium •
29 mg Calcium • 3 gm Fiber

DIABETIC EXCHANGES: 1 Fruit • 1 Vegetable

Broccoli Cashew Salad

I had to test this on friends and family, since my husband continues to pass on broccoli-based dishes. (Nobody's perfect, but he comes very close!) Everyone agreed how nice it was to savor the flavor of cashews even while eating for better health!

⊙ Serves 6 (½ cup)

> 3 cups chopped fresh broccoli
> ½ cup seedless raisins
> ¼ cup finely chopped onion
> 6 tablespoons chopped cashews
> ¼ cup purchased real bacon bits
> ½ cup fat-free mayonnaise
> 1 tablespoon white distilled vinegar
> ¼ cup SPLENDA® Granular

In a large bowl, combine broccoli, raisins, onion, cashews, and bacon bits. In a small bowl, combine mayonnaise, vinegar, and SPLENDA®. Add dressing mixture to broccoli mixture. Toss gently to coat. Cover and refrigerate for at least 30 minutes. Gently stir again just before serving.

HINT: To plump up raisins without "cooking," place in a glass measuring cup and microwave on HIGH for 20 seconds.

Each serving equals:

> HE: 1 Vegetable • ⅔ Fruit • ½ Fat • ¼ Protein •
> ¼ Slider • 11 Optional Calories
> ___
> 133 Calories • 5 gm Fat • 5 gm Protein •
> 17 gm Carbohydrate • 306 mg Sodium •
> 29 mg Calcium • 2 gm Fiber
> ___
> DIABETIC EXCHANGES: 1 Fruit • 1 Fat • ½ Vegetable

Wilted Green Bean
& Lettuce Salad

It's kind of a funny name for an appealing dish, isn't it? In this case "wilted" doesn't mean the kind of soggy, spoiled vegetables you'd avoid at the store, but what happens to crisp greens when they're treated to a heated dressing—yum!   ☻   Serves 4 (1 cup)

  ½ cup chopped red onion
  ¼ cup apple cider vinegar
  ¼ cup SPLENDA® Granular
  3 cups frozen cut green beans, thawed
  ¼ cup purchased real bacon bits
  2 cups shredded lettuce

In a large skillet sprayed with butter-flavored cooking spray, sauté onion for 5 minutes or until tender. Stir in vinegar and SPLENDA®. Add green beans and bacon bits. Mix well to combine. Lower heat and simmer for 10 minutes or just until green beans are tender, stirring often. Remove from heat. Stir in lettuce. Serve at once.

HINT: Thaw green beans by placing in a colander and rinsing under hot water for 1 minute.

Each serving equals:

HE: 2¼ Vegetable • ¼ Slider • 11 Optional Calories

78 Calories • 2 gm Fat • 4 gm Protein •
11 gm Carbohydrate • 230 mg Sodium •
51 mg Calcium • 3 gm Fiber

DIABETIC EXCHANGES: 1 Vegetable • ½ Meat

Pennsylvania Hot Slaw

Here's another classic dish with a special twist! First brought to the United States by European immigrants, it takes something just plain good and makes it special.   ☽   Serves 4 (½ cup)

> ¼ cup SPLENDA® Granular
> 1 tablespoon finely chopped onion
> ¼ cup white distilled vinegar
> 2 tablespoons purchased real bacon bits
> 3 cups thinly sliced cabbage
> ½ cup thinly sliced celery

In a small bowl, combine SPLENDA®, onion, and vinegar. Pour into a large skillet sprayed with butter-flavored cooking spray. Stir in bacon bits. Add cabbage and celery. Mix gently to combine. Cook over medium heat for 5 minutes, or until heated through, stirring often. Serve at once.

Each serving equals:

HE: 1 Vegetable • 18 Optional Calories

41 Calories • 1 gm Fat • 2 gm Protein •
6 gm Carbohydrate • 150 mg Sodium •
38 mg Calcium • 2 gm Fiber

DIABETIC EXCHANGES: 1 Vegetable

Kraut Salad

Cliff and I enjoy this sauerkraut-based dish with several of our favorite pork entrees. It's pretty on the plate and the perfect complement to the "other white meat." ● Serves 4 (¾ cup)

> 1 (15-ounce) can sauerkraut, well drained
> ½ cup chopped green bell pepper
> ½ cup chopped celery
> ½ cup chopped onion
> ½ cup SPLENDA® Granular
> ½ cup white distilled vinegar
> 1 tablespoon vegetable oil

In a medium bowl, combine sauerkraut, green pepper, celery, and onion. In a small bowl, combine SPLENDA®, vinegar, and oil. Drizzle dressing mixture evenly over sauerkraut mixture. Mix gently to combine. Cover and refrigerate for at least 4 hours. Gently stir again just before serving.

HINT: Place sauerkraut in a colander and press juice out with a sturdy spoon.

Each serving equals:

HE: 1¾ Vegetable • ¾ Fat • 12 Optional Calories

88 Calories • 4 gm Fat • 1 gm Protein •
12 gm Carbohydrate • 617 mg Sodium •
43 mg Calcium • 3 gm Fiber

DIABETIC EXCHANGES: 1½ Vegetable • 1 Fat

Best Three-Bean Salad

Nearly every Midwestern farmwife has a family recipe for three-bean salad passed down from generations past. Is this one the best you've ever tried? My recipe testers voted a resounding and unanimous yes! ◐ Serves 6 (⅔ cup)

> 2 (15-ounce) cans cut green beans, rinsed and drained
> 1 (15-ounce) can cut wax beans, rinsed and drained
> 1 (15-ounce) can red kidney beans, rinsed and drained
> ¼ cup finely chopped onion
> 1 (2-ounce) jar chopped pimiento, undrained
> ⅓ cup white distilled vinegar
> ⅓ cup SPLENDA® Granular
> 2 tablespoons vegetable oil
> 1 teaspoon dried parsley flakes
> ⅛ teaspoon black pepper

In a large bowl, combine green beans, wax beans, kidney beans, onion, and undrained pimiento. In a small bowl, combine vinegar, SPLENDA®, and vegetable oil. Stir in parsley flakes and black pepper. Add dressing mixture to vegetable mixture. Mix gently to combine. Cover and refrigerate for at least 30 minutes. Gently stir again just before serving.

Each serving equals:

HE: 2 Vegetable • 1 Fat • ½ Bread • ½ Protein • 5 Optional Calories

125 Calories • 5 gm Fat • 4 gm Protein • 16 gm Carbohydrate • 506 mg Sodium • 41 mg Calcium • 5 gm Fiber

DIABETIC EXCHANGES: 2 Vegetable • 1 Fat • ½ Starch • ½ Meat

Farmers Market Stuffed Tomatoes

Here's a splendid way to serve summer's sweet harvest, whether the ruby-hued tomatoes come directly from your garden or the nearest farm stand. And those bits of egg and bacon just give this dish extra pizzazz! ☻ Serves 4

4 (medium-sized) ripe fresh tomatoes
¼ cup finely chopped celery
½ cup finely chopped unpeeled cucumber
2 tablespoons finely chopped onion
2 tablespoons finely chopped green bell pepper
⅓ cup fat-free mayonnaise
2 tablespoons SPLENDA® Granular
1 teaspoon dried parsley flakes
⅛ teaspoon black pepper
2 tablespoons purchased real bacon bits
3 hard-boiled eggs, chopped

Cut tops off tomatoes. Cut tomatoes into quarters, being careful not to cut all the way through the bottom. Spread wedges slightly apart. In a medium bowl, combine celery, cucumber, onion, and green pepper. Add mayonnaise, SPLENDA®, parsley flakes, and black pepper. Mix gently to combine. Stir in bacon bits and chopped egg. Spoon about ½ cup filling mixture into center of each tomato. Serve at once or cover and refrigerate until ready to serve.

Each serving equals:

HE: 1 Vegetable • ¾ Protein • ¼ Slider •
13 Optional Calories
_____
105 Calories • 5 gm Fat • 7 gm Protein •
8 gm Carbohydrate • 342 mg Sodium •
30 mg Calcium • 2 gm Fiber
_____
DIABETIC EXCHANGES: 1 Vegetable • 1 Meat

Pam's Potato Salad

My daughter-in-law Pam tried this take on a classic potato salad and claimed it as her own! She told me how her mom always put the egg yolks in the dressing. It's a totally different approach to this favorite, and I think it tastes great.   ☻   Serves 8 (¾ cup)

> 2 hard-boiled eggs
> ½ cup fat-free mayonnaise
> 1 teaspoon prepared yellow mustard
> 2 tablespoons white distilled vinegar
> ¼ cup SPLENDA® Granular
> ⅛ teaspoon black pepper
> 3 full cups diced cooked potatoes
> 1¼ cups chopped celery
> ¾ cup chopped onion

Cut eggs in half and remove yolks. In a large bowl, mash egg yolks. Stir in mayonnaise, mustard, vinegar, SPLENDA®, and black pepper. Add potatoes, celery, and onion. Mix well to combine. Dice egg whites and gently fold into potato mixture. Cover and refrigerate for at least 30 minutes. Gently stir again just before serving.

Each serving equals:

HE: ¾ Bread • ½ Vegetable • ¼ Protein •
13 Optional Calories

94 Calories • 2 gm Fat • 3 gm Protein •
16 gm Carbohydrate • 161 mg Sodium •
21 mg Calcium • 2 gm Fiber

DIABETIC EXCHANGES: 1 Starch/Carbohydrate •
½ Vegetable

Grandma's Hot German Potato Salad

If you've never tasted a true "hot" potato salad, I'm thrilled to think that this one will awaken your taste buds to a fantastic taste treat! It's a savory superstar at our house, and soon (I hope) will be at yours. ☻ Serves 6 (½ cup)

> 3 cups diced cooked potatoes
> 3 tablespoons purchased real bacon bits
> ⅛ teaspoon celery seed
> ¼ cup apple cider vinegar
> ¼ cup water
> ¼ cup SPLENDA® Granular
> 1 tablespoon prepared yellow mustard
> 1 tablespoon dried onion flakes

In a large bowl, combine potatoes, bacon bits, and celery seed. In a small saucepan, combine vinegar and water. Stir in SPLENDA®, mustard, and onion flakes. Cook over medium heat until mixture is hot, but not boiling, stirring often. Pour hot mixture over potato mixture. Toss well to coat. Serve at once.

Each serving equals:

HE: ¾ Bread • 16 Optional Calories

93 Calories • 1 gm Fat • 3 gm Protein •
18 gm Carbohydrate • 159 mg Sodium •
9 mg Calcium • 1 gm Fiber

DIABETIC EXCHANGES: 1 Starch

Fantastic Chicken Macaroni Salad

Creativity in the kitchen can produce splendid results—if you let your imagination roam a bit! In this appetizing blend, I've joined juicy fruit with chunks of chicken and a few crunchy nuts for a magnificent macaroni delight. ☻ Serves 6 (⅔ cup)

1 (8-ounce) can pineapple
    tidbits, packed in fruit
    juice, drained and
    ¼ cup liquid reserved
½ cup fat-free mayonnaise
2 tablespoons SPLENDA®
    Granular
1½ cups cooked elbow
    macaroni, rinsed
    and drained

1 full cup (6 ounces) diced
    cooked chicken breast
½ cup seedless green grapes,
    halved
¼ cup finely chopped
    onion
½ cup chopped celery
3 tablespoons chopped
    pecans

In a large bowl, combine reserved pineapple liquid, mayonnaise, and SPLENDA®. Add macaroni, chicken, pineapple tidbits, grapes, onion, and celery. Mix well to combine. Stir in pecans. Cover and refrigerate for at least 30 minutes. Gently stir again just before serving.

HINTS: 1. Usually 1 cup uncooked macaroni cooks to about 1½ cups.
       2. If you don't have leftovers, purchase a chunk of cooked chicken breast from your local deli.

Each serving equals:

HE: 1 Protein • ½ Bread • ½ Fruit • ½ Fat •
½ Vegetable • 15 Optional Calories

168 Calories • 4 gm Fat • 11 gm Protein •
22 gm Carbohydrate • 193 mg Sodium •
17 mg Calcium • 2 gm Fiber

DIABETIC EXCHANGES: 1 Meat • 1 Starch/Carbohydrate •
½ Fruit • ½ Fat

Vivacious Veggies and Succulent Sides

If your family has been microwaving frozen dinners or grabbing fast food instead of sitting down to a home-cooked meal five nights out of seven, it's likely that they've been missing out on well-rounded meals that include delicious side dishes and healthy veggies. I'm aiming to bring some much-needed nutrition back into your menus with this splendid collection of recipes born to share the dinner plate with the usual meat and potatoes. I think you'll agree that these tasty and inventive dishes turn an ordinary meal into a feast!

For everyone who's oh-so-tired of the same old green bean dishes, I've created some delectable versions that will persuade you that you're dining in Rome or Kauai (**Green Beans in Italian Tomato Sauce, Hawaiian Green Beans**). I've introduced some savory spices to their ideal veggie partners (**Rosemary Stewed Tomatoes**), headed South of the Border for a lively taste sensation (**Mexican Succotash Side Dish**), and even offered recipes for veggies that never seem to get equal time (**Butter Bean and Apple Skillet**). You'll find wonderful ways to combine pasta with vegetables (**Cabbage & Green Beans with Noodles**) and dishes so creamy they ought to be illegal (but they're not!). Enjoy!

Pickled Beets

Never had these ruby treats before? They look so beautiful on the plate, and the lemon pepper gives them a little something extra.

◐ Serves 4 (½ cup)

½ cup white distilled vinegar
½ cup water
½ cup SPLENDA® Granular
1 teaspoon lemon pepper
1 (15-ounce) can sliced beets, rinsed and drained

In a large saucepan, combine vinegar, water, SPLENDA®, and lemon pepper. Bring mixture to a boil. Continue boiling for 2 minutes. Stir in beets. Remove from heat. Place saucepan on a wire rack and allow to cool to room temperature. Pour mixture into a medium bowl. Cover and refrigerate for at least 12 hours. Gently stir again just before serving.

Each serving equals:

HE: 1 Vegetable • 12 Optional Calories

---

40 Calories • 0 gm Fat • 1 gm Protein •
9 gm Carbohydrate • 201 mg Sodium •
0 mg Calcium • 1 gm Fiber

DIABETIC EXCHANGES: 1 Vegetable

Harvard Carrots & Green Beans

This cozy blend is inspired by a palace of learning that's more than 350 years old! There's a good reason that university is tops in its class—and the same is true for this recipe.

Serves 4 (½ cup)

> 1 tablespoon cornstarch
> ¼ cup white distilled vinegar
> ¼ cup water
> ¼ cup SPLENDA® Granular
> 2 teaspoons reduced-calorie margarine
> 1 teaspoon dried onion flakes
> 1 teaspoon dried parsley flakes
> 1 (8-ounce) can sliced carrots, rinsed and drained
> 1 (8-ounce) can cut green beans, rinsed and drained

In a medium saucepan sprayed with butter-flavored cooking spray, combine cornstarch, vinegar, and water. Stir in SPLENDA®, margarine, onion flakes, and parsley flakes. Cook over medium heat until mixture thickens and starts to boil, stirring often. Add carrots and green beans. Mix well to combine. Lower heat and simmer for 6 to 8 minutes or until mixture is heated through, stirring often. Good served warm or cold.

Each serving equals:

HE: 1 Vegetable • ¼ Fat • 14 Optional Calories

45 Calories • 1 gm Fat • 1 gm Protein •
8 gm Carbohydrate • 268 mg Sodium •
22 mg Calcium • 2 gm Fiber

DIABETIC EXCHANGES: 1 Vegetable

Old-Fashioned Sweet-Sour Red Cabbage

I confess that my mouth waters whenever I prepare old-world style recipes like this one. I can close my eyes and imagine sharing it with my ancestors in Bohemia many years ago.

○ Serves 4 (½ cup)

3 cups finely shredded red cabbage
½ teaspoon caraway seed
½ cup water
2 tablespoons SPLENDA® Granular
2 tablespoons apple cider vinegar

In a large skillet, combine red cabbage, caraway seed, and water. Cook over medium heat for 6 to 8 minutes, stirring occasionally. Add SPLENDA® and vinegar. Mix well to combine. Lower heat and simmer for 5 minutes or until cabbage is tender, stirring occasionally. Good served warm or cold.

Each serving equals:

HE: ¾ Vegetable • 3 Optional Calories

24 Calories • 0 gm Fat • 1 gm Protein •
5 gm Carbohydrate • 9 mg Sodium • 38 mg Calcium •
2 gm Fiber

DIABETIC EXCHANGES: 1 Vegetable

Summer Skillet Cabbage

Here's another luscious and amazingly fat-free daily product that can turn a plain old veggie into a velvety mouth pleaser. I like knowing I'm getting some calcium along with the cozy goodness.

❍ Serves 6 (1 cup)

2 tablespoons reduced-calorie margarine
9 cups shredded cabbage
1 teaspoon lemon pepper
¼ cup fat-free half & half
3 tablespoons SPLENDA® Granular

In a large skillet sprayed with butter-flavored cooking spray, melt margarine. Add cabbage and lemon pepper. Mix well to combine. Cover and cook over medium heat for 6 minutes, stirring occasionally. Stir in half & half and SPLENDA®. Continue cooking, uncovered, for 2 to 3 minutes, stirring often.

Each serving equals:

HE: 1½ Vegetable • ½ Fat • 9 Optional Calories

62 Calories • 2 gm Fat • 2 gm Protein •
9 gm Carbohydrate • 156 mg Sodium •
80 mg Calcium • 3 gm Fiber

DIABETIC EXCHANGES: 1 Vegetable • ½ Fat

Skillet au Gratin Cabbage

French cooking offers many vegetable dishes served au gratin, meaning that they're baked with cheese and *tres delicieux* (very delicious). Here, I've used a bit of flour (another cook's trick) to thicken up the cheesy sauce surrounding the cabbage.

◑ Serves 4 (¾ cup)

> 1 cup grated carrots
> ½ cup chopped onion
> 4 cups shredded cabbage
> 1 (12-fluid-ounce) can evaporated fat-free milk
> 3 tablespoons all-purpose flour
> 1 tablespoon SPLENDA® Granular
> ¾ cup shredded reduced-fat Cheddar cheese
> 1 tablespoon chopped fresh parsley or 1 teaspoon dried parsley
>   flakes
> ⅛ teaspoon black pepper

In a large skillet sprayed with butter-flavored cooking spray, sauté carrots and onion for 5 minutes. Stir in cabbage. Continue sautéing for 5 minutes. Meanwhile, in a covered jar, combine evaporated milk, flour, and SPLENDA®. Shake well to blend. Add milk mixture, Cheddar cheese, parsley, and black pepper to cabbage mixture. Mix well to combine. Lower heat and simmer for 5 minutes or until mixture thickens and cheese melts, stirring often.

Each serving equals:

HE: 1¾ Vegetable • 1 Protein • ¾ Fat-Free Milk • ¼ Bread • 2 Optional Calories

200 Calories • 4 gm Fat • 14 gm Protein • 27 gm Carbohydrate • 326 mg Sodium • 436 mg Calcium • 3 gm Fiber

DIABETIC EXCHANGES: 2 Vegetable • 1 Meat • 1 Fat-Free Milk

Hawaiian Green Beans

Harmony in music means a perfect balance, and harmony in cooking usually means finding just the right balance of ingredients. Here, the sweet fruit combines with a little vinegar for a true delight. ☻ Serves 4 (½ cup)

> 1 (8-ounce) can pineapple tidbits, packed in fruit juice, drained and ¼ cup liquid reserved
>
> 2 tablespoons white distilled vinegar
>
> 2 tablespoons SPLENDA® Granular
>
> 1 tablespoon cornstarch
>
> ⅛ teaspoon black pepper
>
> 1 teaspoon dried onion flakes
>
> 1 (15-ounce) can cut green beans, rinsed and drained

In a large skillet sprayed with butter-flavored cooking spray, combine reserved pineapple liquid, vinegar, SPLENDA®, cornstarch, black pepper, and onion flakes. Bring mixture to a boil, stirring often. Stir in green beans and pineapple. Lower heat and simmer for 5 minutes or until mixture is heated through, stirring occasionally.

Each serving equals:

HE: 1 Vegetable • ½ Fruit • 11 Optional Calories

68 Calories • 0 gm Fat • 1 gm Protein •
16 gm Carbohydrate • 301 mg Sodium •
30 mg Calcium • 2 gm Fiber

DIABETIC EXCHANGES: 1 Vegetable • ½ Fruit

Green Beans in
Italian Tomato Sauce

My husband loves green beans, so I've probably invented more recipes starring them than any other cook around! This is a simple but wonderfully savory dish.   Serves 6 (⅔ cup)

> 1 (8-ounce) can tomatoes, undrained and coarsely chopped
> ½ cup chopped onion
> ¼ cup water
> 2 tablespoons SPLENDA® Granular
> 1 teaspoon Italian seasoning
> 3 cups frozen cut green beans, thawed

In a large skillet, combine undrained tomatoes, onion, water, SPLENDA®, and Italian seasoning. Stir in green beans. Cover and cook over medium heat for 30 minutes, stirring occasionally.

HINT: Thaw green beans by placing in a colander and rinsing under hot water for 1 minute.

Each serving equals:

HE: 1½ Vegetable • 2 Optional Calories

36 Calories • 0 gm Fat • 1 gm Protein •
8 gm Carbohydrate • 55 mg Sodium •
35 mg Calcium • 3 gm Fiber

DIABETIC EXCHANGES: 1½ Vegetable

Green Beans Oriental

Many health-conscious cooks resist the notion of cooking with peanut butter, thinking that it's too "fattening." Well, a little goes a long way in making this exotically tangy temptation!

Serves 6 (½ cup)

> *3 cups fresh or frozen cut green beans, thawed*
> *1 cup sliced fresh mushrooms*
> *½ cup sliced green onions*
> *1 tablespoon reduced-fat creamy peanut butter*
> *1 tablespoon SPLENDA® Granular*
> *2 tablespoons reduced-sodium soy sauce*
> *¼ cup chopped dry-roasted peanuts*

In an 8-cup glass measuring bowl, combine green beans, mushrooms, and green onions. Cover and microwave on HIGH (100% power) for 8 to 10 minutes or until green beans are just tender, stirring after 5 minutes. Add peanut butter, SPLENDA®, soy sauce, and peanuts. Mix gently to combine. Re-cover and continue to cook on HIGH for 1 minute. Gently stir again. Serve at once.

HINT: If using frozen green beans, thaw by placing in a colander and rinsing under hot water for 1 minute.

Each serving equals:

HE: 1½ Vegetable • ½ Fat • ⅓ Protein

79 Calories • 3 gm Fat • 3 gm Protein • 10 gm Carbohydrate • 190 mg Sodium • 29 mg Calcium • 2 gm Fiber

DIABETIC EXCHANGES: 1 Vegetable • ½ Fat

Rising Sun Carrots

What a sunny plate pleaser this microwave vegetable dish is! It's visually appealing and shows off the natural sweetness of the carrot.

😊 Serves 6 (⅔ cup)

> 3 cups frozen cut carrots, thawed
> ½ cup chopped green bell pepper
> ¼ cup chopped onion
> 2 tablespoons water
> 1 (10¾-ounce) can reduced-fat tomato soup
> 1 (8-ounce) can sliced water chestnuts, drained
> 2 tablespoons SPLENDA® Granular
> 1½ teaspoons Oriental or five-Spice seasoning

In an 8-cup glass measuring bowl, combine carrots, green pepper, onion, and water. Cover and microwave on HIGH (100% power) for 8 to 10 minutes or until carrots are just tender, stirring after 5 minutes. Stir in tomato soup, water chestnuts, SPLENDA®, and Oriental seasoning. Re-cover and continue to microwave on HIGH for 3 to 4 minutes or until mixture is heated through. Gently stir again. Serve at once.

HINT: Thaw carrots by placing in a colander and rinsing under hot water for 1 minute.

Each serving equals:

HE: 1¾ Vegetable • ¼ Slider • 12 Optional Calories

81 Calories • 1 gm Fat • 1 gm Protein •
17 gm Carbohydrate • 228 mg Sodium •
24 mg Calcium • 3 gm Fiber

DIABETIC EXCHANGES: 1½ Vegetable • ½ Carbohydrate

Mexican Succotash Side Dish

If you've been in the habit of peeling your zucchini before cooking, please stop! There are so many good-for-you nutrients in the peel—I don't want you to miss a single one.   ☻   Serves 4 (1 cup)

> *½ cup chopped onion*
> *2 cups chopped unpeeled zucchini*
> *1 (15-ounce) can diced tomatoes, undrained*
> *1½ cups frozen whole-kernel corn, thawed*
> *2 tablespoons SPLENDA® Granular*
> *1 teaspoon chili seasoning*
> *⅛ teaspoon black pepper*

In a large skillet sprayed with butter-flavored cooking spray, sauté onion and zucchini for 10 minutes or just until vegetables are tender. Stir in undrained tomatoes. Add corn, SPLENDA®, chili seasoning, and black pepper. Mix well to combine. Lower heat and simmer for 5 minutes or until mixture is heated through, stirring occasionally.

HINT: Thaw corn by placing in a colander and rinsing under hot water for 1 minute.

Each serving equals:

HE: 2¼ Vegetable • ¾ Bread • 3 Optional Calories

104 Calories • 0 gm Fat • 4 gm Protein •
22 gm Carbohydrate • 146 mg Sodium •
35 mg Calcium • 4 gm Fiber

DIABETIC EXCHANGES: 2 Vegetable • 1 Starch

Tex-Mex Veggie Skillet

Cliff likes this spicy mix alongside his favorite meat loaf, but his "favorite" changes all the time. (A good thing, too, since he's my primary taste tester!) ☻ Serves 4 (¾ cup)

> 2 cups frozen cut green beans, thawed
> 1 cup chopped red pepper
> ½ cup chopped onion
> 1 cup frozen whole-kernel corn, thawed
> 1 (8-ounce) can tomato sauce
> 2 tablespoons SPLENDA® Granular
> 1 teaspoon chili seasoning

In a large skillet sprayed with butter-flavored cooking spray, sauté green beans, red pepper, and onion for 10 minutes or just until vegetables are tender. Stir in corn. Add tomato sauce, SPLENDA®, and chili seasoning. Mix well to combine. Lower heat and simmer for 6 to 8 minutes, stirring occasionally.

HINT: Thaw green beans and corn by placing in a colander and rinsing under hot water for 1 minute.

Each serving equals:

HE: 2¾ Vegetable • ½ Bread • 3 Optional Calories

104 Calories • 0 gm Fat • 4 gm Protein •
22 gm Carbohydrate • 381 mg Sodium •
45 mg Calcium • 5 gm Fiber

DIABETIC EXCHANGES: 2½ Vegetable • ½ Starch

Kraut and Tomato Bake

Most people have never done anything with sauerkraut except spoon it on top of hot dogs, but I saw greater potential in its tangy taste. Surprise yourself tonight with this splendid dish.

○ Serves 4

> 1 (15-ounce) can diced tomatoes, drained and ⅓ cup liquid
>   reserved
> 20 Ritz reduced-fat crackers, made into crumbs
> 1 (15-ounce) can sauerkraut, well drained
> 2 tablespoons SPLENDA® Granular
> 1 teaspoon dried onion flakes
> ⅛ teaspoon black pepper

Preheat oven to 350 degrees. Spray an 8-by-8-inch baking dish with butter-flavored cooking spray. Arrange tomatoes in prepared baking dish. Sprinkle half of cracker crumbs over tomatoes. Arrange sauerkraut evenly over cracker crumbs. Stir SPLENDA®, onion flakes, and black pepper into reserved tomato liquid. Pour liquid mixture evenly over top. Sprinkle remaining cracker crumbs over top. Lightly spray top of crumbs with butter-flavored cooking spray. Bake for 30 minutes. Place baking dish on a wire rack and let set for 5 minutes. Divide into 4 servings.

HINTS: 1. A self-seal sandwich bag works great for crushing crackers.
2. Place sauerkraut in a colander and press juice out with a sturdy spoon.

Each serving equals:

HE: 2 Vegetable • 1 Bread • 3 Optional Calories

---

98 Calories • 2 gm Fat • 2 gm Protein •
18 gm Carbohydrate • 522 mg Sodium •
50 mg Calcium • 3 gm Fiber

DIABETIC EXCHANGES: 2 Vegetable • 1 Starch

Baked Kraut Side Dish

It's savory and a bit of a surprise, but you'll soon discover that noodles and sauerkraut can be delicious partners in culinary pleasure. Keep your pantry well-stocked, and you've got some easy veggie dishes in your repertoire now.   ☺   Serves 6

> 1/2 cup chopped onion
> 1 (15-ounce) can diced tomatoes, undrained
> 1/2 cup SPLENDA® Granular
> 1 (15-ounce) can sauerkraut, well drained
> 1 1/2 cups cooked noodles, rinsed and drained
> 1/4 cup purchased real bacon bits

Preheat oven to 350 degrees. Spray an 8-by-8-inch baking dish with butter-flavored cooking spray. In a large skillet sprayed with butter-flavored cooking spray, sauté onion for 5 minutes or until tender. Stir in undrained tomatoes and SPLENDA®. Add sauerkraut, noodles, and bacon bits. Mix well to combine. Spread mixture into prepared baking dish. Bake for 30 minutes. Place baking dish on a wire rack and let set for 5 minutes. Divide into 6 servings.

HINT: Place sauerkraut in a colander and press juice out with a sturdy spoon.

Each serving equals:

HE: 1 1/2 Vegetable • 1/2 Bread • 1/4 Slider •
5 Optional Calories

---

101 Calories • 1 gm Fat • 5 gm Protein •
18 gm Carbohydrate • 404 mg Sodium •
29 mg Calcium • 2 gm Fiber

DIABETIC EXCHANGES: 1 1/2 Vegetable • 1 Starch

Rosemary Stewed Tomatoes

This aromatic blend will perfume your kitchen as it simmers, inspiring your taste buds to happy dreams of dinner!

○ Serves 4 (½ cup)

¾ cup finely chopped celery
¾ cup finely chopped onion
2 (15-ounce) cans diced tomatoes, undrained
¼ cup SPLENDA® Granular
1 teaspoon dried rosemary
2 teaspoons reduced-calorie margarine
⅛ teaspoon black pepper

In a medium saucepan sprayed with butter-flavored cooking spray, sauté celery and onion for 6 to 8 minutes or just until vegetables are tender. Stir in undrained tomatoes. Add SPLENDA®, rosemary, margarine, and black pepper. Mix well to combine. Lower heat and simmer for 10 minutes or until mixture is heated through, stirring occasionally.

Each serving equals:

HE: 2¾ Vegetable • ¼ Fat • 6 Optional Calories

---

77 Calories • 1 gm Fat • 2 gm Protein •
15 gm Carbohydrate • 313 mg Sodium •
55 mg Calcium • 4 gm Fiber

DIABETIC EXCHANGES: 2½ Vegetable

Corn in Mustard-Butter Sauce

Make every meal just a bit more special by adding a yummy sauce to your canned veggies. This one is simple but absolutely superb.

● Serves 4 (⅓ cup)

> *2 teaspoons reduced-calorie margarine*
> *1 tablespoon prepared yellow mustard*
> *1 teaspoon dried parsley flakes*
> *1 (15-ounce) can whole-kernel corn, rinsed and drained*
> *1 tablespoon SPLENDA® Granular*

In a medium saucepan, combine margarine, mustard, and parsley flakes. Stir in corn and SPLENDA®. Cover and simmer for 6 to 8 minutes or until mixture is heated through, stirring occasionally.

Each serving equals:

HE: 1 Bread • ¼ Fat • 2 Optional Calories

82 Calories • 2 gm Fat • 2 gm Protein •
14 gm Carbohydrate • 178 mg Sodium •
8 mg Calcium • 1 gm Fiber

DIABETIC EXCHANGES: 1 Starch

Corn-Tomato Skillet

Garden-fresh tomatoes can be deliciously combined with a handy bag of frozen corn for a summery sweet taste that is downright irresistible. (You could scrape the kernels off fresh corn if you wanted, but it would take quite a few ears!)   ☻   Serves 6 (½ cup)

> ¾ cup chopped green bell pepper
> ¾ cup chopped onion
> 3 cups peeled and chopped fresh tomatoes
> 2 cups frozen whole-kernel corn, thawed
> ¼ cup SPLENDA® Granular
> 1½ teaspoons dried basil
> ⅛ teaspoon black pepper

In a large skillet sprayed with butter-flavored cooking spray, sauté green pepper and onion for 6 to 8 minutes or just until vegetables are tender. Add tomatoes, corn, SPLENDA®, basil, and black pepper. Mix well to combine. Lower heat and simmer for 12 to 15 minutes, stirring occasionally.

Each serving equals:

HE: 1½ Vegetable • ⅔ Bread • 4 Optional Calories

88 Calories • 0 gm Fat • 2 gm Protein •
20 gm Carbohydrate • 10 mg Sodium •
11 mg Calcium • 3 gm Fiber

DIABETIC EXCHANGES: 1½ Vegetable • 1 Starch

Onion Patties

If you've got onion lovers in the family, here's a fresh and interesting way to provide a savory side dish that celebrates their special spirit! And if chopping all those onions seems like too big a job, use a bag of frozen chopped onions (but thaw and drain them well first).

☉ Serves 6 (5 each)

¾ cup all-purpose flour	½ teaspoon table salt
⅔ cup nonfat dry milk powder	1 teaspoon dried parsley flakes
2 teaspoons baking powder	1 tablespoon yellow cornmeal
1 tablespoon SPLENDA®	½ cup water
Granular	3 cups finely diced onion

In a medium bowl, combine flour, dry milk powder, baking powder, SPLENDA®, salt, parsley flakes, and cornmeal. Stir in water. Add onion. Mix well to combine. Drop by tablespoon onto hot griddle or skillet sprayed with butter-flavored cooking spray to make 30 patties. Brown for about 2 to 3 minutes on each side.

HINTS: 1. Respray griddle with butter-flavored cooking spray between browning each batch.
2. Cover plate of browned patties with foil to keep patties warm while browning other batches.

Each serving equals:

HE: 1 Vegetable • ⅔ Bread • ⅓ Fat-Free Milk •
6 Optional Calories

116 Calories • 0 gm Fat • 5 gm Protein •
24 gm Carbohydrate • 400 mg Sodium •
209 mg Calcium • 2 gm Fiber

DIABETIC EXCHANGES: 1 Vegetable •
1 Starch/Carbohydrate

Quick & Easy Veggie Side Dish

On one of those nights where you and the kids just want something tasty and fast, here's a dish that will satisfy in just a few minutes! Instead of calling for takeout, make your own.

● Serves 4 (1 cup)

> 1 cup chopped onion
> 1½ cups chopped celery
> 1 (15-ounce) can diced tomatoes, undrained
> 1 (8-ounce) can tomato sauce
> 2 tablespoons SPLENDA® Granular
> 2 tablespoons reduced-sodium soy sauce
> ⅛ teaspoon black pepper
> 1½ cups cooked elbow macaroni, rinsed and drained

In a large skillet sprayed with butter-flavored cooking spray, sauté onion and celery for 6 to 8 minutes or just until tender. Add undrained tomatoes, tomato sauce, SPLENDA®, soy sauce, and black pepper. Mix well to combine. Stir in macaroni. Lower heat and simmer for 5 minutes or until mixture is heated through, stirring occasionally.

HINT: Usually 1 full cup uncooked elbow macaroni cooks to about 1½ cups.

Each serving equals:

HE: 3¼ Vegetable • ¾ Bread • 3 Optional Calories

---

144 Calories • 0 gm Fat • 5 gm Protein •
31 gm Carbohydrate • 706 mg Sodium •
55 mg Calcium • 5 gm Fiber

DIABETIC EXCHANGES: 3 Vegetable • 1 Starch

Broccoli Corn Bake

There are so many health benefits from eating broccoli, I won't take the time to list them here. If you've never been a fan of this great green veggie, why not give this dish a try? The cheesy sauce transforms a simple side dish into something grand!

● Serves 6

> 3 cups frozen cut broccoli, thawed and
>   finely chopped
> 2 cups water
> 1 (12-fluid-ounce) can evaporated fat-free milk
> 3 tablespoons all-purpose flour
> ¾ cup (3 ounces) shredded reduced-fat
>   Cheddar cheese
> 1 (4-ounce) can sliced mushrooms, drained
> 2½ cups frozen whole-kernel corn, thawed
> 2 tablespoons SPLENDA® Granular
> ⅛ teaspoon black pepper

Preheat oven to 350 degrees. Spray an 8-by-8-inch baking dish with butter-flavored cooking spray. In a medium saucepan, cook broccoli in water just until tender. Drain well. In a covered jar, combine evaporated milk and flour. Shake well to blend. Pour milk mixture into same saucepan. Add Cheddar cheese and mushrooms. Mix well to combine. Cook over medium heat until mixture thickens and cheese melts, stirring often. Stir in broccoli and corn. Add SPLENDA® and black pepper. Mix well to combine. Pour into prepared baking dish. Bake for 45 to 50 minutes. Place baking dish on a wire rack and let set for 5 minutes. Divide into 6 servings.

HINT: Thaw frozen vegetables by placing in a colander and rinsing under hot water for 1 minute.

Each serving equals:

HE: 1⅓ Vegetable • 1 Bread • ⅔ Protein •
½ Fat-Free Milk • 2 Optional Calories

207 Calories • 3 gm Fat • 13 gm Protein •
32 gm Carbohydrate • 331 mg Sodium •
303 mg Calcium • 4 gm Fiber

DIABETIC EXCHANGES: 1 Vegetable • 1 Starch •
½ Meat • ½ Fat-Free Milk

Corn Bread Pudding

My heart beats fast when I see the words "bread pudding," but usually it's not until the dessert course! Here, I've taken that special treat and made it savory instead of sweet. I bet one taste will make you shout, "Wow!"   ☺   Serves 6

> 1 (15-ounce) can cream-style corn
> 1 (12-fluid-ounce) can evaporated fat-free milk
> 1 egg or equivalent in egg substitute
> ¼ cup no-fat sour cream
> 1 tablespoon SPLENDA® Granular
> 1 teaspoon dried parsley flakes
> ⅛ teaspoon black pepper
> 4 slices reduced-calorie white bread, torn into small pieces

Preheat oven to 325 degrees. Spray an 8-by-8-inch baking dish with butter-flavored cooking spray. In a large bowl, combine cream-style corn, evaporated milk, egg, and sour cream. Stir in SPLENDA®, parsley flakes, and black pepper. Add bread pieces. Mix well to combine. Spread mixture into prepared baking dish. Bake for 60 minutes or until center is firm. Place baking dish on a wire rack and let set for 5 minutes. Divide into 6 servings.

Each serving equals:

HE: 1 Bread • ½ Fat-Free Milk • ¼ Slider •
3 Optional Calories

161 Calories • 1 gm Fat • 8 gm Protein •
30 gm Carbohydrate • 423 mg Sodium •
192 mg Calcium • 1 gm Fiber

DIABETIC EXCHANGES: 1 Starch • ½ Fat-Free Milk

Boarding House Scalloped Corn

Extra! Extra! Read all about it! Creamed corn is actually a healthy ingredient and shouldn't be eliminated from your diet, even if its name sounds all too lush. Here, it provides delectable creaminess to a baked corn pudding.　　❍　　Serves 6

> 1 (15-ounce) can cream-style corn
> ⅔ cup nonfat dry milk powder
> ¾ cup water
> 2 eggs, beaten, or equivalent in egg substitute
> 1 teaspoon dried parsley flakes
> 1 teaspoon dried onion flakes
> 1 tablespoon SPLENDA® Granular
> ⅛ teaspoon black pepper
> 14 small fat-free soda crackers, made into crumbs

Preheat oven to 350 degrees. Spray an 8-by-8-inch baking dish with butter-flavored cooking spray. In a large bowl, combine cream-style corn, dry milk powder, and water. Stir in eggs, parsley flakes, onion flakes, SPLENDA®, and black pepper. Add cracker crumbs. Mix well to combine. Pour mixture into prepared baking dish. Bake for 35 to 40 minutes. Place baking dish on a wire rack and let set for 5 minutes. Divide into 6 servings.

HINT: A self-seal sandwich bag works great for crushing soda crackers.

Each serving equals:

HE: 1 Bread • ⅓ Fat-Free Milk • ⅓ Protein • 1 Optional Calorie

---

146 Calories • 2 gm Fat • 7 gm Protein • 25 gm Carbohydrate • 390 mg Sodium • 116 mg Calcium • 1 gm Fiber

---

DIABETIC EXCHANGES: 1½ Starch

Spanish Butter Beans

Tired of eating green beans night after night? Here's an easy way to add variety to your vegetable menu! ☺ Serves 4 (⅔ cup)

½ cup chopped onion

1 (15-ounce) can diced tomatoes, undrained

2 tablespoons SPLENDA® Granular

⅛ teaspoon black pepper

1 (15-ounce) can butter beans, rinsed and drained

In a large skillet sprayed with butter-flavored cooking spray, sauté onion for 5 minutes or just until tender. Add undrained tomatoes, SPLENDA®, and black pepper. Stir in butter beans. Lower heat and simmer for 10 minutes, stirring occasionally.

Each serving equals:

HE: 1¼ Vegetable • ¾ Protein • ½ Bread • 3 Optional Calories

88 Calories • 0 gm Fat • 4 gm Protein • 18 gm Carbohydrate • 307 mg Sodium • 46 mg Calcium • 5 gm Fiber

DIABETIC EXCHANGES: 1 Vegetable • ½ Starch • ½ Meat

Butter Bean and Apple Skillet

I created this recipe when a basket of fresh-picked apples was sitting on my kitchen counter. "Why not apples and butter beans?" I asked myself. This recipe is the mouthwatering answer to that question. ☻ Serves 4 (½ cup)

½ cup finely chopped onion
1 (15-ounce) can butter beans, rinsed and drained
1 cup (2 small) cored, peeled, and coarsely chopped
    cooking apples
½ cup unsweetened apple juice
1 tablespoon + 1 teaspoon reduced-calorie margarine
2 tablespoons SPLENDA® Granular
1 tablespoon apple cider vinegar

In a large skillet sprayed with butter-flavored cooking spray, sauté onion for 5 minutes or just until tender. Add butter beans, apples, and apple juice. Mix well to combine. Stir in margarine, SPLENDA®, and vinegar. Bring mixture to a boil. Lower heat and simmer for 15 minutes or until apples are tender and most of liquid is absorbed, stirring occasionally.

Each serving equals:

HE: ¾ Protein • ¾ Fruit • ½ Bread • ½ Fat •
¼ Vegetable • 3 Optional Calories

114 Calories • 2 gm Fat • 4 gm Protein •
20 gm Carbohydrate • 209 mg Sodium •
32 mg Calcium • 4 gm Fiber

DIABETIC EXCHANGES: 1 Fruit • ½ Meat • ½ Starch •
½ Fat

Better-Than-Baked-Beans Side Dish

Ever made your own baked beans, or have you always told yourself that the canned kind was "good enough"? Well, I decided that good enough could always be made better, and I think you'll agree when you taste this version. ◐ Serves 4

½ cup finely chopped onion
1 (15-ounce) can diced
    tomatoes, undrained
1 (8-ounce) can tomato sauce
¼ cup SPLENDA® Granular
1 teaspoon prepared yellow
    mustard

1 teaspoon dried parsley flakes
1 (15-ounce) can great
    northern beans, rinsed
    and drained
1½ cups cooked rice
¼ cup purchased real
    bacon bits

Preheat oven to 350 degrees. Spray an 8-by-8-inch baking dish with butter-flavored cooking spray. In a large skillet sprayed with butter-flavored cooking spray, sauté onion for 5 minutes or just until tender. Stir in undrained tomatoes, tomato sauce, SPLENDA®, mustard, and parsley flakes. Add great northern beans, rice, and bacon bits. Mix well to combine. Spread mixture into pre-pared baking dish. Bake for 30 minutes. Place baking dish on a wire rack and let set for 5 minutes. Divide into 4 servings.

HINT: Usually 1 cup uncooked instant rice cooks to about 1½ cups.

Each serving equals:

HE: 2¼ Vegetable • 1 Bread • 1 Protein • ¼ Slider • 11 Optional Calories

202 Calories • 2 gm Fat • 11 gm Protein • 35 gm Carbohydrate • 674 mg Sodium • 72 mg Calcium • 6 gm Fiber

DIABETIC EXCHANGES: 2 Vegetable • 1½ Starch • 1 Meat

Carrot Rice Side Dish

Talk about luscious—this baked veggie casserole is as pretty to look at as it is cozy and warm. It's a festive luncheon dish that all will enjoy. ☺ Serves 6

> 1 (12-fluid-ounce) can evaporated fat-free milk
> 1 egg, beaten, or equivalent in egg substitute
> 1 tablespoon SPLENDA® Granular
> 1 teaspoon dried parsley flakes
> 1 teaspoon dried onion flakes
> ⅛ teaspoon black pepper
> 1½ cups cooked rice
> 1 (15-ounce) can sliced carrots, rinsed and drained
> 1 tablespoon + 1 teaspoon reduced-calorie margarine

Preheat oven to 350 degrees. Spray an 8-by-8-inch baking dish with butter-flavored cooking spray. In a large bowl, combine evaporated milk, egg, and SPLENDA®. Stir in parsley flakes, onion flakes, and black pepper. Add rice, carrots, and margarine. Mix well to combine. Spread mixture into prepared baking dish. Bake for 45 to 50 minutes. Place baking dish on a wire rack and let set 5 minutes. Divide into 6 servings.

HINT: Usually 1 cup uncooked instant rice cooks to about 1½ cups.

Each serving equals:

HE: ⅔ Vegetable • ½ Fat-Free Milk • ½ Bread • ⅓ Fat • 11 Optional Calories

---

126 Calories • 2 gm Fat • 6 gm Protein • 21 gm Carbohydrate • 228 mg Sodium • 182 mg Calcium • 1 gm Fiber

---

DIABETIC EXCHANGES: 1 Starch • ½ Fat-Free Milk • ½ Vegetable • ½ Fat

Pasta Broccoli Side Dish

Broccoli makes a beautiful contrast when served with pasta, so if you're making chicken cutlets or a pale-colored entrée, consider this dish to jazz up the plate. ☻ Serves 4 (1 full cup)

½ cup chopped onion

3 cups frozen chopped broccoli, thawed

1 (15-ounce) can diced tomatoes, undrained

2 tablespoons SPLENDA® Granular

1 (2½-ounce) jar sliced mushrooms, drained

1 teaspoon Italian seasoning

2 cups cooked spaghetti, rinsed and drained

¼ cup grated fat-free Parmesan cheese

In a large skillet sprayed with butter-flavored cooking spray, sauté onion and broccoli for 5 minutes or just until vegetables are tender, stirring often. Stir in undrained tomatoes, SPLENDA®, mushrooms, and Italian seasoning. Add spaghetti. Mix well to combine. Lower heat and simmer for 10 minutes or until mixture is heated through, stirring occasionally. Just before serving, stir in Parmesan cheese.

HINT: Usually 1½ cups broken uncooked spaghetti cooks to about 2 cups.

Each serving equals:

HE: 3 Vegetable • 1 Bread • ¼ Protein •
3 Optional Calories

186 Calories • 2 gm Fat • 8 gm Protein •
34 gm Carbohydrate • 326 mg Sodium •
125 mg Calcium • 6 gm Fiber

DIABETIC EXCHANGES: 3 Vegetable • 1½ Starch

Cabbage & Green Beans with Noodles

Many cost-conscious shoppers move right on by the packages of precut veggies at the market, but when time is a concern, grab one! Not everyone has the urge or inclination to finely shred a bowl of cabbage for a dish like this one, but with a little "kitchen help," you can still serve it up!   ☻   Serves 4 (¾ cup)

2 teaspoons reduced-calorie margarine
2 cups finely shredded cabbage
1 cup frozen cut green beans, thawed
½ cup finely chopped onion
1 cup cooked noodles
1 tablespoon SPLENDA® Granular
⅛ teaspoon black pepper

In a large skillet sprayed with butter-flavored cooking spray, melt margarine. Stir in cabbage, green beans, and onion. Sauté for 6 to 8 minutes or just until vegetables are tender. Add noodles, SPLENDA®, and black pepper. Mix well to combine. Lower heat and simmer for 5 minutes or until mixture is heated through, stirring occasionally.

HINT: 1. Thaw green beans by placing in a colander and rinsing under hot water for one minute.
2. Usually a scant 1 cup uncooked noodles cooks to about 1 cup.

Each serving equals:

HE: 1¼ Vegetable • ½ Bread • ¼ Fat • 2 Optional Calories

94 Calories • 2 gm Fat • 3 gm Protein • 16 gm Carbohydrate • 38 mg Sodium • 42 mg Calcium • 3 gm Fiber

DIABETIC EXCHANGES: 1 Vegetable • 1 Starch

Angie's Rotini Cabbage Side Dish

My daughter-in-law Angie prefers colorful, crunchy dishes that will please everyone in the family. Sure, you could make this with plain rotini, but why settle for "okay" when you can have a little more color on your plate?　　❂　　Serves 4 (¾ cup)

> 4 cups finely shredded cabbage
> 2 cups cooked tricolored rotini pasta, rinsed and drained
> 1 tablespoon + 1 teaspoon reduced-calorie margarine
> 1 tablespoon SPLENDA® Granular
> ½ teaspoon lemon pepper

In a large skillet sprayed with butter-flavored cooking spray, sauté cabbage for 6 to 8 minutes or just until tender. Stir in rotini. Add margarine, SPLENDA®, and lemon pepper. Mix well to combine. Lower heat and simmer for 5 minutes, stirring occasionally.

HINT: Usually 1½ cups uncooked rotini pasta cooks to about 2 cups.

Each serving equals:

> HE: 1 Bread • 1 Vegetable • ½ Fat •
> 2 Optional Calories
> _____
> 122 Calories • 2 gm Fat • 3 gm Protein •
> 23 gm Carbohydrate • 123 mg Sodium •
> 43 mg Calcium • 2 gm Fiber
> _____
> DIABETIC EXCHANGES: 1 Starch • 1 Vegetable • ½ Fat

Creamy Green Beans
and Potatoes Side Dish

This super skillet sensation will remind you just why you should always keep some cans of evaporated fat-free milk on the pantry shelf. With that creamy "magic in a can," you can prepare a feast with very little fuss! 〇 Serves 4 (¾ cup)

2 cups frozen cut green beans,
  thawed
2 cups diced raw potatoes
1½ cups water
1 (12-fluid-ounce) can
  evaporated fat-free milk

3 tablespoons all-purpose flour
1 tablespoon SPLENDA®
  Granular
1 teaspoon dried parsley flakes
1 teaspoon lemon pepper

In a medium saucepan, combine green beans, potatoes, and water. Bring mixture to a boil. Continue cooking for 10 minutes or until beans and potatoes are tender. Drain well. In a covered jar, combine evaporated milk, flour, and SPLENDA®. Shake well to blend. Pour milk mixture into same saucepan. Stir in parsley flakes and lemon pepper. Cook over medium heat until mixture thickens, stirring often. Add drained green beans and potato mixture. Mix well to combine. Continue cooking for 5 minutes or until mixture is heated through, stirring often.

HINT: Thaw green beans by placing in a colander and rinsing under hot water for 1 minute.

Each serving equals:

HE: 1 Vegetable • ¾ Fat-Free Milk • ¾ Bread • 2 Optional Calories

172 Calories • 0 gm Fat • 9 gm Protein • 34 gm Carbohydrate • 184 mg Sodium • 273 mg Calcium • 3 gm Fiber

DIABETIC EXCHANGES: 1 Vegetable • 1 Fat-Free Milk • 1 Starch

Garden Patch Potatoes

Busy moms and dads will love this handy and yet oh-so-appetizing way to serve potatoes and veggies all in one! Grab a package of shredded carrots from the produce section, canned tomatoes from the shelf, and potatoes from your store's freezer, and you're ready to roll. ☻ Serves 4 (1 cup)

> 4½ cups shredded loose-packed frozen potatoes
> 1 cup finely shredded carrots
> ½ cup diced onion
> 1 (15-ounce) can diced tomatoes, undrained
> 1½ teaspoons prepared yellow mustard
> 2 tablespoons SPLENDA® Granular
> ⅛ teaspoon black pepper
> 2 tablespoons purchased real bacon bits

In a large skillet sprayed with butter-flavored cooking spray, sauté potatoes, carrots, and onion for 8 to 10 minutes. Stir in undrained tomatoes, mustard, SPLENDA®, and black pepper. Lower heat, cover, and simmer for 15 minutes, stirring occasionally. Add bacon bits. Mix well to combine. Continue simmering for 5 minutes or just until vegetables are tender, stirring often.

HINT: Raw shredded potatoes, rinsed and patted dry, may be used in place of frozen potatoes.

Each serving equals:

HE: 1¾ Vegetable • ¾ Bread • 15 Optional Calories

---

161 Calories • 1 gm Fat • 6 gm Protein •
32 gm Carbohydrate • 291 mg Sodium •
42 mg Calcium • 5 gm Fiber

DIABETIC EXCHANGES: 2 Vegetable • 1 Starch

Marvelous

Main Dishes

No matter how many scrumptious sides and crunchy salads you bring to the table, everyone is waiting for "the main event"—and who can blame them? The star attraction is what our tummies and taste buds yearn for, and all the recipes in this collection deliver spectacular flavor with just that irresistible touch of sweetness that makes each meal something to remember—with pleasure.

Break out of your mealtime rut with some entrées worthy of applause from those gathered at your table. If you're in the mood for seafood, why not spice things up with **Shrimp Creole** or **Spanish Shrimp?** If nothing satisfies like old-fashioned meat loaf, I offer you some delectable versions (**Bali Hai Meat Loaf, Teriyaki Meat Loaf**). And if you want to serve up a few surprises to your family, put **Main Dish Cornbread** or **Ham Florentine Pilaf** on the menu!

Summertime Zucchini Tomato Pie

If your garden is overflowing with zucchini, it must be summer! This great green veggie grows in such abundance, it can be difficult coming up with ways to cook it all! Here's my vote for a fabulous seasonal entrée that the whole family will love. ☻ Serves 6

2½ cups unpeeled chopped zucchini
1½ cups peeled and chopped fresh tomatoes
½ cup chopped onion
½ cup + 1 tablespoon shredded reduced-fat Cheddar cheese
1 (12-fluid-ounce) can evaporated fat-free milk
2 tablespoons SPLENDA® Granular
¾ cup reduced-fat biscuit baking mix
3 eggs or equivalent in egg substitute
1 teaspoon Italian seasoning

Preheat oven to 400 degrees. Spray a deep-dish 10-inch pie plate with olive oil-flavored cooking spray. Layer zucchini, tomatoes, onion, and Cheddar cheese in prepared pie plate. In a blender container, combine evaporated milk, SPLENDA®, baking mix, eggs, and Italian seasoning. Cover and process on HIGH for 20 seconds. Pour milk mixture evenly over top. Bake for 30 to 35 minutes or until a knife inserted in center comes out clean. Place pie plate on a wire rack and let set for 5 minutes. Cut into 6 wedges.

Each serving equals:

HE: 1½ Vegetable • 1 Protein • ½ Fat-Free Milk • ½ Bread • 2 Optional Calories

189 Calories • 5 gm Fat • 12 gm Protein • 24 gm Carbohydrate • 380 mg Sodium • 268 mg Calcium • 1 gm Fiber

DIABETIC EXCHANGES: 1 Vegetable • 1 Meat • ½ Fat-Free Milk • ½ Starch

Pasta with Broccoli & Bacon

If you're wondering why I don't use artificial bacon bits instead of the real thing, here are my reasons: I think real bacon tastes better, real bacon has better texture, and it doesn't get spongy when heated or combined with sauces.　　○　Serves 4 (scant 1 cup)

1 cup chopped fresh broccoli

1 (12-fluid-ounce) can evaporated fat-free milk

3 tablespoons all-purpose flour

1 tablespoon SPLENDA® Granular

1 teaspoon dried parsley flakes

½ cup water

1 cup + 2 tablespoons shredded reduced-fat mozzarella cheese

¼ cup purchased real bacon bits

1½ cups cooked rotini or rigatoni pasta, rinsed and drained

In a large skillet sprayed with butter-flavored cooking spray, sauté broccoli for 5 minutes. In a covered jar, combine evaporated milk, flour, SPLENDA®, and parsley flakes. Shake well to blend. Pour milk mixture into skillet with broccoli. Add water. Mix well to combine. Stir in mozzarella cheese, bacon bits, and rotini pasta. Lower heat and simmer for 5 to 6 minutes or until mixture is heated through and cheeses are melted, stirring occasionally.

HINT: Usually a full 1 cup uncooked rotini pasta cooks to about 1½ cups.

Each serving equals:

HE: 1½ Protein • 1 Bread • ¾ Fat-Free Milk •
½ Vegetable • ¼ Slider • 6 Optional Calories

300 Calories • 8 gm Fat • 24 gm Protein •
33 gm Carbohydrate • 629 mg Sodium •
532 mg Calcium • 1 gm Fiber

DIABETIC EXCHANGES: 2 Meat • 1 Starch •
1 Fat-Free Milk • ¼ Vegetable

Shrimp Creole

Do you find you're eating shrimp more often now that the big-box stores like Costco offer such great prices on bags of frozen shrimp? Even if you live nowhere near a harbor, you can still satisfy your urge for healthy, spicy seafood! ☻ Serves 4 (1 cup)

½ cup finely chopped onion
½ cup finely chopped green
    bell pepper
1 (14½-ounce) can stewed
    tomatoes
1 tablespoon white distilled
    vinegar
1 tablespoon SPLENDA®
    Granular

2 to 3 drops hot sauce
⅛ teaspoon ground oregano
⅛ teaspoon black pepper
1½ cups cooked rice
1 (5-ounce) package frozen
    shrimp, cooked and
    drained

In a large skillet sprayed with butter-flavored cooking spray, sauté onion and green pepper for 6 to 8 minutes or just until vegetables are tender. Add stewed tomatoes, vinegar, SPLENDA®, hot sauce, oregano, and black pepper. Mix well to combine. Lower heat and simmer for 15 minutes, stirring occasionally. Stir in rice and shrimp. Continue simmering for 5 minutes or until mixture is heated through, stirring occasionally.

HINT: Usually 1 cup uncooked instant rice cooks to about 1½ cups.

Each serving equals:

HE: 1½ Vegetable • 1¼ Protein • ¾ Bread •
2 Optional Calories

---

141 Calories • 1 gm Fat • 10 gm Protein •
23 gm Carbohydrate • 310 mg Sodium •
54 mg Calcium • 2 gm Fiber

DIABETIC EXCHANGES: 1½ Vegetable • 1 Meat •
1 Starch

Spanish Shrimp

Notice that I suggest 2 to 3 drops of hot sauce in this zesty recipe! Anyone who wants it hotter can add a bit more (or a lot more) at the table. By sampling hot sauces from different parts of the country and from all over the world, you can vary this dish every time you make it. ☻ Serves 4 (1 cup)

1 (8-ounce) can tomato sauce
1 (15-ounce) can diced tomatoes, undrained
2 to 3 drops hot sauce
½ cup frozen peas, thawed
1 cup uncooked instant rice
1 (5-ounce) package frozen shrimp, cooked and drained
1½ teaspoons chili seasoning
1 tablespoon SPLENDA® Granular
1 tablespoon chopped fresh parsley or 1 teaspoon dried parsley
    flakes

In a large skillet sprayed with butter-flavored cooking spray, combine tomato sauce, undrained tomatoes, and hot sauce. Bring mixture to a boil. Add peas, uncooked rice, shrimp, chili seasoning, SPLENDA®, and parsley. Mix well to combine. Lower heat, cover, and simmer for 10 minutes, stirring occasionally.

Each serving equals:

HE: 2 Vegetable • 1¼ Protein • 1 Bread •
2 Optional Calories

177 Calories • 1 gm Fat • 12 gm Protein •
30 gm Carbohydrate • 531 mg Sodium •
48 mg Calcium • 4 gm Fiber

DIABETIC EXCHANGES: 2 Vegetable • 1 Meat • 1 Starch

Chicken with Caribbean Pecan Sauce

Sweet, sensuous, and utterly enchanting, this scrumptious supper dish that celebrates the culinary charms of the Caribbean is just a treat! A tiny amount of my favorite nut lends this recipe real tropical magic. ☻ Serves 4

> 16 ounces skinned and boned uncooked chicken breast,
>   cut into 4 pieces
> ½ cup unsweetened orange juice
> 2 tablespoons cornstarch
> ⅓ cup SPLENDA® Granular
> 1 (8-ounce) can crushed pineapple, packed in fruit juice,
>   undrained
> 1 (11-ounce) can mandarin oranges, rinsed and
>   drained
> 2 tablespoons chopped pecans
> 1½ teaspoons dried parsley flakes
> 1½ teaspoons dried onion flakes

In a large skillet sprayed with butter-flavored cooking spray, brown chicken pieces for 4 to 5 minutes on each side. Meanwhile, in a covered jar, combine orange juice, cornstarch, and SPLENDA®. Shake well to blend. Pour mixture into a medium saucepan sprayed with butter-flavored cooking spray. Stir in undrained pineapple. Cook over medium heat until mixture thickens, stirring constantly. Remove from heat. Add mandarin oranges, pecans, parsley flakes, and onion flakes. Mix well to combine. Evenly spoon sauce mixture over browned chicken pieces. Lower heat and simmer for 5 minutes. When serving, evenly spoon sauce over chicken pieces.

Each serving equals:

HE: 3 Protein • 1¼ Fruit • ¼ Fat • ¼ Slider •
3 Optional Calories

253 Calories • 5 gm Fat • 24 gm Protein •
28 gm Carbohydrate • 61 mg Sodium •
26 mg Calcium • 1 gm Fiber

DIABETIC EXCHANGES: 3 Meat • 1 Fruit • ½ Starch •
½ Fat

Sweet and Sour Chicken

Forget about the overly sweet and sticky version you may have tasted in a Chinese restaurant—this dish takes an appealing idea and makes it genuinely great! It's a winner for kids of all ages.

○ Serves 4 (1 cup)

> 16 ounces skinned and boned uncooked chicken breast, cut into bite-size pieces
> 1 cup sliced carrots
> 1 cup coarsely chopped green bell pepper
> 1 cup coarsely chopped onion
> 1 (8-ounce) can tomato sauce
> 1 (8-ounce) can pineapple tidbits, packed in fruit juice, undrained
> 2 tablespoons SPLENDA® Granular
> ⅛ teaspoon dried minced garlic
> ½ cup unsweetened orange juice
> 2 tablespoons cornstarch

In a large skillet sprayed with butter-flavored cooking spray, sauté chicken, carrots, green pepper, and onion for 6 to 8 minutes. Add tomato sauce, undrained pineapple, SPLENDA®, and garlic. Mix well to combine. In a small bowl, combine orange juice and cornstarch. Stir orange juice mixture into chicken mixture. Continue cooking for 5 minutes or until mixture thickens, stirring often.

HINT: Good over rice or toast or as is.

Each serving equals:

HE: 3 Protein • 2½ Vegetable • ¾ Fruit •
18 Optional Calories

235 Calories • 3 gm Fat • 25 gm Protein •
27 gm Carbohydrate • 438 mg Sodium •
43 mg Calcium • 3 gm Fiber

DIABETIC EXCHANGES: 3 Meat • 2 Vegetable • 1 Fruit

Easy Chicken Cacciatore Skillet

If you love good old-fashioned Italian cooking but feel you don't always have the time to prepare the "real thing," I suggest this dish that has all the taste of the original but can be ready in much less time.   ☻   Serves 4 (full 1 cup)

16 ounces skinned and boned
    uncooked chicken breast,
    cut into bite-size pieces
¾ cup chopped onion
¾ cup chopped green
    bell pepper
1 (8-ounce) can tomato sauce
1 (15-ounce) can diced
    tomatoes, undrained

2 tablespoons SPLENDA®
    Granular
1 (2½-ounce) jar sliced
    mushrooms, drained
¼ cup sliced ripe olives
1½ teaspoons Italian seasoning
⅛ teaspoon black pepper
1½ cups hot cooked noodles,
    rinsed and drained

In a large skillet sprayed with olive oil-flavored cooking spray, sauté chicken, onion, and green pepper for 6 to 8 minutes. Stir in tomato sauce, undrained tomatoes, and SPLENDA®. Add mushrooms, olives, Italian seasoning, and black pepper. Mix well to combine. Stir in noodles. Lower heat and simmer for 10 to 12 minutes, stirring occasionally.

HINT: Usually 1¼ cups uncooked noodles cooks to about 1½ cups.

Each serving equals:

HE: 3 Protein • 3 Vegetable • ¾ Bread • ¼ Fat •
3 Optional Calories

265 Calories • 5 gm Fat • 28 gm Protein •
27 gm Carbohydrate • 604 mg Sodium •
62 mg Calcium • 4 gm Fiber

DIABETIC EXCHANGES: 3 Meat • 2 Vegetable • 1 Starch

Baked Italian Chicken

If you don't always feel like turning on your oven in the warmer months, consider upgrading your toaster oven to one that's roomy enough to handle my favorite baking dish, the 8-by-8-inch pan. You may have to adjust cooking times for your new oven, but you'll be pleased how much cooler your house is. ☻   Serves 4

> 16 ounces skinned and boned uncooked chicken breast, cut into 4 pieces
> 1 (8-ounce) can tomato sauce
> 1 (8-ounce) can tomatoes, finely chopped and undrained
> 1½ teaspoons Italian seasoning
> 2 tablespoons SPLENDA® Granular
> ¼ cup grated reduced-fat Parmesan cheese
> 1 (4-ounce) jar sliced mushrooms, drained

Preheat oven to 350 degrees. Spray an 8-by-8-inch baking dish with olive oil-flavored cooking spray. Evenly arrange chicken pieces in prepared baking dish. In a medium bowl, combine tomato sauce, undrained tomatoes, Italian seasoning, and SPLENDA®. Stir in Parmesan cheese and mushrooms. Spoon sauce mixture evenly over chicken pieces. Bake for 45 minutes or until chicken is tender. When serving, evenly spoon sauce mixture over chicken pieces.

Each serving equals:

HE: 3¼ Protein • 2 Vegetable • 3 Optional Calories

176 Calories • 4 gm Fat • 25 gm Protein •
10 gm Carbohydrate • 706 mg Sodium •
67 mg Calcium • 2 gm Fiber

DIABETIC EXCHANGES: 3 Meat • 1½ Vegetable

Bali Hai Meat Loaf

Don't you want to believe that Bali Hai is a real place, not a figment of James Michener's imagination? The island paradise, said to be home to beautiful women and fabulous feasts, was celebrated in song in the musical, *South Pacific*. (It turns out that it's based on a real Tahitian volcanic island called Ambae.)   ☺   Serves 6

> 16 ounces extra-lean ground sirloin beef or turkey breast
> 3/4 cup purchased graham cracker crumbs or 12 (2 1/2-inch)
>   graham cracker squares, made into crumbs
> 3/4 cup finely chopped onion
> 3/4 cup finely chopped green bell pepper
> 1 (8-ounce) can crushed pineapple, packed in fruit juice,
>   undrained
> 1/4 cup SPLENDA® Granular
> 1/2 teaspoon ground ginger
> 1 teaspoon dried parsley flakes

Preheat oven to 350 degrees. Spray a 9-by-5-inch loaf pan with butter-flavored cooking spray. In a large bowl, combine meat, graham cracker crumbs, onion, green pepper, undrained pineapple, SPLENDA®, ginger, and parsley flakes. Mix well to combine. Pat mixture into prepared loaf pan. Bake for 55 to 60 minutes. Place loaf pan on a wire rack and let set for 5 minutes. Cut into 6 servings.

Each serving equals:

> HE: 2 Protein • 1/2 Bread • 1/2 Vegetable • 1/3 Fruit •
> 4 Optional Calories
> _____
> 160 Calories • 4 gm Fat • 16 gm Protein •
> 15 gm Carbohydrate • 108 mg Sodium •
> 14 mg Calcium • 1 gm Fiber
> _____
> DIABETIC EXCHANGES: 2 Meat • 1/2 Starch •
> 1/2 Vegetable

Teriyaki Meat Loaf

Here's a perfect mix of East and West—an all-American dish like meat loaf, but served with a sauce that invites the diner to gaze with affection toward exotic Japan. The word "teriyaki" actually means "glossy roast"—which is a pretty good way to describe the look and taste of this dish.   ☻   Serves 6

> 16 ounces extra-lean ground sirloin beef or turkey breast
> ½ cup + 1 tablespoon dried fine bread crumbs
> 1 cup finely chopped onion
> ½ cup finely chopped green bell pepper
> ¼ teaspoon dried minced garlic
> ¼ cup reduced-sodium soy sauce
> 2 tablespoons SPLENDA® Granular
> 2 teaspoons lemon juice

Preheat oven to 350 degrees. Spray a 9-by-5-inch loaf pan with butter-flavored cooking spray. In a large bowl, combine meat, bread crumbs, onion, green pepper, garlic, soy sauce, SPLENDA®, and lemon juice. Mix well to combine. Pat mixture into prepared loaf pan. Bake for 45 to 50 minutes. Place loaf pan on a wire rack and let set for 5 minutes. Cut into 6 servings.

Each serving equals:

HE: 2 Protein • ½ Bread • ½ Vegetable •
2 Optional Calories

---

156 Calories • 4 gm Fat • 17 gm Protein •
13 gm Carbohydrate • 465 mg Sodium •
30 mg Calcium • 1 gm Fiber

DIABETIC EXCHANGES: 2 Meat • ½ Starch •
½ Vegetable

Becky's Porcupine Meat Loaf

My daughter, Becky, never actually asked for a porcupine as a pet, but ever since she was a little girl, she's been a fan of "porcupine-style" meat loaf that blends rice with the meat to give the dish lots of tasty texture. Don't be afraid to get close enough to taste it—you'll be so glad you did. ☺ Serves 6

16 ounces extra-lean ground sirloin beef or turkey breast

½ cup uncooked instant rice

1 cup finely chopped onion

1 (8-ounce) can tomato sauce ☆

¼ cup fat-free milk

¼ cup SPLENDA® Granular ☆

1½ teaspoons dried parsley flakes

⅛ teaspoon black pepper

¼ cup reduced-sodium ketchup

Preheat oven to 350 degrees. Spray an 8-by-8-inch baking dish with butter-flavored cooking spray. In a large bowl, combine meat, uncooked rice, onion, ¾ cup tomato sauce, milk, 1 tablespoon SPLENDA®, parsley flakes, and black pepper. Mix well to combine. Pat mixture into prepared baking dish. Bake for 15 minutes. In a small bowl, combine remaining ¼ cup tomato sauce, ketchup, and remaining 3 tablespoons SPLENDA®. Evenly spoon sauce mixture over partially baked meat loaf. Continue baking for 30 to 35 minutes. Place baking dish on a wire rack and let set for 5 minutes. Divide into 6 servings.

Each serving equals:

HE: 2 Protein • 1 Vegetable • ¼ Bread • 17 Optional Calories

160 Calories • 4 gm Fat • 16 gm Protein • 15 gm Carbohydrate • 281 mg Sodium • 28 mg Calcium • 1 gm Fiber

DIABETIC EXCHANGES: 2 Meat • 1 Vegetable • ½ Starch

Veggie Lovers Meat Loaf

Clever cooks have always s-t-r-e-t-c-h-e-d their meat by blending it with a variety of other tasty ingredients. Here, I've "bulked" up a traditional meat loaf with lots of good-for-you vegetables that produce a culinary winner. ◑ Serves 6

> 16 ounces extra-lean ground sirloin beef or
>   turkey breast
> 2 cups shredded cabbage
> 1 cup shredded carrots
> 1 cup finely chopped onion
> 1 cup + 2 tablespoons dried fine bread crumbs
> 1½ teaspoons Worcestershire sauce
> 1 (8-ounce) can tomato sauce ☆
> 1 (8-ounce) can tomatoes, finely chopped and
>   undrained
> 2 tablespoons SPLENDA® Granular
> 1 tablespoon chopped fresh parsley or
>   1 teaspoon dried parsley flakes

Preheat oven to 350 degrees. Spray a 9-by-5-inch loaf pan with butter-flavored cooking spray. In a large bowl, combine meat, cabbage, carrots, onion, bread crumbs, Worcestershire, ¼ cup tomato sauce, and undrained tomatoes. Mix well to combine. Pat mixture into prepared loaf pan. Bake for 30 minutes. Stir SPLENDA® and parsley into remaining ¾ cup tomato sauce. Evenly spoon sauce mixture over partially baked meat loaf. Continue baking for 20 to 25 minutes. Place loaf pan on a wire rack and let set for 5 minutes. Cut into 6 servings.

Each serving equals:

HE: 2 Protein • 2 Vegetable • 1 Bread •
2 Optional Calories

217 Calories • 5 gm Fat • 18 gm Protein •
25 gm Carbohydrate • 546 mg Sodium •
75 mg Calcium • 3 gm Fiber

DIABETIC EXCHANGES: 2 Meat • 1½ Vegetable •
1 Starch

Meat Loaf Patties with Grande Sauce

Want to dazzle your loved ones with a dish that actually deserves its grand and glorious name? These meaty patties are succulent and juicy, perfect for a weekend supper or a summer evening meal on the patio. ☻ Serves 6

> 16 ounces extra-lean ground sirloin beef or
>   turkey breast
> ½ cup + 1 tablespoon dried fine bread crumbs
> ½ cup chopped onion
> ½ cup finely chopped green bell pepper
> ¼ cup water
> ⅛ teaspoon dried minced garlic
> ⅛ teaspoon black pepper
> 1 (8-ounce) can tomato sauce
> 1 tablespoon SPLENDA® Granular
> 1 teaspoon taco seasoning
> 1 tablespoon finely chopped cilantro or
>   parsley

In a large bowl, combine meat, bread crumbs, onion, green pepper, water, garlic, and black pepper. Mix well to combine. Using a ½ cup measuring cup as a guide, form into 6 patties. Evenly arrange patties in a large skillet sprayed with butter-flavored cooking spray. Brown patties for 4 to 5 minutes on each side. Meanwhile, in a small bowl, combine tomato sauce, SPLENDA®, taco seasoning, and cilantro. Spoon sauce mixture evenly over patties. Lower heat, cover, and simmer for 6 to 8 minutes or until patties are cooked through to desired doneness. When serving, evenly spoon sauce mixture over patties.

Each serving equals:

HE: 2 Protein • 1 Vegetable • ½ Bread •
1 Optional Calorie

156 Calories • 4 gm Fat • 17 gm Protein •
13 gm Carbohydrate • 416 mg Sodium •
33 mg Calcium • 1 gm Fiber

DIABETIC EXCHANGES: 2 Meat • 1 Vegetable •
½ Starch

Pizza "Steaks"

Remember when menus used to call their burgers "hamburger steaks"? That old-style terminology reminds us that the beef patties we love are made from an excellent cut of beef. Here, I've taken that ground steak and created a truly spectacular pizza burger your entire family will enjoy!　◐　Serves 6

> 16 ounces extra-lean ground sirloin beef or
>   turkey breast
> ½ cup + 1 tablespoon dried fine bread crumbs ☆
> ½ cup + 1 tablespoon shredded reduced-fat
>   mozzarella cheese
> ½ cup finely chopped onion
> 2 teaspoons pizza or Italian seasoning ☆
> 1 (8-ounce) can tomato sauce ☆
> 1 (15-ounce) can diced tomatoes, undrained
> 2 tablespoons SPLENDA® Granular

In a large bowl, combine meat, ½ cup bread crumbs, mozzarella cheese, onion, 1 teaspoon pizza seasoning, and ¼ cup tomato sauce. Mix well to combine. Using a ½ cup measuring cup as a guide, form into 6 patties. Place patties in a large skillet sprayed with olive oil-flavored cooking spray. Brown patties for 4 to 5 minutes on each side. In a medium bowl, combine remaining ¾ cup tomato sauce, undrained tomatoes, SPLENDA®, remaining 1 tablespoon bread crumbs, and remaining 1 teaspoon pizza seasoning. Spoon sauce mixture evenly over patties. Lower heat, cover, and simmer for 6 to 8 minutes or until "steaks" are cooked through to desired doneness. When serving, evenly spoon sauce over patties.

Each serving equals:

HE: 2½ Protein • 1½ Vegetable • ½ Bread •
2 Optional Calories

185 Calories • 5 gm Fat • 20 gm Protein •
15 gm Carbohydrate • 507 mg Sodium •
111 mg Calcium • 2 gm Fiber

DIABETIC EXCHANGES: 2½ Meat • 1½ Vegetable •
½ Starch

German Skillet Dinner

Sometimes a simple stovetop recipe with a bit of ethnic flair is exactly what you want for a relaxed evening meal. This is just one more creative way to enjoy eating sauerkraut!

○ Serves 6 (1 cup)

16 ounces *extra-lean ground sirloin beef or turkey breast*
1/2 cup *chopped onion*
1 (15-ounce) can *sauerkraut, well drained*
1/4 cup *water*
1 (8-ounce) can *tomato sauce*
2 tablespoons *SPLENDA® Granular*
1/8 teaspoon *black pepper*
2/3 cup *uncooked instant rice*

In a large skillet sprayed with butter-flavored cooking spray, brown meat and onion. Stir in sauerkraut, water, tomato sauce, SPLENDA®, and black pepper. Add uncooked rice. Mix well to combine. Lower heat, cover, and simmer for 15 minutes or until rice is tender, stirring occasionally.

HINT: Place sauerkraut in a colander and press juice out with a sturdy spoon.

Each serving equals:

HE: 2 Protein • 1½ Vegetable • ⅓ Bread •
2 Optional Calories

---

164 Calories • 4 gm Fat • 17 gm Protein •
15 gm Carbohydrate • 706 mg Sodium •
33 mg Calcium • 3 gm Fiber

DIABETIC EXCHANGES: 2 Meat • 1½ Vegetable •
½ Starch

Mexican Cabbage Beef Skillet

Even if Mexico's culinary tradition features many "wrapped" dishes (such as tacos and burritos), it's not a requirement! Keeping that in mind, I liberated the delectable contents of what could have been a stuffed cabbage-type recipe and instead invited the filling and the cabbage to mingle. You'll enjoy a fiesta of flavors in every bite.

○ Serves 4 (1 full cup)

8 ounces extra-lean ground sirloin beef or turkey breast
1 cup chopped onion
½ cup chopped green bell pepper
1 (15-ounce) can diced tomatoes, undrained
2 tablespoons SPLENDA® Granular
1 tablespoon chili seasoning
1 (15-ounce) can pinto beans, rinsed and drained
3 cups shredded cabbage
⅓ cup uncooked instant rice
¾ cup shredded reduced-fat Cheddar cheese

In a large skillet sprayed with butter-flavored cooking spray, brown meat, onion, and green pepper. Stir in undrained tomatoes, SPLENDA®, and chili seasoning. Add pinto beans, cabbage, and uncooked rice. Mix well to combine. Lower heat, cover, and simmer for 15 minutes or until rice is tender, stirring occasionally. Stir in Cheddar cheese. Continue simmering for 2 to 3 minutes or until cheese melts, stirring often.

Each serving equals:

HE: 3 Protein • 2½ Vegetable • ¾ Bread •
3 Optional Calories

275 Calories • 7 gm Fat • 23 gm Protein •
30 gm Carbohydrate • 588 mg Sodium •
234 mg Calcium • 6 gm Fiber

DIABETIC EXCHANGES: 3 Meat • 2 Vegetable • 1 Starch

Skillet Chili Casserole

You don't have hours to wait as your chili simmers on the stove? No problem. This skillet version supplies plenty of classic chili charm without the long cooking time. If you like it spicier, add a bit more chili seasoning to taste. ● Serves 6 (1 cup)

> 16 ounces extra-lean ground sirloin beef or turkey breast
> ½ cup chopped onion
> 1 (8-ounce) can tomato sauce
> 1 (15-ounce) can diced tomatoes, undrained
> ¼ cup SPLENDA® Granular
> 1 cup uncooked elbow macaroni
> 1 (8-ounce) can kidney beans, rinsed and drained
> 1 teaspoon chili seasoning

In a large skillet sprayed with butter-flavored cooking spray, brown meat and onion. Stir in tomato sauce, undrained tomatoes, and SPLENDA®. Add uncooked macaroni, kidney beans, and chili seasoning. Mix well to combine. Lower heat, cover, and simmer for 15 to 20 minutes or until macaroni is tender, stirring occasionally.

Each serving equals:

HE: 2 Protein • 1½ Vegetable • 1 Bread •
4 Optional Calories

212 Calories • 4 gm Fat • 19 gm Protein •
25 gm Carbohydrate • 403 mg Sodium •
31 mg Calcium • 3 gm Fiber

DIABETIC EXCHANGES: 2 Meat • 1½ Vegetable •
1 Starch

Calico Beef Pepper Bake

Are you one of those people who dig out the stuffing from traditional stuffed peppers? Don't feel badly, there are lots of "you" out there! This colorful casserole is so pretty on the plate.

● Serves 4

> 8 ounces extra-lean ground sirloin beef or turkey breast
> 1½ cups diced green bell pepper
> ½ cup finely chopped onion
> 1 (8-ounce) can tomato sauce
> 2 tablespoons SPLENDA® Granular
> 1 cup frozen whole-kernel corn
> ⅓ cup uncooked instant rice
> ¾ cup shredded reduced-fat Cheddar cheese

Preheat oven to 350 degrees. Spray an 8-by-8-inch baking dish with butter-flavored cooking spray. In a large skillet sprayed with butter-flavored cooking spray, brown meat, green pepper, and onion. Stir in tomato sauce and SPLENDA®. Add corn, uncooked rice, and Cheddar cheese. Mix well to combine. Spread mixture into prepared baking dish. Bake for 25 to 30 minutes. Place baking dish on a wire rack and let set for 5 minutes. Divide into 4 servings.

Each serving equals:

HE: 2½ Protein • 2 Vegetable • ¾ Bread •
2 Optional Calories

234 Calories • 6 gm Fat • 20 gm Protein •
25 gm Carbohydrate • 557 mg Sodium •
161 mg Calcium • 3 gm Fiber

DIABETIC EXCHANGES: 2 Meat • 2 Vegetable • 1 Starch

Main Dish Butter Bean Barbeque

If you're choosing to limit the amount of beef you eat but you still love meat, this dish will surprise you with its mighty meaty flavor! By using the best ground sirloin—but only a small amount—you still get the hearty goodness as well as the high fiber that comes from eating beans. ☻ Serves 6

> 8 ounces extra-lean ground sirloin beef or
>   turkey breast
> ½ cup finely chopped onion
> ½ cup finely chopped green bell pepper
> 1 (8-ounce) can tomato sauce
> 1 teaspoon poultry seasoning
> ½ teaspoon ground sage
> ½ teaspoon garlic powder
> 2 tablespoons SPLENDA® Granular
> 2 tablespoons apple cider vinegar
> 1 teaspoon Worcestershire sauce
> 2 (15-ounce) cans butter beans, rinsed
>   and drained

Preheat oven to 375 degrees. Spray an 8-by-8-inch baking dish with butter-flavored cooking spray. In a large skillet sprayed with butter-flavored cooking spray, brown meat, onion, and green pepper. Stir in tomato sauce, poultry seasoning, sage, and garlic powder. Add SPLENDA®, vinegar, and Worcestershire sauce. Mix well to combine. Stir in butter beans. Spread mixture into prepared baking dish. Bake for 25 to 30 minutes. Place baking dish on a wire rack and let set for 5 minutes. Divide into 6 servings.

Each serving equals:

HE: 2 Protein • 1 Vegetable • ½ Bread •
2 Optional Calories

159 Calories • 3 gm Fat • 13 gm Protein •
20 gm Carbohydrate • 515 mg Sodium •
45 mg Calcium • 5 gm Fiber

DIABETIC EXCHANGES: 1½ Meat • 1 Vegetable •
½ Starch

Creole Hamburger

Here's a succulent Southern-style supper dish that supplies loads and loads of flavor. It's a saucy blend that satisfies with every single bite! ◐ Serves 4

> 8 ounces extra-lean ground sirloin beef or turkey breast
> ¾ cup chopped onion
> ½ cup chopped celery
> ¼ cup chopped green bell pepper
> 1 (15-ounce) can diced tomatoes, undrained
> 1½ teaspoons Worcestershire sauce
> 1 tablespoon SPLENDA® Granular
> 1 teaspoon dried parsley flakes
> ⅛ teaspoon black pepper
> 2 cups hot cooked rice

In a large skillet sprayed with butter-flavored cooking spray, brown meat, onion, celery, and green pepper. Stir in undrained tomatoes, Worcestershire sauce, SPLENDA®, parsley flakes, and black pepper. Lower heat and simmer for 10 minutes, stirring occasionally. For each serving, place ½ cup rice on a plate and spoon about ¾ cup meat mixture over top.

HINT: Usually 1⅓ cups uncooked instant rice cooks to about 2 cups.

Each serving equals:

> HE: 1¾ Vegetable • 1½ Protein • 1 Bread •
> 3 Optional Calories
> _____
> 191 Calories • 3 gm Fat • 14 gm Protein •
> 27 gm Carbohydrate • 184 mg Sodium •
> 37 mg Calcium • 3 gm Fiber
> _____
> DIABETIC EXCHANGES: 2 Vegetable • 1½ Meat •
> 1½ Starch

James's Beef Taco Supper

My son James is a magnificent cook in his own right, and he loves a meaty main dish like this one, which I created with his particular tastes in mind.   ●   Serves 6 (Scant 1 cup)

16 ounces extra-lean ground sirloin beef or turkey breast
½ cup chopped onion
1 (8-ounce) can tomato sauce
1 cup chunky salsa (mild, medium, or hot)
1 cup reduced-sodium tomato juice
6 (6-inch) flour tortillas, cut into 1-inch pieces
½ cup + 1 tablespoon shredded reduced-fat Cheddar cheese ☆
1 tablespoon SPLENDA® Granular
1½ teaspoons taco seasoning
1 teaspoon dried parsley flakes

In a large skillet sprayed with butter-flavored cooking spray, brown meat and onion. Stir in tomato sauce, salsa, and tomato juice. Add tortilla pieces and ¼ cup Cheddar cheese. Mix well to combine. Stir in SPLENDA®, taco seasoning, and parsley flakes. Bring mixture to a boil. Lower heat, cover, and simmer for 5 minutes, stirring occasionally. Just before serving, stir in remaining 5 tablespoons Cheddar cheese.

Each serving equals:

HE: 2½ Protein • 1½ Vegetable • 1 Bread •
1 Optional Calorie

---

283 Calories • 7 gm Fat • 23 gm Protein •
32 gm Carbohydrate • 827 mg Sodium •
101 mg Calcium • 4 gm Fiber

DIABETIC EXCHANGES: 2½ Meat • 1½ Vegetable •
1½ Starch

BBQ Loose Meat Sandwiches

SPLENDA® is sensational for creating homemade sauces, especially spicy-sweet ones like this! If you prefer your barbecue a bit less sweet, vary the amount of SPLENDA® you use until the flavor is just right for you. ☻ Serves 6

16 ounces extra-lean ground sirloin beef or turkey breast
½ cup finely chopped onion
½ cup finely chopped green bell pepper
1 (8-ounce) can tomato sauce
2 tablespoons apple cider vinegar
¼ cup SPLENDA® Granular
⅛ teaspoon black pepper
6 small hamburger buns

In a large skillet sprayed with butter-flavored cooking spray, brown meat, onion, and green pepper. Add tomato sauce, vinegar, SPLENDA®, and black pepper. Mix well to combine. Lower heat and simmer for 8 to 10 minutes, stirring occasionally. For each sandwich, spoon about ½ cup meat mixture into a bun.

Each serving equals:

HE: 2 Protein • 1 Bread • 1 Vegetable •
4 Optional Calories

---

188 Calories • 4 gm Fat • 18 gm Protein •
20 gm Carbohydrate • 452 mg Sodium •
12 mg Calcium • 2 gm Fiber

DIABETIC EXCHANGES: 2 Meat • 1 Starch • 1 Vegetable

Simple Swiss Steak

Most of my recipes are remarkably easy, but this is one of the quickest and easiest ever! Time and heat combine with this tomato-based sauce to produce a rich and hearty delight. ☻ Serves 4

> 3 tablespoons all-purpose flour
> 4 (4-ounce) lean tenderized minute or cube steaks
> 1 cup chopped onion
> 1 cup chopped celery
> 1 (15-ounce) can diced tomatoes, undrained
> 2 tablespoons SPLENDA® Granular
> 1½ teaspoons dried parsley flakes

Place flour in a shallow dish. Coat meat pieces on both sides in flour. Evenly arrange coated meat pieces in a large skillet sprayed with butter-flavored cooking spray. Brown for 3 to 4 minutes on both sides. Sprinkle onion and celery evenly over meat. In a small bowl, combine undrained tomatoes, SPLENDA®, and parsley flakes. Spoon tomato mixture evenly over top. Lower heat, cover, and simmer for 30 to 35 minutes or until meat and vegetables are tender. When serving, evenly spoon sauce mixture over meat pieces.

Each serving equals:

HE: 3 Protein • 2 Vegetable • ¼ Bread •
3 Optional Calories

212 Calories • 4 gm Fat • 29 gm Protein •
15 gm Carbohydrate • 214 mg Sodium •
44 mg Calcium • 3 gm Fiber

DIABETIC EXCHANGES: 3 Meat • 2 Vegetable

Pepper Steak

This classic dish now features a superb sweet-tangy sauce and is sure to win over your toughest critics. I always keep minute steaks in the freezer, so I can whip up this supper dish in minutes.

☻ Serves 4 (¾ cup)

16 ounces lean tenderized minute steaks, cut into bite-size pieces
1½ cups coarsely chopped green bell pepper
½ cup chopped onion
2 tablespoons reduced-sodium soy sauce
1 tablespoon SPLENDA® Granular
1 cup peeled and coarsely chopped fresh tomatoes
⅛ teaspoon ground ginger
¼ teaspoon dried minced garlic
⅛ teaspoon black pepper

In a large skillet sprayed with butter-flavored cooking spray, brown steak pieces, green pepper, and onion for 8 to 10 minutes. In a small bowl, combine soy sauce and SPLENDA®. Stir soy sauce mixture into meat mixture. Add tomatoes, ginger, garlic, and black pepper. Mix well to combine. Lower heat and simmer for 6 to 8 minutes or until meat is tender, stirring often.

HINT: Good as is or served over hot rice.

Each serving equals:

HE: 3 Protein • 1½ Vegetable • 2 Optional Calories

177 Calories • 5 gm Fat • 24 gm Protein •
9 gm Carbohydrate • 321 mg Sodium •
12 mg Calcium • 2 gm Fiber

DIABETIC EXCHANGES: 3 Meat • 1 Vegetable

Sweet-Sour Cabbage with Pork

Why did I use pork instead of beef in my sweet-sour cabbage? I don't need a better reason than the fact that Cliff and I love the taste of pork! Besides, it's so widely available in lean tenderloins. Don't get stuck in a rut—try something new!

☻ Serves 4 (1 cup)

> 16 ounces extra-lean pork tenderloin, cut into bite-size pieces
> 1/2 cup chopped onion
> 4 cups shredded cabbage
> 1 cup water ☆
> 1/2 cup SPLENDA® Granular
> 1/2 cup apple cider vinegar
> 3 tablespoons all-purpose flour
> 1/8 teaspoon black pepper

In a large skillet sprayed with butter-flavored cooking spray, brown meat and onion for 6 to 8 minutes. Add cabbage and 3/4 cup water. Mix well to combine. Continue cooking for 5 to 6 minutes or until cabbage is just tender. Stir in SPLENDA® and vinegar. In a small bowl, combine remaining 1/4 cup water, flour, and black pepper. Add flour mixture to cabbage mixture. Mix well to combine. Continue cooking for 5 minutes or until mixture thickens, stirring often.

Each serving equals:

HE: 3 Protein • 1 1/4 Vegetable • 1/4 Bread • 12 Optional Calories

200 Calories • 4 gm Fat • 27 gm Protein • 14 gm Carbohydrate • 70 mg Sodium • 53 mg Calcium • 2 gm Fiber

DIABETIC EXCHANGES: 3 Meat • 1 Vegetable • 1/2 Starch

Main Dish Cornbread

Do you love cornbread as much as I do? I'm glad, because here's a terrific way to serve it as an entrée—mixing in lots of meat and veggies for a splendidly satisfying supper dish. (And, of course, cleanup will be a one-dish breeze.)   ☻   Serves 8

1 (10¾-ounce) can reduced-fat
    cream of mushroom soup
⅓ cup fat-free milk
1 egg, slightly beaten, or
    equivalent in egg substitute
1¼ cups reduced-fat biscuit
    baking mix
½ cup yellow cornmeal
¼ cup SPLENDA® Granular

½ cup frozen whole-kernel
    corn, thawed
1 cup frozen chopped broccoli,
    thawed
1½ cups diced extra-lean ham
⅛ cup shredded reduced-fat
    Cheddar cheese
1 teaspoon dried parsley flakes

Preheat oven to 350 degrees. Spray an 8-by-8-inch baking dish with butter-flavored cooking spray. In a large bowl, combine mushroom soup, milk, and egg. Stir in baking mix, cornmeal, and SPLENDA®. Add corn, broccoli, ham, Cheddar cheese, and parsley flakes. Mix well to combine. Spread mixture evenly into prepared baking dish. Bake for 30 to 35 minutes or until a toothpick inserted in center comes out clean. Place baking dish on a wire rack and let set for 5 minutes. Cut into 8 servings.

HINT: Thaw corn and broccoli by placing in a colander and rinsing under hot water for 1 minute.

Each serving equals:

HE: 1½ Bread • 1⅓ Protein • ¼ Vegetable •
6 Optional Calories

205 Calories • 5 gm Fat • 12 gm Protein •
28 gm Carbohydrate • 723 mg Sodium •
147 mg Calcium • 2 gm Fiber

DIABETIC EXCHANGES: 1½ Meat • 1½ Starch

Spanish Ham Rice

If your kids love ham as much as mine do, here's a fast and fun way to serve it. And if you're economizing (aren't we all?), don't you love the fact that you can feed four using less than a pound of ham?

● Serves 4 (1 cup)

> 1 cup chopped onion
> 1 cup chopped celery
> 1 (15-ounce) can diced tomatoes, undrained
> 1 cup water
> 2 tablespoons SPLENDA® Granular
> ½ teaspoon chili seasoning
> 1 teaspoon dried parsley flakes
> 1½ cups diced extra-lean ham
> 1 cup uncooked instant rice

In a large skillet sprayed with butter-flavored cooking spray, sauté onion and celery for 8 minutes or just until celery is tender. Stir in undrained tomatoes, water, SPLENDA®, chili seasoning, and parsley flakes. Add ham and uncooked rice. Mix well to combine. Lower heat, cover, and simmer for 15 minutes or until vegetables and rice are tender, stirring occasionally.

Each serving equals:

HE: 2 Vegetable • 1½ Protein • ¾ Bread •
3 Optional Calories

194 Calories • 2 gm Fat • 14 gm Protein •
30 gm Carbohydrate • 673 mg Sodium •
46 mg Calcium • 3 gm Fiber

DIABETIC EXCHANGES: 2 Vegetable • 2 Meat • 1 Starch

Ham Florentine Pilaf

If you're an avid menu reader, you already know that any dish called "Florentine" features spinach, but I think I added something fresh and creative to that notion by combining that iron-rich green with ham and rice and then topping it with yummy cheese.

☻ Serves 4

> ³⁄4 cup chopped red bell pepper
> ¹⁄4 cup chopped green onion
> 1 (14-ounce) can lower-sodium fat-free chicken broth
> ¹⁄2 teaspoon dried dill weed
> 1¹⁄3 cups uncooked instant rice
> 1¹⁄2 cups diced extra-lean ham
> 2 cups shredded fresh spinach leaves
> 1 tablespoon SPLENDA® Granular
> ¹⁄4 cup grated reduced-fat Parmesan cheese

In a large skillet sprayed with olive oil-flavored cooking spray, sauté red pepper and onion for 2 minutes. Stir in chicken broth, dill weed, and uncooked rice. Bring mixture to a boil, stirring often. Add ham. Mix well to combine. Lower heat, cover, and simmer for 12 minutes. Stir in spinach and SPLENDA®. Continue simmering for 3 minutes or until rice is tender, stirring often. For each serving, place 1 cup pilaf mixture on a plate and sprinkle 1 tablespoon Parmesan cheese over top.

Each serving equals:

HE: 1³⁄4 Protein • 1 Bread • 1 Vegetable •
9 Optional Calories

190 Calories • 2 gm Fat • 15 gm Protein •
28 gm Carbohydrate • 727 mg Sodium •
28 mg Calcium • 2 gm Fiber

DIABETIC EXCHANGES: 2 Meat • 1¹⁄2 Starch •
1 Vegetable

Baked Ham Slices with Hawaiian Sauce

Talk about a piquant culinary vacation! This sweet and pungent dish is almost as good as a plane ticket to boost your spirits out of those midwinter doldrums. It's tender and sweet but with a little kick. ☻ Serves 4

> 4 (4½-ounce) slices extra-lean ham
> 1 (8-ounce) can crushed pineapple, packed in fruit juice, undrained
> 2 tablespoons SPLENDA® Granular
> ½ teaspoon Worcestershire sauce
> 1 teaspoon prepared yellow mustard
> 3 tablespoons purchased graham cracker crumbs or
>   3 (2½-inch) graham crackers, made into crumbs

Preheat oven to 350 degrees. Spray an 8-by-8-inch baking dish with butter-flavored cooking spray. Evenly arrange ham slices in prepared baking dish. In a blender container, combine undrained pineapple, SPLENDA®, Worcestershire sauce, and mustard. Cover and process on BLEND for 10 seconds or until mixture is smooth. Pour mixture evenly over ham slices. Evenly sprinkle graham cracker crumbs over top. Bake for 30 minutes. Place baking dish on a wire rack and let set 5 minutes. Divide into 4 servings.

HINTS: 1. A ¾-inch slice of ham usually weighs 4½ ounces.
2. A self-seal sandwich bag works great for crushing graham crackers.

Each serving equals:

HE: 3 Protein • ½ Fruit • ¼ Bread •
3 Optional Calories

188 Calories • 4 gm Fat • 22 gm Protein •
16 gm Carbohydrate • 948 mg Sodium •
11 mg Calcium • 1 gm Fiber

DIABETIC EXCHANGES: 3 Meat • ½ Fruit

Franks & Kraut

Octoberfest, here we come! Every fall, it just seems natural to serve sauerkraut and hot dogs, but I thought I'd stir in a bit of the sweet fall apple harvest to produce a dish that is definitely worth throwing a party for! ☻ Serves 6 (scant 1 cup)

1 (16-ounce) package reduced-fat frankfurters, cut into ½-inch
   pieces
½ cup chopped onion
1 (15-ounce) can diced tomatoes, undrained
1 (15-ounce) can sauerkraut, well drained
1½ cups (3 small) cored, peeled, and finely chopped cooking
   apples
2 tablespoons SPLENDA® Granular
1 teaspoon dried parsley flakes

In a large skillet sprayed with butter-flavored cooking spray, sauté frankfurters and onion for 5 minutes. Stir in undrained tomatoes and sauerkraut. Add apples, SPLENDA®, and parsley flakes. Mix well to combine. Lower heat, cover, and simmer for 20 minutes, stirring occasionally.

HINT: Place sauerkraut in a colander and press juice out with a sturdy spoon.

Each serving equals:

HE: 1¾ Protein • 1½ Vegetable • ½ Fruit •
2 Optional Calories

143 Calories • 3 gm Fat • 11 gm Protein •
18 gm Carbohydrate • 925 mg Sodium •
37 mg Calcium • 4 gm Fiber

DIABETIC EXCHANGES: 2 Meat • 1½ Vegetable •
½ Fruit

Dazzling Desserts

A delightful dessert sends everyone home (or to bed) happy, so every cook knows that for a grand finale, there's nothing more important than a really good "sweet treat." Dessert is the course that convinces us we're not really on a diet of deprivation—how could we be if we're eating a slice of creamy pie or downing a decadent dish of bread pudding? I've always loved the notion that life is uncertain, so it would be a good idea to eat dessert first, and even if I choose to enjoy it at the meal's end instead of at the beginning, knowing that it's waiting for me just puts me in a great mood!

Here's a luscious selection of desserts to please you as much as your family or friends. They're quick to fix, easy to stir up, and remarkably delicious considering their calorie counts! From my glorious **Caramelized Baked Rice Pudding** to a **Pear Crumble** that could win a ribbon at the State Fair, from a dessert that deserves its own day of celebration (**Holiday Banana Cranberry Meringue Pie**) to a cake that will produce delicious flashbacks to your happy childhood (**Mud Pie Cake**), these five-star delights are sure to put smiles on every face around your table.

Baked Vanilla Custard

Though I have one friend who vows never to eat anything vanilla, she knows she's in a tiny minority. Everyone else will love this sweet and velvety dessert that's just like the cozy ones "Grandma used to make." ☻ Serves 4

2 eggs, or equivalent in egg
   substitute
½ cup + 1 tablespoon
   SPLENDA® Granular ☆
1 (12-fluid-ounce) can
   evaporated fat-free milk

¼ cup water
2 teaspoons vanilla extract
¼ teaspoon ground nutmeg
Hot water

Preheat oven to 350 degrees. Spray 4 (12-ounce) custard cups with butter-flavored cooking spray. In a medium bowl, combine eggs and ½ cup SPLENDA®. Mix well using a wire whisk. Blend in evaporated milk and water. Add vanilla extract. Mix gently just to combine. Evenly pour mixture into prepared custard cups. In a small bowl, combine nutmeg and remaining 1 tablespoon SPLENDA®. Lightly sprinkle tops with nutmeg mixture. Place filled custard cups in a 9-by-9-inch cake pan. Carefully pour hot water into cake pan to almost the height of the cups. Bake for 50 minutes or until a knife inserted near the edge of the cups comes out clean. Remove cups from cake pan and cool on a wire rack for at least 10 minutes. Refrigerate for at least 30 minutes.

HINT: Good served warm or cold.

Each serving equals:

HE: ¾ Fat-Free Milk • ½ Protein •
13 Optional Calories

118 Calories • 2 gm Fat • 9 gm Protein •
16 gm Carbohydrate • 151 mg Sodium •
252 mg Calcium • 0 gm Fiber

DIABETIC EXCHANGES: 1 Fat-Free Milk • ½ Meat

Aunt Rita's
Rice and Raisin Pudding

I've depended on "Aunt" Rita for years to help me test dozens of recipes every month for my books and newsletter. She's a great cook with a special fondness for old-fashioned desserts like this creamy-smooth one. ☻ Serves 4

1 (12-fluid-ounce) can
    evaporated fat-free milk
½ cup water
1 tablespoon cornstarch
¼ cup SPLENDA® Granular
2 cups cold cooked rice

2 teaspoons vanilla extract
¼ cup seedless raisins
½ teaspoon ground cinnamon
¼ cup reduced-calorie whipped
    topping

In a medium saucepan, combine evaporated milk, water, and cornstarch. Mix well using a wire whisk. Stir in SPLENDA® and rice. Cook over medium heat until mixture comes to a boil, stirring often. Continue cooking for 1 minute, stirring constantly. Remove from heat. Add vanilla extract and raisins. Mix gently to combine. Evenly spoon mixture into 4 dessert dishes. Lightly sprinkle ⅛ teaspoon cinnamon over top of each. Refrigerate for at least 1 hour. When serving, top each with 1 tablespoon whipped topping.

HINT: Usually 1⅓ cups uncooked instant rice cooks to about 2 cups.

Each serving equals:

HE: 1 Bread • ¾ Fat-Free Milk • ½ Fruit • ¼ Slider • 3 Optional Calories

192 Calories • 0 gm Fat • 8 gm Protein • 40 gm Carbohydrate • 124 mg Sodium • 256 mg Calcium • 1 gm Fiber

DIABETIC EXCHANGES: 1 Starch • 1 Fat-Free Milk • ½ Fruit

Caramelized Baked Rice Pudding

So many men love rice pudding, I've discovered—maybe because it reminds them of happy days when they were children. My grandsons really enjoyed the sweet, browned top of this baked-in-the-oven variation.   ♥   Serves 4

1 (12-fluid-ounce) can
     evaporated fat-free milk
1 egg, or equivalent in egg
     substitute
¼ cup SPLENDA® Granular
1 teaspoon vanilla extract

1 cup cooked rice
hot water
½ cup reduced-calorie whipped
     topping
½ teaspoon ground cinnamon

Preheat oven to 350 degrees. Spray 4 (12-ounce) custard cups with butter-flavored cooking spray. In a large bowl, combine evaporated milk, egg, SPLENDA®, and vanilla extract. Add rice. Mix gently to combine. Evenly spoon mixture into prepared custard cups. Place custard cups in a 9-by-9-inch cake pan. Carefully pour hot water into pan to almost the height of the cups. Bake for 30 to 35 minutes. Remove cups from cake pan and cool on a wire rack for at least 10 minutes. When serving, top each with 2 tablespoons whipped topping and sprinkle ⅛ teaspoon cinnamon over top of each.

HINTS: 1. Usually ⅔ cup uncooked instant rice cooks to about
             1 cup.
          2. Good served warm or cold.

Each serving equals:

HE: ¾ Fat-Free Milk • ½ Bread • ¼ Protein •
¼ Slider • 6 Optional Calories

150 Calories • 2 gm Fat • 9 gm Protein •
24 gm Carbohydrate • 138 mg Sodium •
256 mg Calcium • 1 gm Fiber

DIABETIC EXCHANGES: 1 Fat-Free Milk • 1 Starch

Apricot-Pecan Bread Pudding

If a dessert can be said to make a person merry, I'd say that this one does it for me. I adore pecans, and the creamy sauce that transforms plain old white bread into perfection tastes like heaven on a spoon!

◐ Serves 6

3 cups fat-free milk
¼ cup water
2 tablespoons cornstarch
¾ cup SPLENDA® Granular
⅔ cup finely chopped dried
    apricots

1 tablespoon vanilla extract
1 teaspoon ground cinnamon
9 slices reduced-calorie white
    bread, cubed
3 tablespoons chopped pecans

Preheat oven to 350 degrees. Spray an 8-by-8-inch baking dish with butter-flavored cooking spray. In a large saucepan sprayed with butter-flavored cooking spray, combine milk, water, cornstarch, and SPLENDA®. Stir in apricots. Cook over medium heat until mixture thickens and starts to boil, stirring constantly. Remove from heat. Add vanilla extract and cinnamon. Mix well to combine. Fold in bread cubes and pecans. Spread mixture evenly into prepared baking dish. Bake for 35 to 40 minutes or until golden brown and center springs back when lightly touched. Place baking dish on a wire rack and let set for at least 5 minutes. Cut into 6 servings.

HINT: Good warm or cold.

Each serving equals:

HE: ¾ Bread • ¾ Fruit • ½ Fat-Free Milk • ½ Fat • ¼ Slider • 2 Optional Calories

207 Calories • 3 gm Fat • 9 gm Protein • 36 gm Carbohydrate • 237 mg Sodium • 191 mg Calcium • 2 gm Fiber

DIABETIC EXCHANGES: 1 Starch • 1 Fruit • ½ Fat-Free Milk • ½ Fat

Sour Cream Rhubarb Cobbler

Too often, rhubarb is only served in partnership with another fruit (usually strawberries!), but it has its own special delights that this recipe highlights. Isn't a cozy cobbler just the ideal dessert for a chilly winter's eve?　❂　Serves 6

3 cups diced fresh or frozen rhubarb, thawed
1¾ cups + 2 tablespoons SPLENDA® Granular ☆
1 cup + 2 tablespoons reduced-fat biscuit baking mix
¾ cup no-fat sour cream
2 tablespoons fat-free half & half
½ teaspoon vanilla extract

Preheat oven to 350 degrees. Spray an 8-by-8-inch baking dish with butter-flavored cooking spray. Evenly arrange rhubarb in prepared baking dish. Sprinkle 1 cup SPLENDA® evenly over top. In a medium bowl, combine baking mix, ¾ cup SPLENDA®, sour cream, half & half, and vanilla extract. Carefully spread batter evenly over rhubarb. Lightly spray top with butter-flavored cooking spray. Evenly sprinkle remaining 2 tablespoons SPLENDA® over top. Bake for 28 to 32 minutes. Place baking dish on a wire rack and let set for at least 10 minutes. Cut into 6 servings.

Each serving equals:

HE: 1 Bread • ½ Vegetable • ¾ Slider •
3 Optional Calories

154 Calories • 2 gm Fat • 3 gm Protein •
31 gm Carbohydrate • 303 mg Sodium •
115 mg Calcium • 2 gm Fiber

DIABETIC EXCHANGES: 2 Starch/Carbohydrate

Pear Crumble

Here's a dream of a dessert that will warm you body and soul! Talk about comfort food—this crumb-topped pear pleaser is easy and special. ☻ Serves 6

4½ cups peeled and thinly sliced ripe Bartlett pears
¾ cup all-purpose flour
½ cup SPLENDA® Granular
1 teaspoon apple pie spice
¼ cup reduced-calorie margarine
¾ cup fat-free half & half

Preheat oven to 350 degrees. Spray an 8-by-8-inch baking dish with butter-flavored cooking spray. Evenly layer pear slices in prepared baking dish. In a large bowl, combine flour, SPLENDA®, and apple pie spice. Add margarine. Using a pastry blender or fork, mix until mixture resembles coarse crumbs. Sprinkle crumb mixture evenly over pears. Bake for 18 to 20 minutes or until pears are tender and top is browned. Place baking dish on a wire rack and let set for at least 5 minutes. Divide into 6 servings. For each serving, spoon warm pear crumble in a dessert dish and drizzle 2 tablespoons half & half over top. Serve at once.

Each serving equals:

HE: 1½ Fruit • 1 Fat • ⅔ Bread • ¼ Slider •
8 Optional Calories

188 Calories • 4 gm Fat • 3 gm Protein •
35 gm Carbohydrate • 121 mg Sodium •
67 mg Calcium • 3 gm Fiber

DIABETIC EXCHANGES: 1½ Fruit • 1 Fat •
1 Starch/Carbohydrate

Ruby Razz Crunch

What a delectable combination—the tartness of rhubarb coupled with the richness of raspberries! Thank heavens for SPLENDA®'s power to make the fruit sweeter and the topping terrific.

Serves 8

> 2 cups chopped fresh or frozen rhubarb, thawed
> 3 cups frozen unsweetened raspberries, thawed
> 1 cup water
> 1¾ cups SPLENDA® Granular ☆
> 3 tablespoons cornstarch
> 1 cup + 2 tablespoons all-purpose flour
> ½ cup quick oats
> ½ teaspoon ground cinnamon
> ½ cup reduced-calorie margarine, melted

Preheat oven to 325 degrees. Spray a 7-by-11-inch biscuit pan with butter-flavored cooking spray. In a large bowl, combine rhubarb and raspberries. In a medium saucepan, combine water, ¾ cup SPLENDA®, and cornstarch. Cook over medium heat until mixture thickens and starts to boil, stirring constantly. Remove from heat and set saucepan on a wire rack. Stir in rhubarb and raspberry mixture. In another large bowl, combine flour, oats, remaining 1 cup SPLENDA®, and cinnamon. Add margarine. Using a pastry blender or fork, mix well until mixture resembles coarse crumbs. Press ⅔ cup of crumb mixture into prepared pan. Spoon fruit mixture evenly over crumbs. Evenly sprinkle remaining crumb mixture over top. Bake for 55 to 60 minutes. Place pan on a wire rack and let set for at least 5 minutes. Cut into 8 servings.

HINT: Good warm as is or cold with Cool Whip Lite, but don't forget to count the few additional calories.

Each serving equals:

HE: 1½ Fat • 1 Bread • ½ Fruit • ¼ Vegetable •
¼ Slider • 12 Optional Calories

---

190 Calories • 6 gm Fat • 3 gm Protein •
31 gm Carbohydrate • 139 mg Sodium •
58 mg Calcium • 4 gm Fiber

DIABETIC EXCHANGES: 1½ Starch • 1½ Fat • 1 Fruit

Pumpkin Patch Pie Squares

Not every pumpkin pie has to be round, I decided, and not every pie has to be served in a traditional crust to be good, right? Right! So I cooked up this rectangular version to serve a crowd with panache! ☻ Serves 12

½ cup + 1 tablespoon all-
   purpose flour
¾ cup quick oats
1 cup SPLENDA® Granular ☆
⅓ cup + 2 teaspoons reduced-
   calorie margarine
1 (15-ounce) can solid pack
   pumpkin

1 cup nonfat dry milk powder
¾ cup water
2 eggs or equivalent in egg
   substitute
2 teaspoons pumpkin pie spice
¼ cup chopped walnuts

Preheat oven to 350 degrees. Spray a 9-by-13-inch cake pan with butter-flavored cooking spray. In a medium bowl, combine flour, oats, ½ cup SPLENDA®, and margarine. Mix with a fork until crumbly. Pat mixture into prepared pan. Bake for 8 minutes. Meanwhile, in a large bowl, combine pumpkin, dry milk powder, and water. Add eggs, pumpkin pie spice, walnuts, and remaining ½ cup SPLENDA®. Mix well to combine. Pour pumpkin mixture evenly over partially baked crust. Continue baking for 25 to 30 minutes or until filling is set. Place pan on a wire rack and let set for at least 15 minutes. Cut into 12 servings.

HINT: Place hand in a plastic bag when patting crust into pan.

Each serving equals:

HE: ¾ Fat • ½ Bread • ⅓ Vegetable •
¼ Fat-Free Milk • ¼ Protein • 14 Optional Calories

129 Calories • 5 gm Fat • 5 gm Protein •
16 gm Carbohydrate • 104 mg Sodium •
98 mg Calcium • 2 gm Fiber

DIABETIC EXCHANGES: 1 Starch • 1 Fat

Apple Pizza Dessert

Fruit pizzas are loads of fun and remarkably simple to stir up! I've made them while my grandkids were visiting, and they were over-joyed to help Grandma spread the scrumptious filling across the top of the dough. They were also energetic tasters of everything that emerged from the kitchen that day!   ☻   Serves 12

1 (8-ounce) can reduced-fat crescent rolls
2 (20-ounce) cans no-sugar-added apple pie filling
1½ teaspoons apple pie spice
¾ cup purchased graham cracker crumbs
½ cup SPLENDA® Granular
¼ cup reduced-calorie margarine

Preheat oven to 375 degrees. Unroll crescent rolls and pat into a rimmed 10-by-15-inch baking sheet, being sure to seal perfora-tions. Bake for 5 minutes. In a medium bowl, combine both cans of apple pie filling and apple pie spice. Evenly spread apple mixture over partially baked crust. In a small bowl, combine graham cracker crumbs, SPLENDA®, and margarine. Mix gently with a pas-try cutter or 2 forks to form soft crumbs. Sprinkle crumb mixture evenly over apple pie filling mixture. Continue baking for 15 min-utes. Place baking sheet on a wire rack and let set for at least 10 min-utes. Cut into 12 servings.

Each serving equals:

HE: 1 Bread • ½ Fruit • ½ Fat • 3 Optional Calories

141 Calories • 5 gm Fat • 2 gm Protein •
22 gm Carbohydrate • 299 mg Sodium •
8 mg Calcium • 1 gm Fiber

DIABETIC EXCHANGES: 1 Starch • ½ Fruit • ½ Fat

Rhubarb Cream Pie

Are you shocked to see such a short list of ingredients for this luscious pie? In this case, simplicity is the key to something spectacularly good. ● Serves 8

1 refrigerated unbaked 9-inch
    piecrust
4 cups chopped fresh or frozen
    rhubarb, thawed

1½ cups SPLENDA® Granular
3 tablespoons all-purpose flour
¾ cup fat-free half & half

Let piecrust set at room temperature for 20 minutes. Cut the room temperature piecrust in half on the folded line. Gently roll each half into a ball. Wipe counter with a wet cloth and place a sheet of waxed paper over damp spot. Place one of the balls on the waxed paper. Cover with another piece of waxed paper and roll out into a 9-inch circle with rolling pin. Carefully remove waxed paper from one side and place crust into an 8- or 9-inch pie plate. Remove other piece of waxed paper. In a large bowl, combine rhubarb, SPLENDA®, and flour. Add half & half. Mix gently to combine. Spoon rhubarb mixture into prepared piecrust. Repeat process of rolling out remaining piecrust half. Place on top of pie. Flute edges. Lightly spray top crust with butter-flavored cooking spray. Make about 8 slashes with a knife to allow steam to escape. Bake at 350 degrees for 50 to 60 minutes or until done. Place pie plate on a wire rack and let set for at least 30 minutes. Refrigerate for at least 1 hour. Cut into 8 servings.

HINT: Place piece of uncooked elbow macaroni upright in center of pie to keep filling from cooking out of crust.

Each serving equals:

HE: 1 Bread • ½ Fat • ½ Vegetable • ½ Slider •
4 Optional Calories

175 Calories • 7 gm Fat • 3 gm Protein •
25 gm Carbohydrate • 124 mg Sodium •
76 mg Calcium • 1 gm Fiber

DIABETIC EXCHANGES: 1½ Starch/Carbohydrate • 1 Fat

Blue Ribbon
Apple Raisin Crumb Pie

Did you know that besides the usual state fair baking contests, they hold an annual pie contest for best-in-the-land bragging rights? I watched a competition on the Food Network recently, and the ingenuity of cooks young and old was dazzling. They have a separate category for apple pie, and I might just have to submit this one next year.   ◐   Serves 8

1 refrigerated unbaked
   9-inch piecrust
4 cups (8 small) cored,
   peeled and sliced cooking
   apples
1/2 cup seedless raisins
1 cup SPLENDA® Granular ☆

2 tablespoons fat-free half &
   half
1/2 cup + 2 tablespoons all-
   purpose flour ☆
1 teaspoon ground cinnamon
3 tablespoons reduced-calorie
   margarine

Preheat oven to 400 degrees. Place piecrust in a 9-inch pie plate and flute edges. In a large bowl, combine apples, raisins, 3/4 cup SPLENDA®, half & half, 2 tablespoons flour, and cinnamon. Evenly spoon mixture into prepared piecrust. In a medium bowl, combine remaining 1/4 cup SPLENDA® and remaining 1/2 cup flour. With a fork or pastry blender, cut margarine into mixture until crumbly. Sprinkle crumb mixture evenly over apple mixture. Bake for 35 to 45 minutes or until apples are tender and crust is golden brown. Place pie plate on a wire rack and allow to cool completely. Cut into 8 servings.

Each serving equals:

HE: 1 1/2 Bread • 1 1/2 Fruit • 1 Fat •
15 Optional Calories

241 Calories • 9 gm Fat • 2 gm Protein •
38 gm Carbohydrate • 157 mg Sodium •
21 mg Calcium • 2 gm Fiber

DIABETIC EXCHANGES: 1 1/2 Starch • 1 1/2 Fruit • 1 Fat

Apple and Peanut Butter Crumb Pie

Remember how good it tasted to dunk an apple slice into the jar of peanut butter when you were a kid? Well, it still does, and this is a neater way to enjoy the treat!   ☻   Serves 8

> 3 cups (6 small) cored, peeled, and sliced
>   cooking apples
> 1 (6-ounce) purchased graham cracker piecrust
> 2 tablespoons cornstarch
> ½ cup SPLENDA® Granular
> 1 cup unsweetened apple juice
> ¼ cup water
> 6 tablespoons reduced-fat peanut butter ☆
> 6 tablespoons purchased graham cracker crumbs or
>   6 (2½-inch) graham cracker squares made
>   into crumbs

Preheat oven to 350 degrees. Evenly arrange apple slices in piecrust. In a medium saucepan, combine cornstarch, SPLENDA®, apple juice, and water. Add ¼ cup peanut butter. Mix well to combine. Cook over medium heat until mixture thickens and starts to boil, stirring constantly. Evenly spoon hot mixture over apples. In a medium bowl, combine graham cracker crumbs and remaining 2 tablespoons peanut butter until mixture is crumbly. Evenly sprinkle crumb mixture over top of pie. Bake for 25 to 30 minutes. Place pie plate on a wire rack and let set for at least 1 hour. Cut into 8 servings.

HINT: A self-seal sandwich bag works great for crushing graham crackers.

Each serving equals:

HE: 1 Bread • 1 Fruit • 1 Fat • ¾ Protein • ¼ Slider • 10 Optional Calories

---

246 Calories • 10 gm Fat • 4 gm Protein • 35 gm Carbohydrate • 253 mg Sodium • 6 mg Calcium • 2 gm Fiber

---

DIABETIC EXCHANGES: 1½ Starch • 1 Fruit • 1 Fat • ½ Meat

Holiday Banana Cranberry Meringue Pie

Bananas aren't the first fruit that comes to mind when you're baking for the holidays, but maybe that needs to change. Bananas are widely available all year round, and when they're ripe and ready, they make everything sweeter than sweet. In this pie, they "invite" those tart cranberries to dance up a storm! ☺ Serves 8

> 2 tablespoons cornstarch ☆
> 1 cup SPLENDA® Granular ☆
> ¾ cup water
> 2 cups fresh or frozen whole cranberries
> 2 cups (2 medium) sliced bananas
> 1 (6-ounce) purchased graham cracker piecrust
> 6 egg whites
> ½ teaspoon vanilla extract
> 1 tablespoon purchased graham cracker crumbs or 1 (2½-inch)
>   graham cracker square made into fine crumbs

Preheat oven to 375 degrees. In a medium saucepan, combine cornstarch, ½ cup SPLENDA®, and water. Stir in cranberries. Cook over medium heat until mixture thickens and cranberries soften, stirring often. Remove from heat. Carefully mash cranberries using a potato masher or fork. Gently fold in bananas. Place piecrust on a wire rack. Carefully spoon hot mixture into piecrust. In a large bowl, beat egg whites with an electric mixer on HIGH until soft peaks form. Add remaining ½ cup SPLENDA® and vanilla extract. Continue beating on HIGH until stiff peaks form. Spread meringue mixture evenly over filling mixture, being sure to seal to edges of piecrust. Evenly sprinkle graham cracker crumbs over top. Bake for 10 to 12 minutes or until meringue starts to turn golden brown. Place pie plate on a wire rack and let set for 30 minutes. Refrigerate for at least 1 hour. Cut into 8 servings.

HINTS: 1. Egg whites beat best at room temperature.
        2. Meringue pie cuts easily if you dip a sharp knife in warm water before slicing.

Each serving equals:

HE: 1 Bread • ¾ Fruit • ½ Fat • ¼ Protein •
¼ Slider • 2 Optional Calories

185 Calories • 5 gm Fat • 4 gm Protein •
31 gm Carbohydrate • 180 mg Sodium •
6 mg Calcium • 2 gm Fiber

DIABETIC EXCHANGES: 1 Starch • 1 Fruit • 1 Fat

Luscious Lemon Meringue Pie

Close your eyes, let the flavors roll across your tongue with every bite, and you'll know what paradise tastes like!

○ Serves 8

> 1 refrigerated unbaked 9-inch piecrust
> 2 cups SPLENDA® Granular ☆
> 6 tablespoons cornstarch
> 1¾ cups diet lemon-lime soda pop
> 2 egg yolks
> 2 tablespoons + 2 teaspoons reduced-calorie margarine
> ½ cup lemon juice
> 4 to 6 drops yellow food coloring
> 6 egg whites
> ½ teaspoon vanilla extract

Preheat oven to 425 degrees. Place piecrust in a 9-inch pie plate. Flute edges and prick bottom and sides with tines of a fork. Bake for 8 to 10 minutes or until lightly browned. Place pie plate on a wire rack and allow to cool completely. Lower heat to 350 degrees. Meanwhile, in a medium saucepan, combine 1½ cups SPLENDA® and cornstarch. Gradually stir in soda pop. Cook over medium-high heat until mixture thickens and starts to boil, stirring constantly. Lower heat and simmer for 2 minutes. Remove from heat. Place egg yolks in a large bowl. Stir 1 cup of hot filling mixture into yolks. Stir yolk mixture into mixture in saucepan. Continue cooking for 2 minutes or until mixture comes to a boil, stirring constantly. Remove from heat. Add margarine, lemon juice, and food coloring. Mix well to combine. Pour hot mixture into cooled piecrust. In a large bowl, beat egg whites with an electric mixer until soft peaks form. Add remaining ½ cup SPLENDA® and vanilla extract. Continue beating until stiff peaks form. Spread meringue mixture evenly over filling mixture, being sure to seal to edges of piecrust. Bake for 12 to 14 minutes until meringue starts to turn golden brown. Place pie plate on a wire rack and let set for 45 minutes. Refrigerate for at least 2 hours. Cut into 8 servings.

HINTS: 1. Egg whites beat best at room temperature.

2. Meringue pie cuts easily if you dip a sharp knife in warm water before slicing.

Each serving equals:

HE: 1 Bread • 1 Fat • ½ Protein • ½ Slider •
7 Optional Calories

---

210 Calories • 10 gm Fat • 4 gm Protein •
26 gm Carbohydrate • 194 mg Sodium •
9 mg Calcium • 1 gm Fiber

DIABETIC EXCHANGES: 1½ Starch/Carbohydrate •
1 Fat • ½ Meat

Baked Almond Cheesecake

Too full for dessert? Some guests might insist they are, but when you bring out this luscious cheesecake, they're sure to find room! This recipe makes it easy to be elegant. ☻ Serves 8

> ¾ cup purchased graham cracker crumbs or
> > 12 (2½-inch) graham cracker squares
> > made into crumbs
>
> 1¾ cups SPLENDA® Granular ☆
> ¼ cup reduced-calorie margarine
> 4 (8-ounce) packages fat-free
> > cream cheese
>
> 4 eggs, or equivalent in egg substitute
> 2 teaspoons almond extract ☆
> 1 cup no-fat sour cream
> 2 tablespoons sliced almonds, toasted

Preheat oven to 350 degrees. In a medium bowl, combine graham cracker crumbs, ¼ cup SPLENDA®, and margarine. Mix well to combine. Press mixture into an ungreased 9-inch springform pan. Set aside. In a large bowl, stir cream cheese with a sturdy spoon until softened. Add 1¼ cups SPLENDA® and eggs. Using an electric mixer on LOW, mix until mixture is blended and creamy. Fold in 1 teaspoon almond extract. Pour batter evenly over crust in springform pan. Bake for 55 to 60 minutes. Remove from oven and place on a wire rack. In a small bowl, combine sour cream, remaining ¼ cup SPLENDA® and remaining 1 teaspoon almond extract. Spread mixture evenly over filling. Continue baking for 5 minutes. Return pan to wire rack and allow to cool for 30 minutes. Evenly sprinkle almonds over top. Refrigerate for at least 8 hours. Remove sides from pan. Cut into 8 servings.

Each serving equals:

HE: 2½ Protein • ¾ Fat • ½ Bread • ½ Slider •
11 Optional Calories

---

260 Calories • 8 gm Fat • 22 gm Protein •
25 gm Carbohydrate • 647 mg Sodium •
379 mg Calcium • 0 gm Fiber

DIABETIC EXCHANGES: 2½ Meat •
1½ Starch/Carbohydrate • 1 Fat

Individual Chocolate Pudding Cakes

One of the most popular fancy restaurant desserts in recent years has been the soft-centered pudding cake or soufflé. I decided to create my own magnificent entry with this warm and wonderful treat. What a terrific way to show friends how much they are treasured!

○ Serves 8

> 1 cup cake flour
> 1¾ cups SPLENDA® Granular ☆
> 6 tablespoons unsweetened cocoa powder ☆
> 2 teaspoons baking powder
> ½ teaspoon baking soda
> ½ cup fat-free milk
> 2 tablespoons + 2 teaspoons vegetable oil
> 2 tablespoons unsweetened applesauce
> 1 teaspoon vanilla extract
> 1½ cups boiling water

Preheat oven to 350 degrees. Spray 8 (8-ounce) custard cups with butter-flavored cooking spray. In a large bowl, combine flour, 1 cup SPLENDA®, ¼ cup cocoa, baking powder, and baking soda. Add milk, vegetable oil, applesauce, and vanilla extract. Mix gently just to combine. (Batter will be thick.) Spread batter evenly into prepared custard cups. In a small bowl, combine remaining ¾ cup SPLENDA® and 2 tablespoons cocoa. Evenly sprinkle a full tablespoon of mixture over top of each cup. Spoon 3 tablespoons boiling water evenly over top of each. Place custard cups on a baking sheet. Bake for 25 minutes or until each is set around the sides and the top is soft and slightly bubbly. Place custard cups on a wire rack and let set for at least 10 minutes.

HINT: Good warm with sugar- and fat-free ice cream or cold with reduced-calorie whipped topping.

Each serving equals:

HE: 1 Fat • ⅔ Bread • ¼ Slider • 16 Optional Calories

129 Calories • 5 gm Fat • 2 gm Protein •
19 gm Carbohydrate • 209 mg Sodium •
93 mg Calcium • 1 gm Fiber

DIABETIC EXCHANGES: 1 Starch • 1 Fat

Devil's Food Cupcakes

You might think this recipe is just for a child's birthday party, but in fact, cupcakes are now seen at trendy weddings, replacing the formal wedding cake with a multitiered display of gorgeously decorated treats! ❍ Serves 8

2 tablespoons no-fat
   sour cream
⅓ cup reduced-calorie
   margarine
1 egg, or equivalent in egg
   substitute
1 teaspoon vanilla extract
½ cup fat-free milk

1½ teaspoons white distilled
   vinegar
1½ cups cake flour
½ cup unsweetened cocoa
   powder
1 cup SPLENDA® Granular
1 teaspoon baking soda
½ cup boiling water

Preheat oven to 350 degrees. Spray 8 wells of a 12-hole muffin pan with butter-flavored cooking spray or line with paper liners. In a large bowl, combine sour cream, margarine, egg, and vanilla extract. Stir in milk and vinegar. Add flour, cocoa, SPLENDA®, baking soda, and boiling water. Mix well to combine. Evenly spoon batter into each prepared well. Bake for 10 to 12 minutes or until a toothpick inserted in center comes out clean. Place muffin pan on a wire rack and allow to cool completely.

HINTS: 1. Fill unused muffin wells with water. It protects the muffin pan and ensures even cooking.
2. The tops turn darker chocolate, almost like they "frost" themselves.

Each serving equals:

HE: 1 Bread • 1 Fat • ¼ Slider • 13 Optional Calories

153 Calories • 5 gm Fat • 4 gm Protein •
23 gm Carbohydrate • 269 mg Sodium •
38 mg Calcium • 2 gm Fiber

DIABETIC EXCHANGES: 1 Starch • 1 Fat

Basic White Layer Cake

Every cook should have this classic in her repertoire. It's the ideal birthday or anniversary cake, the perfect graduation treat, the bakery basic that delivers a luscious result. ☻ Serves 8

1½ cups + 2 teaspoons reduced-fat biscuit baking mix ☆
¾ cup SPLENDA® Granular
⅔ cup fat-free milk
1 egg, or equivalent in egg substitute
2 tablespoons + 2 teaspoons reduced-calorie margarine
1½ teaspoons vanilla extract

Preheat oven to 350 degrees. Spray a 9-by-9-inch cake pan with butter-flavored cooking spray. Sprinkle 2 teaspoons baking mix into prepared pan. Gently pat pan to coat. In a large bowl, combine remaining 1½ cups baking mix and SPLENDA®. Add milk, egg, margarine, and vanilla extract. Mix gently just to combine. Spread batter evenly into prepared pan. Bake for 18 to 22 minutes or until a toothpick inserted in center comes out clean. Place pan on a wire rack and allow to cool completely. Cut into 8 servings.

Each serving equals:

HE: 1 Bread • ½ Fat • 18 Optional Calories

128 Calories • 4 gm Fat • 3 gm Protein •
20 gm Carbohydrate • 332 mg Sodium •
52 mg Calcium • 1 gm Fiber

DIABETIC EXCHANGES: 1 Starch • ½ Fat

Hawaiian Pineapple Cake

Pineapple inside plus pineapple on top—an excellent equation that adds up to impressively good flavor! If you can't jump on a plane for Hawaii, at the very least invite your taste buds to journey somewhere delectable. ◐ Serves 8

> 1½ cups reduced-fat biscuit baking mix
> ¾ cup SPLENDA® Granular
> 2 (8-ounce) cans crushed pineapple, packed
>   in fruit juice ☆
> 2 tablespoons fat-free half & half
> 1 egg, or equivalent in egg substitute
> 2 tablespoons reduced-calorie margarine
> ¼ cup chopped pecans ☆
> 1½ teaspoons coconut extract ☆
> 1 cup reduced-calorie whipped topping ☆
> 2 tablespoons flaked coconut

Preheat oven to 350 degrees. Spray a 9-inch round cake pan with butter-flavored cooking spray. In a large bowl, combine baking mix and SPLENDA®. Add 1 can undrained pineapple, half & half, egg, margarine, 2 tablespoons pecans, and 1 teaspoon coconut extract. Mix gently just to combine. Spread batter evenly into prepared pan. Bake for 18 to 22 minutes or until a toothpick inserted in center comes out clean. Place pan on a wire rack and allow to cool completely. Drain remaining can crushed pineapple well. In a medium bowl, gently combine crushed pineapple and whipped topping. Stir in remaining ½ teaspoon coconut extract. Sprinkle remaining 2 tablespoons pecans and coconut evenly over top. Cut into 8 servings. Refrigerate leftovers.

Each serving equals:

HE: 1 Bread • 1 Fat • ½ Fruit • ½ Slider •
6 Optional Calories

204 Calories • 8 gm Fat • 3 gm Protein •
30 gm Carbohydrate • 321 mg Sodium •
43 mg Calcium • 1 gm Fiber

DIABETIC EXCHANGES: 1½ Starch/Carbohydrate •
1 Fat • ½ Fruit

Cranberry-Walnut Sour Cream Cake

I'd like to give a standing ovation to the culinary chemistry whiz who figured out how to make a no-fat sour cream that tastes and bakes so beautifully! This cake would probably taste pretty good without it, but it's (as Mary Poppins might say) supercalifragilistic-expialidocious with it.   ☻   Serves 8

¾ cup no-fat sour cream
¼ cup reduced-calorie margarine
2 eggs, or equivalent in egg substitute
2 tablespoons fat-free half & half
¾ cup SPLENDA® Granular
1½ teaspoons vanilla extract
1½ cups cake flour
1 teaspoon baking powder
½ teaspoon baking soda
1 teaspoon pumpkin pie spice
1 cup sweetened dried cranberries
¼ cup chopped walnuts
½ cup reduced-calorie whipped topping

Preheat oven to 350 degrees. Spray a 9-by-9-inch cake pan with butter-flavored cooking spray. In a large bowl, combine sour cream, margarine, eggs, half & half, SPLENDA®, and vanilla extract. Add flour, baking powder, baking soda, and pumpkin pie spice. Mix gently just to combine. Fold in cranberries and walnuts. Spread batter evenly into prepared pan. Bake for 20 to 25 minutes or until a toothpick inserted in center comes out clean. Place pan on a wire rack and let set for at least 15 minutes. Cut into 8 servings. When serving, top each piece with 1 tablespoon whipped topping.

HINT: Raisins or chopped dried apricots can be used in place of cranberries.

Each serving equals:

HE: 1 Bread • 1 Fruit • 1 Fat • ¼ Protein •
½ Slider • 1 Optional Calorie

205 Calories • 5 gm Fat • 4 gm Protein •
36 gm Carbohydrate • 257 mg Sodium •
81 mg Calcium • 1 gm Fiber

DIABETIC EXCHANGES: 1½ Starch/Carbohydrate •
1 Fruit • 1 Fat

Fruit Cocktail Cake

This is sweeter than sweet, a real old-style cake that you can stir up anytime as long as you've got the right ingredients on your shelf. The nuts give it just the right amount of crunch.

Serves 8

> 1 cup cake flour
> ½ cup purchased graham cracker crumbs
> 1 cup SPLENDA® Granular
> 1 teaspoon baking soda
> 1 teaspoon baking powder
> 2 eggs, beaten, or equivalent in egg substitute
> 1 (8-ounce) can fruit cocktail, packed in fruit juice, undrained
> ¼ cup chopped pecans

Preheat oven to 350 degrees. Spray a 9-by-9-inch cake pan with butter-flavored cooking spray. In a large bowl, combine flour, graham cracker crumbs, SPLENDA®, baking soda, and baking powder. Stir in eggs, undrained fruit cocktail, and pecans. Spread batter evenly into prepared pan. Bake for 16 to 20 minutes or until a toothpick inserted in center comes out clean. Place pan on a wire rack and allow to cool completely. Cut into 8 servings.

HINT: Good served with reduced-calorie whipped topping, but don't forget to count the few additional calories.

Each serving equals:

HE: 1 Bread • ½ Fat • ¼ Protein • ¼ Fruit • 12 Optional Calories

---

140 Calories • 4 gm Fat • 4 gm Protein •
22 gm Carbohydrate • 206 mg Sodium •
14 mg Calcium • 1 gm Fiber

DIABETIC EXCHANGES: 1½ Starch • ½ Fat

Sour Cream Banana Cake

Stop right there! Were you just about to throw out those brown, overripe bananas that no one wants to eat because they're so soft and goodly? Don't do it! They're absolutely perfect for this lush, luxurious cake.   ◐   Serves 12

1½ cups SPLENDA® Granular
1 cup no-fat sour cream
2 eggs, or equivalent in egg
    substitute
1 cup (3 medium) mashed ripe
    bananas

2 cups cake flour
1 teaspoon baking powder
1 teaspoon baking soda
½ teaspoon table salt
½ cup chopped walnuts

Preheat oven to 350 degrees. Spray a 9-by-13-inch cake pan with butter-flavored cooking spray. In a large bowl, combine SPLENDA® and sour cream. Stir in eggs and mashed bananas. Add flour, baking powder, baking soda, and salt. Mix gently just to combine. Fold in walnuts. Spread batter evenly into prepared pan. Bake for 20 to 25 minutes or until a toothpick inserted in center comes out clean. Place pan on a wire rack and allow to cool completely. Cut into 12 servings.

HINT: Good topped with reduced-calorie whipped topping, but
    don't forget to count the few additional calories.

Each serving equals:

HE: ¾ Bread • ¾ Fruit • ⅓ Protein • ⅓ Fat •
½ Slider • 3 Optional Calories

152 Calories • 4 gm Fat • 4 gm Protein •
25 gm Carbohydrate • 280 mg Sodium •
61 mg Calcium • 2 gm Fiber

DIABETIC EXCHANGES: 1 Starch • ½ Fruit • ½ Fat

Snicker Doodles Cake

I figured, if it works for a cookie batter, it'd work for a cake—and I was right! Snickerdoodles are a beloved sugar-style cookie, and this recipe calls for an abundance of sweetness in the form of SPLENDA®. You couldn't make this cake with a calorie-free sweetener before we got SPLENDA®, but now you can!

● Serves 12

> 1 cup fat-free milk
> 1 teaspoon baking soda
> 2½ cups SPLENDA® Granular ☆
> ½ cup reduced-calorie margarine
> ½ cup no-fat sour cream
> 2 eggs, beaten, or equivalent in egg substitute
> 2½ cups cake flour
> 2 teaspoons cream of tartar
> 1 teaspoon ground cinnamon

Preheat oven to 350 degrees. Spray a 9-by-13-inch cake pan with butter-flavored cooking spray. In a small bowl, combine milk and baking soda. Set aside. In a large bowl, combine 2 cups SPLENDA®, margarine, sour cream, and eggs. Stir in milk mixture. Add flour and cream of tartar. Mix gently just to combine. Spread batter evenly into prepared pan. In a small bowl, combine cinnamon and remaining ½ cup SPLENDA®. Evenly sprinkle mixture over batter. Using a fork, swirl cinnamon mixture into batter. Lightly spray top with butter-flavored cooking spray. Bake for 18 to 22 minutes or until a toothpick inserted in center comes out clean. Place pan on a wire rack and allow to cool completely. Cut into 12 servings.

HINT: Good topped with reduced-calorie whipped topping, but don't forget to count the additional calories.

Each serving equals:

HE: 1 Bread • 1 Fat • ½ Slider • 6 Optional Calories

165 Calories • 5 gm Fat • 4 gm Protein •
26 gm Carbohydrate • 231 mg Sodium •
49 mg Calcium • 1 gm Fiber

DIABETIC EXCHANGES: 1½ Starch/Carbohydrate • 1 Fat

Apricot-Pecan Cake

Invite your mother-in-law to dinner and you'll win more than her son's heart when you serve this culinary champion! Its silken texture makes every bite a delight, and the nutty, fruit flavor is a true original.   ❍   Serves 8

¾ cup no-fat sour cream	½ cup SPLENDA® Granular
¼ cup fat-free half & half	1 teaspoon baking powder
2 eggs, or equivalent in egg substitute	½ teaspoon baking soda
1 teaspoon vanilla extract	1 teaspoon ground cinnamon
1½ cups cake flour	1 cup chopped dried apricots
	¼ cup chopped pecans

Preheat oven to 350 degrees. Spray a 9-by-9-inch cake pan with butter-flavored cooking spray. In a large bowl, combine sour cream, half & half, eggs, and vanilla extract. Add flour, SPLENDA®, baking powder, baking soda, and cinnamon. Mix gently just to combine. Fold in apricots and pecans. Spread batter evenly into prepared pan. Bake for 20 to 25 minutes or until a toothpick inserted in center comes out clean. Place pan on a wire rack and let set for at least 5 minutes. Cut into 8 servings.

HINT: Good topped with sugar- and fat-free vanilla ice cream, but don't forget to count the additional calories.

Each serving equals:

HE: 1 Bread • 1 Fruit • ½ Fat • ¼ Protein • ¼ Slider • 13 Optional Calories

---

196 Calories • 4 gm Fat • 5 gm Protein • 35 gm Carbohydrate • 194 mg Sodium • 100 mg Calcium • 2 gm Fiber

---

DIABETIC EXCHANGES: 1½ Starch • 1 Fruit • ½ Fat

Sour Cream Chocolate Cake

Cocoa powder packs a sensational punch. Its intensity delivers a wicked wallop when stirred into any cake batter. Combined with just enough silky sour cream, it produces a dream dessert!

● Serves 12

1 cup boiling water
1 teaspoon baking soda
2 eggs, beaten, or equivalent in egg substitute
2 cups SPLENDA® Granular
1 cup no-fat sour cream
1½ teaspoons vanilla extract
2 cups cake flour
¼ cup unsweetened cocoa powder
½ teaspoon table salt

Preheat oven to 350 degrees. Spray a 9-by-13-inch cake pan with butter-flavored cooking spray. In a small bowl, combine boiling water and baking soda. Set aside. In a large bowl, combine eggs, SPLENDA®, sour cream, and vanilla extract. Add flour, cocoa, and salt. Mix gently just to combine. Stir water mixture into flour mixture. Spread batter evenly in prepared pan. Bake for 14 to 16 minutes or until a toothpick inserted in center comes out clean. Place pan on a wire rack and allow to cool completely. Cut into 12 servings.

Each serving equals:

HE: ¾ Bread • ½ Slider • 13 Optional Calories

113 Calories • 1 gm Fat • 4 gm Protein •
22 gm Carbohydrate • 239 mg Sodium •
36 mg Calcium • 1 gm Fiber

DIABETIC EXCHANGES: 1½ Starch/Carbohydrate

Chocolate Wacky Cake

All I can say is, follow the instructions for preparing this recipe—no matter how strange or peculiar they appear to be! It may seem like a wacky way to make a cake, but a little kitchen magic will convince you. Wacky seems wacky, till wacky works! ☻ Serves 8

1½ cups cake flour

1 cup SPLENDA® Granular

3 tablespoons unsweetened cocoa powder

1 teaspoon baking soda

½ teaspoon table salt

⅓ cup reduced-calorie margarine, melted

1 tablespoon white distilled vinegar

1½ teaspoons vanilla extract

1 cup cold water

Preheat oven to 350 degrees. In an ungreased 9-by-9-inch cake pan, combine flour, SPLENDA®, cocoa, baking soda, and salt. Make 3 depressions in flour mixture. Pour melted margarine in one, vinegar in second, and vanilla extract in third. Pour water evenly over all. Mix gently using a fork, BUT DO NOT BEAT. Bake for 30 to 35 minutes or until a toothpick inserted in center comes out clean. Place pan on a wire rack and allow to cool completely. Cut into 8 servings.

Each serving equals:

HE: 1 Bread • 1 Fat • 17 Optional Calories

124 Calories • 4 gm Fat • 2 gm Protein •
20 gm Carbohydrate • 393 mg Sodium •
7 mg Calcium • 1 gm Fiber

DIABETIC EXCHANGES: 1 Starch • 1 Fat

Red Chocolate Cake

Are you confused yet? It's chocolate, but it's red. Why would you want to do such a crazy thing? First of all, it's fun. Second, it's surprising. And third, it tastes delicious. If your favorite ball team or high school's colors include red, go for it! ☽ Serves 8

2 cups SPLENDA® Granular
¼ cup reduced-calorie margarine
2 eggs, or equivalent in egg substitute
¾ cup no-fat sour cream
1 teaspoon vanilla extract
1½ cups cake flour

3 tablespoons unsweetened cocoa powder
½ teaspoon baking powder
2 teaspoons baking soda
1 cup boiling water
2 tablespoons red food coloring
1 cup reduced-calorie whipped topping

Preheat oven to 350 degrees. Spray a 9-inch round cake pan with butter-flavored cooking spray. In a large bowl, combine SPLENDA®, margarine, eggs, sour cream, and vanilla extract. Add flour, cocoa, baking powder, and baking soda. Mix gently just to combine. Stir in boiling water and red food coloring. Spread batter evenly into prepared pan. Bake for 35 to 40 minutes or until a toothpick inserted in center comes out clean. Place pan on a wire rack and allow to cool completely. Cut into 12 servings. When serving, top each piece with 2 tablespoons whipped topping.

Each serving equals:

HE: 1 Bread • ¾ Fat • ¼ Protein • ¾ Slider • 10 Optional Calories

177 Calories • 5 gm Fat • 4 gm Protein • 29 gm Carbohydrate • 490 mg Sodium • 76 mg Calcium • 1 gm Fiber

DIABETIC EXCHANGES: 1½ Starch/Carbohydrate • 1 Fat

Hello Dolly Chocolate Cake

Remember that magical scene in the movie musical when Dolly walks down a long staircase while everyone welcomes her home with the title song? It's an unforgettable, thrilling moment that will make hearts beat faster and eyes light up. Well, so will this captivating cake!   ☻   Serves 8

> 1½ cups cake flour
> 1 cup SPLENDA® Granular
> ¼ cup unsweetened cocoa powder
> 2 teaspoons baking powder
> 1 teaspoon baking soda
> ⅔ cup fat-free milk
> ½ cup no-fat sour cream
> 2 tablespoons + 2 teaspoons reduced-calorie margarine
> 2 eggs, or equivalent in egg substitute
> 2 teaspoons vanilla extract
> ½ teaspoon coconut extract
> 2 tablespoons lite chocolate syrup
> ¼ cup chopped pecans
> ¼ cup mini chocolate chips
> 2 tablespoons flaked coconut

Preheat oven to 350 degrees. Spray a 9-by-9-inch cake pan with butter-flavored cooking spray. In a large bowl, combine flour, SPLENDA®, cocoa, baking powder, and baking soda. In a small bowl, combine milk, sour cream, margarine, eggs, vanilla extract, and coconut extract. Add milk mixture to flour mixture. Mix gently just to combine. Spread batter evenly into prepared pan. Evenly drizzle chocolate syrup over batter. Sprinkle pecans, chocolate chips, and coconut evenly over top. Bake for 20 to 25 minutes or until a toothpick inserted near center comes out clean. Place pan on a wire rack and allow to cool completely. Cut into 8 servings.

Each serving equals:

HE: 1 Bread • 1 Fat • ¼ Protein • ¾ Slider •
8 Optional Calories

---

199 Calories • 7 gm Fat • 5 gm Protein •
29 gm Carbohydrate • 259 mg Sodium •
62 mg Calcium • 2 gm Fiber

DIABETIC EXCHANGES: 2 Starch/Carbohydrate • 1 Fat

Mud Pie Cake

As kids, we loved to play in the mud, even pretending to make "yummy" pies from dirt and water. Now that we're all grown up, we can't resist the real thing—a chocolate dessert that is marvelously moist and really rich! ☻ Serves 8

1 cup + 2 tablespoons cake
    flour
1¾ cups SPLENDA®
    Granular ☆
½ teaspoon table salt
2 teaspoons baking powder
¼ cup unsweetened cocoa
    powder ☆

½ cup fat-free half & half
2 tablespoons + 2 teaspoons
    reduced-calorie
    margarine, melted
1 teaspoon vanilla extract
¼ cup chopped walnuts
1 cup hot water

Preheat oven to 325 degrees. Spray a deep-dish 9-inch pie plate with butter-flavored cooking spray. In a large bowl, combine flour, ¾ cup SPLENDA®, salt, baking powder, and 1 tablespoon cocoa. Add half & half, melted margarine, and vanilla extract. Mix gently just to combine. Fold in walnuts. Evenly spread batter into prepared pie plate. In a medium bowl, combine remaining 3 tablespoons cocoa, remaining 1 cup SPLENDA®, and hot water. Drizzle water mixture evenly over batter. Bake for 30 to 35 minutes. Place pie plate on a wire rack and let set for at least 10 minutes. Cut into 8 servings.

HINT: Good as is or with sugar- and fat-free vanilla ice cream, but don't forget to count the additional calories.

Each serving equals:

HE: ¾ Bread • ¾ Fat • ½ Slider • 4 Optional Calories

132 Calories • 4 gm Fat • 3 gm Protein •
21 gm Carbohydrate • 328 mg Sodium •
101 mg Calcium • 1 gm Fiber

DIABETIC EXCHANGES: 1 Starch • 1 Fat

Angel Fool's Loaf Cake

Remember to use a completely clean bowl when you're whipping up the egg whites in this frothy cake batter. It's light, it's oh-so-lovely, and it's amazingly low in calories, too. I like to serve it with fresh fruit and a dab of whipped topping, but I bet a little chocolate sauce wouldn't be bad, either. ☺ Serves 12

1 cup cake flour	*12 egg whites*
1½ cups SPLENDA®	*2 tablespoons vanilla extract*
Granular☆	*¼ teaspoon table salt*

Preheat oven to 350 degrees. In a small bowl, combine cake flour and ¾ cup SPLENDA®. Mix well using a wire whisk. Place egg whites in a very large glass mixing bowl. Beat egg whites with an electric mixer on HIGH until foamy. Add vanilla extract and salt. Continue beating until stiff enough to form soft peaks. Add remaining ¾ cup SPLENDA®, 2 tablespoons at a time, while continuing to beat egg whites until stiff peaks form. Add the flour mixture, ½ cup at a time, folding in with spatula or wire whisk. Pour batter into an ungreased 9-by-13-inch metal cake pan. Run a knife through batter to remove air bubbles. Bake for 15 to 18 minutes or until cake springs back when lightly touched. Do not overbake. Place pan on a wire rack and allow to cool. Cut into 12 servings.

HINTS: 1. Garnish any way you would angel food cake.
2. If you prefer, this can be baked in a regular angel food cake pan for 27 to 30 minutes.

Each serving equals:

HE: ⅓ Bread • ⅓ Protein • ¼ Slider •
1 Optional Calorie

64 Calories • 0 gm Fat • 5 gm Protein •
11 gm Carbohydrate • 103 mg Sodium •
3 mg Calcium • 0 gm Fiber

DIABETIC EXCHANGES: ½ Starch • ½ Meat

Magnificent Muffins, Quick Breads, and Coffee Cakes

One of the first items dieters usually give up is their morning muffins or that beloved piece of coffee cake to accompany a much-needed cup of coffee at three in the afternoon (or one in the morning, depending on your schedule!). But I say, why should you give up those little things that make life bearable, even wonderful? You don't have to because I've got muffins, quick breads, and coffee cakes to win your heart with just one bite.

It's 6 a.m. and your eyes aren't quite open yet, but I promise you, if you pop one of my **Start the Day Muffins** into your toaster oven to warm it up, you'll be ready in a jiffy for whatever challenges your day demands. (And my **Southern Delight Muffins** are just peachy keen, believe me!) **Grandma's Black Walnut Banana Bread** is perfect for the 11 a.m. munchies and an ideal offering for the next bake sale fund-raiser at your daughter's school. And when your dearest friends drop by for coffee, show how much their friendship means to you by serving **Cranberry Walnut Coffee Cake** or **Sour Cream Raspberry Coffee Cake**.

Apple Biscuit Breakfast Treat

Here's a fast and easy, crunchy-crispy morning marvel that everyone will adore! It's wonderfully aromatic, sure to call every apple lover for miles around to race toward your kitchen. ☻ Serves 6

> 2 cups cored, peeled, and chopped cooking apples
> 1/4 cup seedless raisins
> 1 (7½-ounce) can refrigerated buttermilk biscuits
> 1/4 cup SPLENDA® Granular
> 1/4 cup sugar-free maple syrup
> 1 teaspoon ground cinnamon
> 2 tablespoons chopped pecans

Preheat oven to 350 degrees. Spray an 8-inch pie plate with butter-flavored cooking spray. Evenly layer apples and raisins in prepared pie plate. Separate biscuits and cut each into 4 pieces. Sprinkle biscuit pieces over raisins. In a small bowl, combine SPLENDA®, maple syrup, cinnamon, and pecans. Drizzle mixture evenly over top. Bake for 25 to 30 minutes. Place serving plate over top of pie plate and invert onto serving plate. Cut into 6 wedges.

Each serving equals:

HE: 1¼ Bread • 1 Fruit • 1/3 Fat •
10 Optional Calories

---

155 Calories • 3 gm Fat • 3 gm Protein •
29 gm Carbohydrate • 321 mg Sodium •
10 mg Calcium • 3 gm Fiber

DIABETIC EXCHANGES: 1 Starch • 1 Fruit

Quick Cinnamon Apricot Biscuit Bread

I just love handy, healthy convenience foods like these blissful buttermilk biscuits! When topped with a fantastic fruity topping, they make every day feel like a holiday. ☻ Serves 6

> 1 (7½-ounce) can refrigerated buttermilk biscuits
> ⅔ cup finely chopped dried apricots
> ½ teaspoon ground cinnamon
> ½ cup hot water
> 2 tablespoons apricot spreadable fruit
> 1 tablespoon reduced-calorie margarine
> ½ cup SPLENDA® Granular

Preheat oven to 425 degrees. Spray an 8-inch pie plate with butter-flavored cooking spray. Separate biscuits and cut each into 2 pieces. Arrange half of biscuit pieces in prepared pie plate. Sprinkle apricots evenly over top. Arrange remaining biscuit pieces over apricots. Lightly spray tops with butter-flavored cooking spray. Sprinkle cinnamon evenly over top. In a small bowl, combine hot water, spreadable fruit, margarine, and SPLENDA®. Carefully pour mixture evenly over top. Bake for 10 to 12 minutes. Place pie plate on a wire rack. Lightly spray top with butter-flavored cooking spray. Let set for at least 5 minutes. Cut into 6 wedges.

Each serving equals:

HE: 1¼ Bread • 1 Fruit • ¼ Fat • 8 Optional Calories

162 Calories • 2 gm Fat • 3 gm Protein •
33 gm Carbohydrate • 326 mg Sodium •
11 mg Calcium • 1 gm Fiber

DIABETIC EXCHANGES: 1 Starch • 1 Fruit

Rise & Shine Peanut Butter & Jelly Muffins

What child (of any age) wouldn't find it easier to get up in the morning when these lip-smacking muffins are on the menu? With all of the flavors of spreadable fruit available, you can try a new one every week or two for a year! ☻ Serves 8

¾ cup water
1 tablespoon white distilled vinegar
⅔ cup nonfat dry milk powder
1½ cups all-purpose flour
⅓ cup SPLENDA® Granular
1½ teaspoons baking powder
½ teaspoon baking soda
2 tablespoons no-fat sour cream
¼ cup reduced-fat peanut butter
1 egg, or equivalent in egg substitute
¼ cup spreadable fruit (any flavor)

Preheat oven to 375 degrees. Spray 8 wells of a 12-hole muffin pan with butter-flavored cooking spray or line with paper liners. In a small bowl, combine water, vinegar, and dry milk powder. Set aside. In a large bowl, combine flour, SPLENDA®, baking powder, and baking soda. Add milk mixture, sour cream, peanut butter, and egg. Mix gently just to combine. Spoon 1 tablespoon batter into each prepared muffin well. Top each with ½ teaspoon spreadable fruit. Evenly spoon remaining batter over top. Bake for 10 to 12 minutes or until a toothpick inserted in center comes out clean. Place muffin pan on a wire rack and let set for 5 minutes. Remove muffins from pan and continue cooling on wire rack.

HINT: Fill unused muffin wells with water. It protects the muffin tin and ensures even baking.

Each serving equals:

HE: 1 Bread • ½ Protein • ½ Fruit • ½ Fat • ¼ Fat-Free Milk • 18 Optional Calories

192 Calories • 4 gm Fat • 7 gm Protein • 32 gm Carbohydrate • 277 mg Sodium • 137 mg Calcium • 1 gm Fiber

DIABETIC EXCHANGES: 1½ Starch/Carbohydrate • ½ Meat • ½ Fruit • ½ Fat

Start the Day Muffins

In a hurry in the morning? (Aren't we all?) Now you can grab a tasty muffin and get your juice in, too. These are remarkably moist and oh-so-sweet.   ☺   Serves 8

⅔ cup dry milk powder

1 cup unsweetened orange juice

¼ cup reduced-calorie margarine

1 egg, or equivalent in egg substitute

⅓ cup SPLENDA® Granular

1½ cups reduced-fat biscuit baking mix

2 tablespoons orange marmalade spreadable fruit

Preheat oven to 375 degrees. Spray 8 wells of a 12-hole muffin pan with butter-flavored cooking spray or line with paper liners. In a large bowl, combine dry milk powder and orange juice. Stir in margarine, egg, and SPLENDA®. Add baking mix. Mix just until combined. Evenly spoon batter into prepared muffin wells. Top each with ¾ teaspoon spreadable fruit. Bake for 16 to 20 minutes or until a toothpick inserted in center comes out clean. Place muffin pan on a wire rack and let set for 5 minutes. Remove muffins from pan and continue cooling on wire rack.

HINT: Fill unused muffin wells with water. It protects the muffin tin and ensures even baking.

Each serving equals:

HE: 1 Bread • ¾ Fat • ½ Fruit • ¼ Fat-Free Milk • 13 Optional Calories

165 Calories • 5 gm Fat • 5 gm Protein • 25 gm Carbohydrate • 369 mg Sodium • 104 mg Calcium • 1 gm Fiber

DIABETIC EXCHANGES: 1 Starch • 1 Fat • ½ Fruit

Banana Bonanza Muffins

Light, lovely, and velvety, these muffins deliver an abundance of rich banana taste. You'll feel as if you've uncovered buried treasure when you enjoy a muffin prepared with this simple recipe.

◐ Serves 8

1½ cups reduced-fat biscuit baking mix
½ cup SPLENDA® Granular
1 teaspoon baking powder
¼ cup reduced-calorie margarine
1 egg, or equivalent in egg substitute
1 cup (3 medium) mashed ripe bananas

Preheat oven to 375 degrees. Spray 8 wells of a 12-hole muffin pan with butter-flavored cooking spray or line with paper liners. In a large bowl, combine baking mix, SPLENDA®, and baking powder. Add margarine, egg, and mashed bananas. Mix gently just to combine. Evenly spoon batter into prepared muffin wells. Bake for 15 to 20 minutes or until a toothpick inserted in center comes out clean. Place muffin pan on a wire rack and let set for 5 minutes. Remove muffins from pan and continue cooling on wire rack.

HINT: Fill unused muffin wells with water. It protects the muffin tin and ensures even baking.

Each serving equals:

HE: 1 Bread • ¾ Fruit • ¾ Fat • 6 Optional Calories

153 Calories • 5 gm Fat • 3 gm Protein •
24 gm Carbohydrate • 398 mg Sodium •
62 mg Calcium • 1 gm Fiber

DIABETIC EXCHANGES: 1 Starch • ½ Fruit • ½ Fat

Chocolate Delight Banana Muffins

Bananas and chocolate make a fantastic culinary partnership! Both are such feel-good flavors you just can't feel sad for a second after munching one of these. 　●　 Serves 8

1½ cups reduced-fat biscuit baking mix
¾ cup SPLENDA® Granular
¼ cup unsweetened cocoa powder
1 teaspoon baking powder
½ teaspoon baking soda
1 cup (3 medium) mashed ripe bananas
1 egg, or equivalent in egg substitute
¼ cup reduced-calorie margarine
¼ cup fat-free milk
2 tablespoons no-fat sour cream
¼ cup mini chocolate chips
¼ cup chopped walnuts

Preheat oven to 375 degrees. Spray 8 wells of a 12-hole muffin pan with butter-flavored cooking spray or line with paper liners. In a large bowl, combine baking mix, SPLENDA®, cocoa, baking powder, and baking soda. In a small bowl, combine mashed bananas, egg, margarine, milk, and sour cream. Add banana mixture to baking mix mixture. Mix gently just to combine. Fold in chocolate chips and walnuts. Evenly spoon batter into prepared muffin wells. Bake for 20 to 25 minutes or until a toothpick inserted in center comes out clean. Place muffin pan on a wire rack and let set for 5 minutes. Remove muffins from pan and continue cooling on wire rack.

HINT: Fill unused muffin wells with water. It protects the muffin tin and ensures even baking.

Each serving equals:

HE: 1 Bread • 1 Fat • ¾ Fruit • ¼ Protein •
¼ Slider • 18 Optional Calories

208 Calories • 8 gm Fat • 4 gm Protein •
30 gm Carbohydrate • 487 mg Sodium •
85 mg Calcium • 2 gm Fiber

DIABETIC EXCHANGES: 1 Starch • 1 Fat • 1 Fruit

Cinnamon Chocolate Chip Muffins

Blending cinnamon and chocolate is a "make it Mexican" flavor tradition, so even if you can't make time for a trip south of the border, these moist and aromatic muffins taste like a mini vacation in every bite. ☻ Serves 8

1½ cups reduced-fat biscuit baking mix
1 teaspoon ground cinnamon
1 teaspoon baking soda
¾ cup SPLENDA® Granular
1 cup fat-free milk
¼ cup reduced-calorie margarine
1 egg, beaten, or equivalent in egg substitute
¼ cup chopped walnuts
¼ cup mini chocolate chips

Preheat oven to 350 degrees. Spray 8 wells of a 12-hole muffin pan with butter-flavored cooking spray or line with paper liners. In a large bowl, combine baking mix, cinnamon, baking soda, and SPLENDA®. Add milk, margarine, and egg. Mix gently just to combine. Fold in walnuts and chocolate chips. Evenly spoon batter into prepared muffin wells. Bake for 20 to 25 minutes or until a toothpick inserted in center comes out clean. Place muffin pan on a wire rack and let set for 5 minutes. Remove muffins from pan and continue cooling on wire rack.

HINT: Fill unused muffin wells with water. It protects the muffin tin and ensures even baking.

Each serving equals:

HE: 1 Bread • 1 Fat • ½ Protein • ½ Slider • 17 Optional Calories

176 Calories • 8 gm Fat • 4 gm Protein • 22 gm Carbohydrate • 489 mg Sodium • 72 mg Calcium • 1 gm Fiber

DIABETIC EXCHANGES: 1½ Starch/Carbohydrate • 1 Fat

Southern Delight Muffins

These are "powerfully" peach in flavor, with just a touch of nutti-ness for an appealing contrast. Y'all will surely love 'em!

● Serves 8

> 1 (15-ounce) can sliced peaches, packed in fruit juice, drained,
>   and ½ cup liquid reserved
> 1½ cups reduced-fat biscuit baking mix
> ½ cup SPLENDA® Granular
> 1 teaspoon baking powder
> 1 tablespoon + 1 teaspoon reduced-calorie margarine
> ¼ cup no-fat sour cream
> 2 tablespoons peach spreadable fruit
> 2 tablespoons chopped pecans

Preheat oven to 375 degrees. Spray 8 wells of a 12-hole muffin pan with butter-flavored cooking spray or line with paper liners. Finely chop peaches. Set aside. In a large bowl, combine baking mix, SPLENDA®, and baking powder. Add margarine, sour cream, reserved fruit juice, and spreadable fruit. Mix gently just to combine. Fold in chopped peaches and pecans. Evenly spoon batter into prepared muffin wells. Bake for 24 to 28 minutes or until a toothpick inserted in center comes out clean. Place muffin pan on a wire rack and let set for 5 minutes. Remove muffins from pan and continue cooling on wire rack.

HINT: Fill unused muffin wells with water. It protects the muffin tin and ensures even baking.

Each serving equals:

HE: 1 Bread • ¾ Fruit • ½ Fat • 13 Optional Calories

155 Calories • 3 gm Fat • 2 gm Protein •
30 gm Carbohydrate • 358 mg Sodium •
68 mg Calcium • 1 gm Fiber

DIABETIC EXCHANGES: 1 Starch • 1 Fruit • ½ Fat

Festive Cranberry Muffins

This colorful berry is as rich in vitamin C as it is terrifically tart. Lucky for us, SPLENDA® sweetens it just enough to make these muffins a passion and a pleasure. ♥ Serves 12

1 cup chopped fresh or frozen cranberries

¾ cup SPLENDA® Granular ☆

¾ cup fat-free milk

2 teaspoons white distilled vinegar

1 egg, or equivalent in egg substitute

¼ cup reduced-calorie margarine

2 cups all-purpose flour

¾ teaspoon baking soda

¼ teaspoon table salt

Preheat oven to 375 degrees. Spray a 12-hole muffin pan with butter-flavored cooking spray or line with paper liners. In a small bowl, combine cranberries and ½ cup SPLENDA®. Let set for 30 minutes. In a large bowl, combine milk and vinegar. Stir in egg and margarine. Add flour, remaining ¼ cup SPLENDA®, baking soda, and salt. Mix gently just to combine. Fold in cranberry mixture. Evenly spoon batter into prepared muffin wells. Bake for 12 to 15 minutes or until a toothpick inserted in center comes out clean. Place muffin pan on a wire rack and let set for 5 minutes. Remove muffins from pan and continue cooling on wire rack.

HINT: Don't be surprised when the muffins come out of the oven green tinted with the specks of red cranberry peeking through!

Each serving equals:

HE: ¾ Bread • ½ Fat • ¼ Slider • 12 Optional Calories

115 Calories • 3 gm Fat • 3 gm Protein • 19 gm Carbohydrate • 186 mg Sodium • 25 mg Calcium • 1 gm Fiber

DIABETIC EXCHANGES: 1 Starch • ½ Fat

Raisin-Pecan Muffins

Laden with fruit and nuts, these are perfect for a chilly winter morning's brunch. They also freeze beautifully and are even better (I think) a day or two later.   ☻   Serves 8

1½ cups all-purpose flour
½ cup SPLENDA® Granular☆
1½ teaspoons baking powder
½ teaspoon baking soda
¾ cup fat-free milk
2 tablespoons no-fat sour cream

1 tablespoon + 1 teaspoon
   vegetable oil
1½ teaspoons vanilla extract
1 cup seedless raisins
¼ cup chopped pecans
½ teaspoon ground cinnamon

Preheat oven to 375 degrees. Spray 8 wells of a 12-hole muffin pan with butter-flavored cooking spray or line with paper liners. In a small bowl, combine flour, 6 tablespoons SPLENDA®, baking powder, and baking soda. Add milk, sour cream, oil, and vanilla extract. Mix gently just to combine. Fold in raisins and pecans. Evenly spoon batter into prepared muffin wells. In a small bowl, combine remaining 2 tablespoons SPLENDA® and cinnamon. Sprinkle about ¾ teaspoon SPLENDA® mixture evenly over top of each muffin. Bake for 15 to 20 minutes or until a toothpick inserted in center comes out clean. Place muffin pan on a wire rack and let set for 5 minutes. Remove muffins from pan and continue cooling on wire rack.

HINT: Fill unused muffin wells with water. It protects the muffin tin and ensures even baking.

Each serving equals:

HE: 1 Bread • 1 Fruit • ½ Fat • 18 Optional Calories

232 Calories • 8 gm Fat • 4 gm Protein •
36 gm Carbohydrate • 189 mg Sodium •
102 mg Calcium • 2 gm Fiber

DIABETIC EXCHANGES: 1½ Starch/Carbohydrate •
1 Fruit • ½ Fat

Give Me S'More Muffins

Joyful childhood memories live again in these irresistible marvels!
Don't you just love those melted marshmallows?

◑ Serves 8

> ¾ cup purchased graham cracker crumbs or
>> 12 (2½-inch) graham crackers, made into crumbs
>
> ¾ cup reduced-fat biscuit baking mix
> ¼ cup SPLENDA® Granular
> 1 teaspoon baking powder
> ½ teaspoon baking soda
> 1 cup miniature marshmallows
> ¼ cup mini chocolate chips
> ¾ cup fat-free milk
> ¼ cup no-fat sour cream
> 1½ teaspoons vanilla extract

Preheat oven to 375 degrees. Spray 8 wells of a 12-hole muffin
pan with butter-flavored cooking spray or line with paper liners. In
a large bowl, combine graham cracker crumbs, baking mix,
SPLENDA®, baking powder, and baking soda. Stir in marshmallows and chocolate chips. In a small bowl, combine milk, sour
cream, and vanilla extract. Add milk mixture to graham cracker
mixture. Mix gently just to combine. Evenly spoon batter into prepared muffin wells. Bake for 13 to 15 minutes or until a toothpick
inserted in center comes out clean. Place muffin pan on a wire rack
and let set for 5 minutes. Remove muffins from pan and continue
cooling on wire rack.

HINTS: 1. A self-seal sandwich bag works great for crushing graham crackers.
2. Fill unused muffin wells with water. It protects the
muffin tin and ensures even baking.

Each serving equals:

HE: 1 Bread • ½ Slider • 15 Optional Calories

130 Calories • 2 gm Fat • 3 gm Protein •
25 gm Carbohydrate • 343 mg Sodium •
87 mg Calcium • 1 gm Fiber

DIABETIC EXCHANGES: 1½ Starch/Carbohydrate

Cheese & Dill Muffins

A muffin with one cheese will please your taste buds, but one that features two will be hard to resist—so don't! The piquant aroma these produce while baking will send hungry family members racing to the kitchen. ☻ Serves 8

> 1½ cups all-purpose flour
> ¼ cup SPLENDA® Granular
> 1½ teaspoons baking powder
> 1 teaspoon baking soda
> ¼ cup grated reduced-fat Parmesan cheese
> 2 teaspoons dried dill weed
> 1 cup + 2 tablespoons shredded reduced-fat Cheddar cheese
> ⅔ cup fat-free half & half
> 3 tablespoons no-fat sour cream
> 2 tablespoons + 2 teaspoons vegetable oil
> 1 egg, or equivalent in egg substitute
> 2 teaspoons prepared yellow mustard

Preheat oven to 375 degrees. Spray 8 wells of a 12-hole muffin pan with butter-flavored cooking spray or line with paper liners. In a large bowl, combine flour, SPLENDA®, baking powder, baking soda, and Parmesan cheese. Stir in dill weed and Cheddar cheese. In a small bowl, combine half & half, sour cream, vegetable oil, egg, and mustard. Add liquid mixture to dry mixture. Mix gently just to combine. Evenly spoon batter into prepared muffin wells. Bake for 15 to 20 minutes or until a toothpick inserted in center comes out clean. Place muffin pan on a wire rack and let set for 5 minutes. Remove muffins from pan and continue cooling on wire rack.

HINT: Fill unused muffin wells with water. It protects the muffin tin and ensures even baking.

Each serving equals:

HE: 1 Bread • 1 Protein • 1 Fat • ¼ Slider • 1 Optional Calorie

209 Calories • 9 gm Fat • 9 gm Protein • 23 gm Carbohydrate • 485 mg Sodium • 233 mg Calcium • 1 gm Fiber

DIABETIC EXCHANGES: 1 Starch • 1 Meat • 1 Fat

Cornbread "Buttermilk" Muffins

You won't believe how easy it is to make your own buttermilk in this old-fashioned recipe that is perfect for a casual brunch or Sunday supper, served alongside a hearty bowl of homemade soup.

○ Serves 12

> 1 cup nonfat dry milk powder
>
> 1¼ cups water
>
> 1 tablespoon white distilled vinegar
>
> 1 cup yellow cornmeal
>
> ¾ cup reduced-fat biscuit baking mix
>
> 1 teaspoon baking powder
>
> ⅔ cup SPLENDA® Granular
>
> 1 egg, slightly beaten, or equivalent in egg substitute
>
> ¼ cup reduced-calorie margarine

Preheat oven to 375 degrees. Spray a 12-hole muffin pan with butter-flavored cooking spray or line with paper liners. In a small bowl, combine dry milk powder, water, and vinegar. Set aside. In a large bowl, combine cornmeal, baking mix, baking powder, and SPLENDA®. Add milk mixture, egg, and margarine. Mix gently just to combine. Evenly spoon batter into prepared muffin wells. Bake for 12 to 14 minutes or until a toothpick inserted in center comes out clean. Place muffin pan on a wire rack and let set for 5 minutes. Remove muffins from pan and continue cooling on wire rack.

Each serving equals:

HE: 1 Bread • ½ Fat • ¼ Fat-Free Milk •
11 Optional Calories

119 Calories • 3 gm Fat • 4 gm Protein •
19 gm Carbohydrate • 210 mg Sodium •
109 mg Calcium • 1 gm Fiber

DIABETIC EXCHANGES: 1 Starch • ½ Fat

Applesauce Nut Bread

It's one of a healthy baker's best secrets—that applesauce produces a magnificently moist bread. This is a lovely choice for your kids to take for lunch or a snack. ☻ Serves 8

> 1½ cups all-purpose flour
> ¾ cup SPLENDA® Granular
> 2 teaspoons baking powder
> ½ teaspoon baking soda
> ½ teaspoon apple pie spice
> 1 cup unsweetened applesauce
> 1 egg, or equivalent in egg substitute
> 2 tablespoons vegetable oil
> ¼ cup chopped walnuts

Preheat oven to 350 degrees. Spray a 9-by-5-inch loaf pan with butter-flavored cooking spray. In a large bowl, combine flour, SPLENDA®, baking powder, baking soda, and apple pie spice. In a small bowl, combine applesauce, egg, and vegetable oil. Add applesauce mixture to flour mixture. Mix gently just to combine. Gently fold in walnuts. Evenly spread batter into prepared loaf pan. Bake for 30 to 40 minutes or until a toothpick inserted in center comes out clean. Place loaf pan on a wire rack and let set for 10 minutes. Remove bread from pan and continue cooling on wire rack. Cut into 8 slices.

Each serving equals:

HE: 1 Bread • 1 Fat • ¼ Protein • ¼ Fruit • 9 Optional Calories

166 Calories • 6 gm Fat • 4 gm Protein • 24 gm Carbohydrate • 209 mg Sodium • 80 mg Calcium • 1 gm Fiber

DIABETIC EXCHANGES: 1½ Starch/Carbohydrate • 1 Fat

Best Banana Bread

What makes a recipe deserve a medal and to be called the best? In this case, it's a classic, traditional dish in the best sense of the words. Bananas are rich in potassium, and when they're too ripe for eating, they're just perfect for this recipe. ☻ Serves 8

> ¾ cup SPLENDA® Granular
> ⅓ cup reduced-calorie margarine
> 2 eggs, or equivalent in egg substitute
> 1 cup (3 medium) mashed ripe bananas
> 1½ cups all-purpose flour
> 1 teaspoon baking powder
> ½ teaspoon baking soda

Preheat oven to 325 degrees. Spray a 9-by-5-inch glass loaf pan with butter-flavored cooking spray. In a large bowl, combine SPLENDA®, margarine, and eggs. Mix well using a wire whisk. Stir in mashed bananas. Add flour, baking powder, and baking soda. Mix gently using a sturdy spoon. Evenly spread batter into prepared loaf pan. Bake for 45 to 50 minutes or until a toothpick inserted in center comes out clean. Place loaf pan on a wire rack and let set for 10 minutes. Remove bread from pan and continue cooling on wire rack. Cut into 8 slices.

Each serving equals:

HE: 1 Bread • 1 Fat • ¾ Fruit • ¼ Protein • 9 Optional Calories

169 Calories • 5 gm Fat • 4 gm Protein • 27 gm Carbohydrate • 246 mg Sodium • 46 mg Calcium • 1 gm Fiber

DIABETIC EXCHANGES: 1 Starch • 1 Fat • 1 Fruit

Grandma's Black Walnut Banana Bread

If your grandma had a black walnut tree in her yard, your sweetest childhood memories may include a sweet bread like this one. If not, why not start a new tradition that includes it (and maybe plant a tree so future generations can harvest their own walnuts)? Delicious! ☻ Serves 8

¼ cup fat-free milk
½ teaspoon white distilled
   vinegar
1½ cups all-purpose flour
½ cup SPLENDA® Granular
1½ teaspoons baking powder
½ teaspoon baking soda

¼ cup chopped black walnuts
1 cup (3 medium) mashed
   banana
2 tablespoons no-fat sour
   cream
1 egg, or equivalent in egg
   substitute

Preheat oven to 350 degrees. Spray a 9-by-5-inch loaf pan with butter-flavored cooking spray. In a small bowl, combine milk and vinegar. Set aside. In a large bowl, combine flour, SPLENDA®, baking powder, and baking soda. Stir in walnuts. In a medium bowl, combine mashed banana, sour cream, egg, and milk mixture. Add banana mixture to flour mixture. Mix gently just to combine. Evenly spread batter into prepared loaf pan. Bake for 25 to 30 minutes or until a toothpick inserted in center comes out clean. Place loaf pan on a wire rack and let set for 10 minutes. Remove bread from pan and continue cooling on wire rack. Cut into 8 slices.

Each serving equals:

HE: 1 Bread • ¾ Fruit • ¼ Protein • ¼ Fat •
10 Optional Calories

155 Calories • 3 gm Fat • 5 gm Protein •
27 gm Carbohydrate • 187 mg Sodium •
75 mg Calcium • 1 gm Fiber

DIABETIC EXCHANGES: 1 Starch • 1 Fruit • ½ Fat

Maple Banana Quick Bread

What did we do before some clever inventor developed a sugar-free maple syrup? If you're like many dieters, you ate your pancakes dry, or else poured on the sweet syrup you love and gobbled guilt with your food. Here's a great way to enjoy the taste you love—and use up those old bananas! ☻ Serves 8

> 1½ cups reduced-fat biscuit baking mix
> ¼ cup SPLENDA® Granular
> 1½ teaspoons baking powder
> ⅔ cup (2 medium) mashed banana
> ½ cup sugar-free maple syrup
> 2 tablespoons no-fat sour cream
> 1 teaspoon vanilla extract

Preheat oven to 325 degrees. Spray a 9-by-5-inch glass loaf pan with butter-flavored cooking spray. In a large bowl, combine baking mix, SPLENDA®, and baking powder. In a small bowl, combine mashed banana, maple syrup, sour cream, and vanilla extract. Add banana mixture to baking mix mixture. Mix gently just to combine. Evenly spread batter into prepared loaf pan. Bake for 40 to 45 minutes or until a toothpick inserted in center comes out clean. Place loaf pan on a wire rack and let set for 10 minutes. Remove bread from pan and continue cooling on wire rack. Cut into 8 slices.

Each serving equals:

HE: 1 Bread • ½ Fruit • 16 Optional Calories

113 Calories • 1 gm Fat • 2 gm Protein •
24 gm Carbohydrate • 383 mg Sodium •
79 mg Calcium • 1 gm Fiber

DIABETIC EXCHANGES: 1 Starch • ½ Fruit

Banana Spice Bread

My husband, Cliff, loves spice breads and cakes, and who can blame him? They make your house smell good enough to eat while they're baking! This is a cozy, feel-good treat that you (and he) can enjoy without guilt.   ☻   Serves 8

1 cup + 3 tablespoons all-purpose flour
½ cup quick oats
¾ cup SPLENDA® Granular
1 teaspoon baking powder
½ teaspoon baking soda
1 teaspoon ground cinnamon
6 tablespoons seedless raisins
¼ cup chopped walnuts
¼ cup reduced-calorie margarine
½ cup unsweetened applesauce
1 egg, or equivalent in egg substitute
⅔ cup (2 medium) mashed banana
¼ cup fat-free half & half
1½ teaspoons vanilla extract

Preheat oven to 325 degrees. Spray a 9-by-5-inch glass loaf pan with butter-flavored cooking spray. In a large bowl, combine flour, oats, SPLENDA®, baking powder, baking soda, and cinnamon. Stir in raisins and walnuts. In a medium bowl, combine margarine, applesauce, egg, banana, half & half, and vanilla extract. Add margarine mixture to flour mixture. Mix gently just to combine. Evenly spread batter into prepared loaf pan. Bake for 50 to 55 minutes or until a toothpick inserted in center comes out clean. Place loaf pan on a wire rack and let set for 5 minutes. Remove bread from pan and continue cooling on wire rack. Cut into 8 slices.

Each serving equals:

HE: 1 Bread • 1 Fruit • 1 Fat • ¼ Protein • 18 Optional Calories

202 Calories • 6 gm Fat • 5 gm Protein • 32 gm Carbohydrate • 225 mg Sodium • 66 mg Calcium • 2 gm Fiber

DIABETIC EXCHANGES: 1 Starch • 1 Fruit • 1 Fat

Raisin Nut Bread

Raisins just seem to get better in the oven, so they're a wonderful addition to this quick bread batter, which also features good-for-you walnuts. What a winning combination they make!

○ Serves 8

1 cup seedless raisins
1 cup water
1 teaspoon baking soda
1 egg, or equivalent in egg
    substitute

¾ cup SPLENDA® Granular
¼ teaspoon table salt
1 teaspoon vanilla extract
1½ cups all-purpose flour
½ cup chopped walnuts

Preheat oven to 350 degrees. Spray a 9-by-5-inch loaf pan with butter-flavored cooking spray. In a medium saucepan, combine raisins, water, and baking soda. Bring mixture to a boil, stirring often. Remove from heat. Place saucepan on a wire rack and allow to cool completely. In a large bowl, combine egg, SPLENDA®, salt, and vanilla extract. Stir in cooled raisin mixture. Add flour. Mix gently just to combine. Fold in walnuts. Evenly spread batter into prepared loaf pan. Bake for 30 to 35 minutes or until a toothpick inserted in center comes out clean. Place loaf pan on a wire rack and let set for 10 minutes. Remove bread from pan and continue cooling on wire rack. Cut into 8 slices.

Each serving equals:

HE: 1 Bread • 1 Fruit • ½ Fat • ⅓ Protein •
11 Optional Calories

205 Calories • 5 gm Fat • 5 gm Protein •
35 gm Carbohydrate • 240 mg Sodium •
22 mg Calcium • 2 gm Fiber

DIABETIC EXCHANGES: 1 Starch • 1 Fruit • 1 Fat

Apricot-Raisin Sour Cream Bread

Apricots are another dried fruit that gets better when it's baked. Talk about magic from the oven: You won't find a richer-tasting fruit bread than this one! ☻ Serves 8

1½ cups reduced-fat biscuit baking mix
1 teaspoon baking powder
1 teaspoon baking soda
½ cup SPLENDA® Granular
1 teaspoon ground cinnamon
¼ cup chopped pecans

⅔ cup chopped dried apricots
¼ cup seedless raisins
½ cup no-fat sour cream
2 eggs, or equivalent in egg substitute
¼ cup fat-free half & half
1 teaspoon vanilla extract

Preheat oven to 375 degrees. Spray a 9-by-5-inch loaf pan with butter-flavored cooking spray. In a large bowl, combine baking mix, baking powder, baking soda, SPLENDA®, and cinnamon. Stir in pecans, apricots, and raisins. In a small bowl, combine sour cream, eggs, half & half, and vanilla extract. Add sour cream mixture to baking mix mixture. Mix gently just to combine. Evenly spread batter into prepared loaf pan. Bake for 30 to 35 minutes or until a toothpick inserted in center comes out clean. Place loaf pan on a wire rack and let set for 10 minutes. Remove bread from pan and continue cooling on wire rack. Cut into 8 slices.

Each serving equals:

HE: 1 Bread • ¾ Fruit • ½ Fat • ¼ Protein • ¼ Slider • 10 Optional Calories

197 Calories • 5 gm Fat • 5 gm Protein • 33 gm Carbohydrate • 523 mg Sodium • 108 mg Calcium • 2 gm Fiber

DIABETIC EXCHANGES: 1½ Starch/Carbohydrate • ½ Fruit • ½ Fat

Glorious Carrot Pineapple Quick Bread

Here's an impressive and delicious bread that's as moist and luscious as any I've ever tasted! Keep one of these on hand all through the holiday season, and you're always ready for guests.

● Serves 8

> 1½ cups reduced-fat biscuit baking mix
> ¾ cup SPLENDA® Granular
> 1 teaspoon baking powder
> ½ teaspoon baking soda
> 1 teaspoon ground cinnamon
> 1 cup grated carrots
> ¼ cup seedless raisins
> ¼ cup chopped walnuts
> 1 (8-ounce) can crushed pineapple, packed in fruit juice,
>   undrained
> ¼ cup no-fat sour cream
> 1 egg, or equivalent in egg substitute
> 1½ teaspoons vanilla extract

Preheat oven to 350 degrees. Spray a 9-by-5-inch loaf pan with butter-flavored cooking spray. In a large bowl, combine baking mix, SPLENDA®, baking powder, baking soda, and cinnamon. Stir in carrots, raisins, and walnuts. In a medium bowl, combine undrained pineapple, sour cream, egg, and vanilla extract. Add pineapple mixture to baking mix mixture. Mix gently just to combine. Evenly spread batter into prepared loaf pan. Bake for 35 to 40 minutes or until a toothpick inserted in center comes out clean. Place loaf pan on a wire rack and let set for 10 minutes. Remove bread from pan and continue cooling on wire rack. Cut into 8 slices.

Each serving equals:

HE: 1 Bread • ½ Fruit • ¼ Protein • ¼ Fat •
¼ Vegetable • 16 Optional Calories

---

172 Calories • 4 gm Fat • 4 gm Protein •
30 gm Carbohydrate • 503 mg Sodium •
86 mg Calcium • 1 gm Fiber

DIABETIC EXCHANGES: 1½ Starch • ½ Fruit • ½ Fat

Carrot Cake Quick Bread

Take a beloved dessert classic, wave my Healthy Exchanges magic wand over it, and you've got an anytime bread that tastes too good to be good for you—but it is! ☻ Serves 8

1 egg, beaten, or equivalent in
    egg substitute
2 tablespoons vegetable oil
¼ cup unsweetened applesauce
¼ cup fat-free milk
1½ cups all-purpose flour
½ cup SPLENDA® Granular

1 teaspoon baking powder
½ teaspoon baking soda
1 teaspoon ground cinnamon
1 cup grated carrots
¼ cup chopped walnuts
½ cup seedless raisins

Preheat oven to 350 degrees. Spray a 9-by-5-inch loaf pan with butter-flavored cooking spray. In a large bowl, combine egg, oil, applesauce, and milk. Add flour, SPLENDA®, baking powder, baking soda, and cinnamon. Mix gently just to combine. Fold in carrots, walnuts, and raisins. Evenly spread batter into prepared loaf pan. Bake for 30 to 35 minutes or until a toothpick inserted in center comes out clean. Place loaf pan on a wire rack and let set for 10 minutes. Remove bread from pan and continue cooling on wire rack. Cut into 8 slices.

Each serving equals:

HE: 1 Bread • 1 Fat • ½ Fruit • ¼ Protein •
12 Optional Calories

190 Calories • 6 gm Fat • 4 gm Protein •
30 gm Carbohydrate • 236 mg Sodium •
64 mg Calcium • 2 gm Fiber

DIABETIC EXCHANGES: 1½ Starch • 1 Fat • ½ Fruit

Garden Nut Bread

Imagine being able to boost your intake of healthy fruits and vegetables simply by nibbling a piece of this tasty and colorful bread! It's a miracle of flavors that celebrates the glorious rewards nature gives us each year. ☻ Serves 8

1½ cups reduced-fat biscuit
  baking mix
1 cup SPLENDA® Granular
1 teaspoon ground cinnamon
1 teaspoon baking powder
¼ cup reduced-calorie
  margarine
½ cup unsweetened applesauce

1 egg, beaten, or equivalent in
  egg substitute
1 teaspoon vanilla extract
1 cup grated zucchini
1 cup grated carrots
¾ cup seedless raisins
¼ cup chopped walnuts

Preheat oven to 325 degrees. Spray a 9-by-5-inch loaf pan with butter-flavored cooking spray. In a large bowl, combine baking mix, SPLENDA®, cinnamon, and baking powder. In a medium bowl, combine margarine and applesauce. Stir in egg and vanilla extract. Add margarine mixture to baking mix mixture. Mix gently just to combine. Fold in zucchini, carrots, raisins, and walnuts. Evenly spread batter into prepared loaf pan. Bake for 40 to 45 minutes or until a toothpick inserted in center comes out clean. Place loaf pan on a wire rack and let set for 10 minutes. Remove bread from pan and continue cooling on wire rack. Cut into 8 slices.

Each serving equals:

HE: 1 Bread • 1 Fat • ¾ Fruit • ½ Vegetable • ¼ Protein • ¼ Slider • 5 Optional Calories

278 Calories • 10 gm Fat • 5 gm Protein • 42 gm Carbohydrate • 540 mg Sodium • 107 mg Calcium • 2 gm Fiber

DIABETIC EXCHANGES: 1 Starch • 1 Fat • 1 Fruit • ½ Vegetable

Pears Helene Coffee Cake

This impressive combination of sweet chocolate and juicy pears makes a fabulous brunch finale or a festive way to show friends you think they're special. It's a really rich delight that is perfect for a party. ☻ Serves 8

> 1 (15-ounce) can pears, packed in fruit juice, drained,
>   and ½ cup liquid reserved
> 1½ cups reduced-fat biscuit baking mix
> ½ cup SPLENDA® Granular
> ¼ cup unsweetened cocoa powder
> ¼ cup no-fat sour cream
> 1 egg, or equivalent in egg substitute
> 1 teaspoon vanilla extract
> ¼ cup chopped walnuts
> ¼ cup mini chocolate chips

Preheat oven to 375 degrees. Spray an 8-by-8-inch baking dish with butter-flavored cooking spray. Finely chop pears. Set aside. In a large bowl, combine baking mix, SPLENDA®, and cocoa. Add sour cream, egg, reserved pear juice, and vanilla extract. Mix gently just to combine. Fold in pears, walnuts, and chocolate chips. Evenly spread batter into prepared baking dish. Bake for 25 to 30 minutes or until a toothpick inserted in center comes out clean. Place baking dish on a wire rack and let set for at least 15 minutes. Cut into 8 servings.

Each serving equals:

HE: 1 Bread • ½ Fruit • ¼ Protein • ¼ Fat •
¼ Slider • 16 Optional Calories

194 Calories • 6 gm Fat • 4 gm Protein •
31 gm Carbohydrate • 284 mg Sodium •
44 mg Calcium • 2 gm Fiber

DIABETIC EXCHANGES: 1½ Starch • ½ Fruit • ½ Fat

Sour Cream Raspberry Coffee Cake

Just a tiny bit of lemon juice (fresh-squeezed or from the little plastic bottle) packs a scrumptious citrus punch in this recipe. It's a delectable partner for beautiful rosy-red raspberries and helps makes this a sweet dream of a luncheon dessert. ☻ Serves 8

> 1½ cups reduced-fat biscuit baking mix
> ½ cup SPLENDA® Granular
> 1 cup water
> 1 teaspoon lemon juice
> ¼ cup no-fat sour cream
> 1 teaspoon coconut extract
> 1½ cups frozen unsweetened red raspberries
> 2 tablespoons flaked coconut

Preheat oven to 375 degrees. Spray an 8-by-8-inch baking dish with butter-flavored cooking spray. In a large bowl, combine baking mix and SPLENDA®. Add water, lemon juice, sour cream, and coconut extract. Mix gently just to combine. Fold in frozen raspberries. Evenly spread batter into prepared baking dish. Sprinkle coconut evenly over top. Bake for 30 to 35 minutes or until a toothpick inserted in center comes out clean. Place baking dish on a wire rack and let set for at least 15 minutes. Cut into 8 servings.

Each serving equals:

HE: 1 Bread • ¼ Fruit • 18 Optional Calories

114 Calories, 2 gm Fat • 2 gm Protein •
22 gm Carbohydrate • 277 mg Sodium •
38 mg Calcium • 2 gm Fiber

DIABETIC EXCHANGES: 1½ Starch/Carbohydrate

Banana Coffee Cake with Blueberry Glaze

This is a truly luscious way to combine the pleasure of coffee cake with the outrageous goodness of banana bread! Try it with blueberry first, but you'll discover that other flavors of spreadable fruit are also great.   ☺   Serves 8

1½ cups all-purpose flour
1 teaspoon baking powder
½ teaspoon baking soda
½ cup SPLENDA® Granular
1½ teaspoons ground cinnamon
¼ cup chopped walnuts
⅔ cup (2 medium) mashed ripe banana
½ cup no-fat sour cream
1 egg, or equivalent in egg substitute
½ cup fat-free half & half
1½ teaspoons vanilla extract
¼ cup blueberry spreadable fruit

Preheat oven to 350 degrees. Spray an 8-by-8-inch baking dish with butter-flavored cooking spray. In a large bowl, combine flour, baking powder, baking soda, SPLENDA®, and cinnamon. Stir in walnuts. In a medium bowl, combine bananas, sour cream, egg, - half & half, and vanilla extract. Add banana mixture to flour mixture. Mix gently just to combine. Evenly spread batter into prepared baking dish. Bake for 40 to 45 minutes or until a toothpick inserted in center comes out clean. Place baking dish on a wire rack. In a small microwaveable bowl, microwave spreadable fruit on HIGH (100% power) for 15 seconds or until melted. Drizzle melted blueberry spreadable fruit over top. Allow to cool completely. Cut into 8 servings.

Each serving equals:

HE: 1 Bread • 1 Fruit • ¼ Protein • ¼ Fat •
¼ Slider • 11 Optional Calories

---

175 Calories • 3 gm Fat • 4 gm Protein •
33 gm Carbohydrate • 175 mg Sodium •
89 mg Calcium • 2 gm Fiber

DIABETIC EXCHANGES: 1 Starch • 1 Fruit • ½ Fat

Cherry Nut Party Coffee Cake with Chocolate Glaze

No excuse for a party? Invent one! You've been blessed with one more sunrise, you survived your boss's endless demands one more week—whatever makes you feel good is an ideal reason to make this recipe. I've provided the cake—you choose the occasion.

○   Serves 8

> 1½ cups reduced-fat biscuit baking mix
> 1 teaspoon baking powder
> 1¾ cups SPLENDA® Granular ☆
> 8 maraschino cherries, chopped
> ¼ cup chopped walnuts
> ⅔ cup fat-free milk
> 1 egg, well beaten, or equivalent in egg substitute
> 1 tablespoon + 1 teaspoon reduced-calorie margarine
> 1 (1-ounce) square unsweetened chocolate
> 2 tablespoons fat-free sour cream
> 1 teaspoon vanilla extract

Preheat oven to 350 degrees. Spray an 8-by-8-inch baking dish with butter-flavored cooking spray. In a large bowl, combine baking mix, baking powder, ½ cup SPLENDA®, cherries, and walnuts. Add milk and egg. Mix gently just to combine. Evenly spread batter into prepared baking dish. Bake for 20 minutes or until a toothpick inserted in center comes out clean. Place baking dish on a wire rack and let set while preparing chocolate glaze. In a medium saucepan, melt margarine and chocolate square. Remove from heat. Stir in sour cream. Add remaining 1¼ cups SPLENDA® and vanilla extract. Mix well to combine. Drizzle warm mixture evenly over top of warm coffee cake. Let set for at least 15 minutes. Cut into 8 servings.

Each serving equals:

HE: 1 Bread • ½ Fat • ¼ Protein • ½ Slider •
15 Optional Calories

---

187 Calories • 7 gm Fat • 4 gm Protein •
27 gm Carbohydrate • 368 mg Sodium •
96 mg Calcium • 1 gm Fiber

DIABETIC EXCHANGES: 1½ Starch/Carbohydrate • ½ Fat

Pineapple Paradise Coffee Cake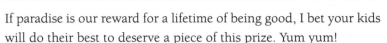

If paradise is our reward for a lifetime of being good, I bet your kids will do their best to deserve a piece of this prize. Yum yum!

● Serves 8

> 1½ cups reduced-fat biscuit baking mix
> ¼ cup SPLENDA® Granular
> 1 (8-ounce) can crushed pineapple, packed in fruit juice, undrained
> 2 tablespoons no-fat sour cream
> 1 egg, or equivalent in egg substitute
> 1 teaspoon coconut extract
> 1 (8-ounce) can pineapple tidbits, packed in fruit juice, drained
> ¼ cup chopped pecans
> ¼ cup flaked coconut

Preheat oven to 375 degrees. Spray a 9-inch round cake pan with butter-flavored cooking spray. In a large bowl, combine baking mix and SPLENDA®. Add undrained crushed pineapple, sour cream, egg, and coconut extract. Mix gently just to combine. Fold in pineapple tidbits, pecans, and coconut. Evenly spread batter into prepared cake pan. Bake for 20 to 30 minutes or until a toothpick inserted in center comes out clean. Place cake pan on a wire rack and let set for at least 15 minutes. Cut into 8 wedges.

HINT: If you can't find tidbits, use chunk pineapple and chop coarsely.

Each serving equals:

> HE: 1 Bread • ½ Fat • ¼ Fruit • 17 Optional Calories
>
> 173 Calories • 5 gm Fat • 3 gm Protein •
> 29 gm Carbohydrate • 280 mg Sodium •
> 42 mg Calcium • 1 gm Fiber
>
> DIABETIC EXCHANGES: 1 Starch • 1 Fat

Cranberry Walnut Coffee Cake

Invite your friends in for coffee and cake, then just sit back and wait for the applause to start! This is such an easy recipe, it's sure to become one of your "old reliables"! ☕ Serves 8

1½ cups reduced-fat biscuit baking mix
½ cup SPLENDA® Granular
½ cup unsweetened orange juice
1 egg, or equivalent in egg substitute
1 tablespoon fat-free half & half
2 tablespoons no-fat sour cream
1 cup chopped fresh or frozen cranberries
¼ cup chopped walnuts

Preheat oven to 350 degrees. Spray an 8-by-8-inch baking dish with butter-flavored cooking spray. In a large bowl, combine baking mix and SPLENDA®. Add orange juice, egg, half & half, and sour cream. Mix gently just to combine. Fold in cranberries and walnuts. Evenly spread batter into prepared baking dish. Bake for 15 to 20 minutes or until a toothpick inserted in center comes out clean. Place baking dish on a wire rack and let set for at least 15 minutes. Cut into 8 servings.

Each serving equals:

HE: 1 Bread • ¼ Protein • ¼ Fruit • ¼ Fat •
11 Optional Calories

136 Calories • 4 gm Fat • 3 gm Protein •
22 gm Carbohydrate • 275 mg Sodium •
39 mg Calcium • 1 gm Fiber

DIABETIC EXCHANGES: 1 Starch • ½ Fat

Candy Coffee Cake

Doesn't the list of ingredients for this splendidly decadent dessert make your mouth water and your eyes light up? Every bite's a treat!

○ Serves 8

> 1 cup reduced-fat biscuit baking mix
> 1/2 cup purchased graham cracker crumbs
> 1/2 cup SPLENDA® Granular
> 1 egg, or equivalent in egg substitute
> 1/2 cup fat-free milk
> 2 tablespoons fat-free half & half
> 2 tablespoons no-fat sour cream
> 1/4 cup chopped dry-roasted peanuts
> 3/4 cup miniature marshmallows
> 1/4 cup mini chocolate chips

Preheat oven to 375 degrees. Spray an 8-by-8-inch baking dish with butter-flavored cooking spray. In a large bowl, combine baking mix, graham cracker crumbs, and SPLENDA®. Add egg, milk, half & half, and sour cream. Mix gently just to combine. Fold in peanuts, marshmallows, and chocolate chips. Evenly spread batter into prepared baking dish. Bake for 18 to 22 minutes or until a toothpick inserted in center comes out clean. Place baking dish on a wire rack and let set for at least 15 minutes. Cut into 8 servings.

Each serving equals:

HE: 1 Bread • 3/4 Protein • 1/4 Fat • 1/2 Slider • 9 Optional Calories

---

157 Calories • 5 gm Fat • 4 gm Protein • 24 gm Carbohydrate • 233 mg Sodium • 52 mg Calcium • 1 gm Fiber

---

DIABETIC EXCHANGES: 1 1/2 Starch/Carbohydrate • 1/2 Fat

Captivating

Candy, Cookies,

and Bars

Whether it's a week until Christmas or the day before Valentine's Day, living the sweet life means enjoying a few treats fresh from the oven or the fridge! Why should you miss out on a "sisters, cousins, and aunts" cookie swap just because you're a diabetic or counting calories? My Healthy Exchanges cookies fit perfectly into your meal plan—just offer a couple to your nutritionist, and see if she or he doesn't ask for the recipe!

If you're one of those people who feel that life without candy just isn't worth living, join the club! I promise to serve **Peanut Butter Candy Balls** at our first meeting, or maybe **Holiday Pecan Fudge**. When you're trying to decide what to send to school for a birthday celebration, consider **Almost "Candy" Cookies** or **Oatmeal Surprise Cookies**. I'm a big fan of all kinds of bar cookies, so I'm sharing some of my best with you: **Lemon Coconut Bars** and **Apricot Meringue Bars** are downright amazing!

Chocolate Peanut Butter Krispy Bites

Isn't it fun to think you get three (count 'em, three) of these marvelous mouthfuls? Clever cooks have mixed up cereal sweets for years, but I think this combo is one of my favorites.

🙂 Serves 8 (3 each)

> ½ cup reduced-fat peanut butter
> ½ cup mini chocolate chips
> ¼ cup SPLENDA® Granular
> 3 cups Rice Krispies cereal

Place a large piece of waxed paper on a baking sheet. In an 8-cup glass microwaveable measuring cup, combine peanut butter, chocolate chips, and SPLENDA®. Microwave on HIGH (100% power) for 40 seconds or until mixture is melted, stirring after 20 seconds. Fold in Rice Krispies cereal. Drop mixture by teaspoonful onto prepared baking sheet to form 24 pieces. Refrigerate for at least 30 minutes or until firm.

Each serving equals:

HE: 1 Protein • 1 Fat • ½ Bread • ¼ Slider • 17 Optional Calories

176 Calories • 8 gm Fat • 5 gm Protein • 21 gm Carbohydrate • 232 mg Sodium • 3 mg Calcium • 1 gm Fiber

DIABETIC EXCHANGES: 1 Starch • 1 Fat • ½ Meat

Chocolate Quickie Clusters

Can you believe that chow mein noodles work amazingly well in a cookie recipe? It's true, they do. These are sweetly crunchy, with just a hint of salty contrast. Reminds me of Phyllis, who always likes a bite of pretzel after her dish of sugar-free, fat-free ice cream!

❂ Serves 12 (2 each)

> ½ cup mini chocolate chips
> ¼ cup SPLENDA® Granular
> 1 tablespoon water
> 1 cup coarsely chopped chow mein noodles
> ½ cup miniature marshmallows

Place a large piece of waxed paper on a baking sheet. Place chocolate chips in an 8-cup glass microwaveable measuring cup. Microwave on HIGH (100% power) for 1½ minutes or until chips are melted, stirring every 30 seconds. Stir in SPLENDA® and water. Add chow mein noodles and marshmallows. Mix gently just to combine. Drop mixture by teaspoonful onto prepared baking sheet to form 24 clusters. Refrigerate for at least 1 hour.

Each serving equals:

HE: ¼ Bread • ¼ Slider • 10 Optional Calories

---

50 Calories • 2 gm Fat • 1 gm Protein •
7 gm Carbohydrate • 18 mg Sodium • 2 mg Calcium •
0 gm Fiber

DIABETIC EXCHANGES: ½ Other Carbohydrate

Peanut Cluster Balls

Microwave cooking is great for candy recipes because it melts foods so beautifully, and you can do everything in just one bowl! These candy charmers are impressively good and ready in very little time.

◐ Serves 8 (2 each)

> ½ cup miniature marshmallows
> ¼ cup mini chocolate chips
> ½ cup SPLENDA® Granular
> 1 tablespoon + 1 teaspoon reduced-calorie margarine
> 1 teaspoon vanilla extract
> ¾ cup dry-roasted peanuts

Place a large piece of waxed paper on a baking sheet. In an 8-cup glass microwaveable measuring cup, combine marshmallows, chocolate chips, SPLENDA®, and margarine. Cover and microwave on HIGH (100% power) for 30 seconds, stirring after 15 seconds. Stir in vanilla extract. Add peanuts. Mix gently to coat peanuts completely. Drop mixture by tablespoonful onto prepared baking sheet to form 16 mounds. Refrigerate for at least 30 minutes or until firm.

Each serving equals:

HE: 1 Fat • ⅓ Protein • ¼ Slider •
13 Optional Calories

107 Calories • 7 gm Fat • 3 gm Protein •
8 gm Carbohydrate • 25 mg Sodium • 7 mg Calcium •
1 gm Fiber

DIABETIC EXCHANGES: 1 Fat • 1 Other Carbohydrate

Peanut Butter Candy Balls

This recipe makes just four servings, but that can be a good thing. I've had readers tell me they were afraid to keep a pie with 8 servings in the fridge because they feared eating all of it at once. While I believe that you're *less* likely to binge, not more, when you don't deprive yourself, I know how it feels to have treats "calling your name." Why not try making this fun food when you've got company coming to share the goodies? ☺ Serves 4 (3 each)

¼ cup reduced-fat peanut butter
2 tablespoons fat-free half & half
1 teaspoon vanilla extract
6 tablespoons purchased graham cracker crumbs or
     6 (2½-inch) graham cracker squares made into crumbs
¼ cup SPLENDA® Granular
⅓ cup nonfat dry milk powder
¼ cup mini chocolate chips

Place a large piece of waxed paper on a baking sheet. In a medium bowl, cream peanut butter, half & half, and vanilla extract until smooth. Add graham cracker crumbs, SPLENDA®, and dry milk powder. Mix gently to combine. Stir in chocolate chips. Form into 12 (1-inch) balls and place on prepared baking sheet. Refrigerate for at least 30 minutes.

HINT: A self-seal sandwich bag works great for crushing graham crackers.

Each serving equals:

HE: 1 Protein • 1 Fat • ½ Bread • ¼ Fat-Free Milk • ½ Slider • 5 Optional Calories

192 Calories • 8 gm Fat • 7 gm Protein • 23 gm Carbohydrate • 212 mg Sodium • 91 mg Calcium • 1 gm Fiber

DIABETIC EXCHANGES: 1 Meat • 1 Fat • 1 Starch/Carbohydrate

Holiday Pecan Fudge

Fudge is such an all-American favorite, especially around the holidays, but most healthy eaters figure it's a definite no-no. I'm so pleased to prove them wrong. This recipe tastes rich and decadent, but because it's made with nonfat milk and a moderate amount of chocolate and nuts, it's a good-for-you choice.

◐ Serves 8 (2 pieces)

> 1⅓ cups nonfat dry milk powder
> 1¼ cups water
> ½ cup cornstarch
> ⅔ cup SPLENDA® Granular
> 1 cup mini chocolate chips
> 1 tablespoon vanilla extract
> ¼ cup coarsely chopped pecans

Spray an 8-by-8-inch baking dish with butter-flavored cooking spray. In a medium saucepan, combine dry milk powder, water, cornstarch, SPLENDA®, and chocolate chips. Cook over medium heat until mixture thickens and chocolate chips are melted, stirring constantly. Place saucepan on a wire rack. Stir in vanilla extract. Using an electric mixer, beat on MEDIUM until mixture is light and fluffy. Fold in pecans, using a sturdy spoon. Spread mixture into prepared baking dish. Refrigerate for at least 6 hours or until firm. Cut into 16 pieces.

Each serving equals:

HE: 1 Bread • 1 Fat • ½ Fat-Free Milk • ½ Slider • 3 Optional Calories

---

208 Calories • 8 gm Fat • 5 gm Protein • 29 gm Carbohydrate • 66 mg Sodium • 161 mg Calcium • 1 gm Fiber

---

DIABETIC EXCHANGES: 1½ Starch/Carbohydrate • 1 Fat • ½ Fat-Free Milk

Stove Top Peanut Butter Cookies

Here's a fun recipe you can make in just minutes and tastes impossibly good! These will keep real well in the refrigerator, but they're so delicious, they probably won't last very long.

○ Serves 12 (2 each)

> ½ cup reduced-calorie margarine
> ½ cup fat-free half & half
> 2 cups SPLENDA® Granular
> ¼ teaspoon table salt
> ¼ cup reduced-fat peanut butter
> 2 teaspoons vanilla extract
> 2 tablespoons unsweetened cocoa powder
> 3 cups quick oats

Place a large piece of waxed paper on a baking sheet. In a large saucepan sprayed with butter-flavored cooking spray, combine margarine and half & half. Stir in SPLENDA® and salt. Bring mixture to a boil, stirring constantly. Remove from heat. Stir in peanut butter and vanilla extract. Add cocoa and oats. Mix well to combine. Drop mixture by tablespoonfuls onto prepared baking sheet to form 24 mounds. Lightly flatten cookies with the tines of a fork. Refrigerate for at least 30 minutes.

Each serving equals:

HE: 1 Bread • 1 Fat • ⅓ Protein • ¼ Slider •
4 Optional Calories

---

167 Calories • 7 gm Fat • 5 gm Protein •
21 gm Carbohydrate • 192 mg Sodium •
29 mg Calcium • 2 gm Fiber

DIABETIC EXCHANGES: 1½ Starch/Carbohydrate • 1 Fat

"Sugar" Drop Cookies

"Wow!" you may think, "she used an entire cup and a half of SPLENDA® to make these sugar cookies." No other sweetener would work, but SPLENDA® isn't like any other—it's a revolution in every teaspoon, and it makes a much-loved sugar cookie not only possible for healthy eaters, but irresistible!

● Serves 12 (2 each)

½ cup reduced-calorie margarine
1½ cups SPLENDA® Granular
¼ cup fat-free half & half
1 egg, or equivalent in egg substitute
2 teaspoons almond extract
1½ cups all-purpose flour
1 teaspoon baking powder
½ teaspoon table salt

Preheat oven to 375 degrees. Spray 2 baking sheets with butter-flavored cooking spray. In a large bowl, cream margarine and SPLENDA®, using a sturdy spoon. Stir in half & half, egg, and almond extract. Add flour, baking powder, and salt. Mix well to combine. Drop batter by tablespoonful onto prepared baking sheets to form 24 cookies. Lightly flatten cookies with the bottom of a glass sprayed with butter-flavored cooking spray. Bake for 12 to 14 minutes. Do not overbake. Place baking sheets on wire racks and let set for 5 minutes. Remove cookies from baking sheets and continue to cool on wire racks.

Each serving equals:

HE: 1 Fat • ⅔ Bread • ¼ Slider • 1 Optional Calorie

104 Calories • 4 gm Fat • 2 gm Protein •
15 gm Carbohydrate • 218 mg Sodium •
36 mg Calcium • 1 gm Fiber

DIABETIC EXCHANGES: 1 Fat • 1 Starch

Almost "Candy" Cookies

The line between cookies and candy is already a little fuzzy, isn't it? Let's just say that these cookies have enough sweet treats in them to deserve a home in "Candyland"! ☻ Serves 8 (2 each)

> 1 cup cake flour
> 1 teaspoon baking powder
> ½ teaspoon baking soda
> ¾ cup SPLENDA® Granular
> ⅓ cup reduced-calorie margarine
> 1 egg, or equivalent in egg substitute
> 1 teaspoon coconut extract
> ¼ cup mini chocolate chips
> 2 tablespoons flaked coconut

Preheat oven to 375 degrees. Spray 2 baking sheets with butter-flavored cooking spray. In a large bowl, combine flour, baking powder, baking soda, and SPLENDA®. Add margarine, egg, and coconut extract. Mix gently just to combine. Fold in chocolate chips and coconut. Drop batter by tablespoonful onto prepared baking sheets to form 16 cookies. Lightly flatten cookies with the bottom of a glass sprayed with butter-flavored cooking spray. Bake for 8 to 10 minutes. Do not overbake. Place baking sheets on wire racks and let set for 5 minutes. Remove cookies from baking sheets and continue to cool on wire racks.

Each serving equals:

HE: 1 Fat • ⅔ Bread • ½ Slider • 1 Optional Calorie

126 Calories • 6 gm Fat • 2 gm Protein •
16 gm Carbohydrate • 201 mg Sodium •
42 mg Calcium • 1 gm Fiber

DIABETIC EXCHANGES: 1 Fat • 1 Starch

Zach's Chocolate Chippers

For a classic grandson, here's a good old reliable cookie recipe that always brings a grin to Zach's face! He likes to help stir these up with Grandma's big wooden spoon.　　○　　Serves 12 (2 each)

> *½ cup reduced-calorie margarine*
> *⅔ cup SPLENDA® Granular*
> *1 egg, beaten, or equivalent in egg substitute*
> *½ teaspoon vanilla extract*
> *1 cup all-purpose flour*
> *½ teaspoon baking soda*
> *¼ teaspoon table salt*
> *½ cup mini chocolate chips*

Preheat oven to 375 degrees. Spray 2 baking sheets with butter-flavored cooking spray. In a large bowl, cream margarine and SPLENDA®, using a sturdy spoon. Stir in egg and vanilla extract. Add flour, baking soda, and salt. Mix gently just to combine. Fold in chocolate chips. Drop batter by tablespoonful onto prepared baking sheets to form 24 cookies. Lightly flatten cookies with the bottom of a glass sprayed with butter-flavored cooking spray. Bake for 8 to 10 minutes. Do not overbake. Place baking sheets on wire racks and let set for 5 minutes. Remove cookies from baking sheets and continue to cool on wire racks.

Each serving equals:

HE: 1 Fat • ½ Bread • ¼ Slider • 14 Optional Calories

101 Calories • 5 gm Fat • 2 gm Protein •
12 gm Carbohydrate • 197 mg Sodium •
7 mg Calcium • 1 gm Fiber

DIABETIC EXCHANGES: 1 Fat • 1 Starch

Pam's Peanut Butter Cookies

When it comes to taking a break from caring for her family, my daughter-in-law Pam likes nothing better than a cup of tea and a couple of these little superstars! She thinks (and I bet you'll agree) that peanut butter is the perfect splurge when you want to treat yourself!   ☻   Serves 12 (2 each)

1 tablespoon + 1 teaspoon reduced-calorie margarine
¾ cup reduced-fat peanut butter
⅔ cup SPLENDA® Granular
⅓ cup fat-free milk
1 egg, or equivalent in egg substitute
1 teaspoon vanilla extract
1½ cups cake flour
1 teaspoon baking powder
¼ teaspoon table salt

Preheat oven to 375 degrees. Spray 2 baking sheets with butter-flavored cooking spray. In a large bowl, cream margarine, peanut butter, and SPLENDA®, using a sturdy spoon. Stir in milk, egg, and vanilla extract. Add flour, baking powder, and salt. Mix gently just to combine. Drop batter by rounded teaspoonful onto prepared baking sheets to form 24 cookies. Flatten cookies with a fork dipped in water. Bake for 8 to 10 minutes. Do not overbake. Place baking sheets on wire racks and let set for 5 minutes. Remove cookies from baking sheets and continue to cool on wire racks.

Each serving equals:

HE: 1 Protein • 1 Fat • ⅔ Bread •
19 Optional Calories

---

163 Calories • 7 gm Fat • 6 gm Protein •
19 gm Carbohydrate • 238 mg Sodium •
35 mg Calcium • 1 gm Fiber

DIABETIC EXCHANGES: 1 Meat • 1 Fat • 1 Starch

Raisin Sugar Cookies

Take two favorite cookie styles and stir them into a wonderfully inviting combination—you've got a treat that celebrates the best of each! To keep them soft and spectacular, do not overbake.

● Serves 12 (3 each)

> ½ cup reduced-calorie margarine
> ¾ cup SPLENDA® Granular
> 1 egg, or equivalent in egg substitute
> 1 tablespoon fat-free milk
> 1 teaspoon lemon juice
> 1½ cups cake flour
> ½ teaspoon baking powder
> ½ teaspoon baking soda
> 1 cup seedless raisins

In a large bowl, combine margarine, SPLENDA®, egg, milk, and lemon juice. Add flour, baking powder, and baking soda. Mix gently just to combine. Fold in raisins. Cover and refrigerate dough for at least 30 minutes. Just before baking, preheat oven to 400 degrees. Spray 3 baking sheets with butter-flavored cooking spray. Form chilled dough into 36 (1-inch) balls. Place balls on prepared baking sheets. Lightly flatten cookies with the bottom of a glass sprayed with butter-flavored cooking spray and then dipped into more SPLENDA®. Bake for 5 to 7 minutes. Do not overbake. Place baking sheets on wire racks and let set for 5 minutes. Remove cookies from baking sheets and continue to cool on wire racks.

Each serving equals:

HE: 1 Fat • ⅔ Bread • ⅔ Fruit • 12 Optional Calories

132 Calories • 4 gm Fat • 2 gm Protein •
22 gm Carbohydrate • 191 mg Sodium •
35 mg Calcium • 1 gm Fiber

DIABETIC EXCHANGES: 1 Fat • 1 Fruit • ½ Starch

Graham Cracker Cookies

I prefer using the commercial graham cracker crumbs for this recipe, even though I've experimented with grinding graham crackers in my blender (a messy job to clean up!). They taste great, they're easy to use, and they're just right for this particular cookie.

● Serves 8 (3 each)

> 1⅓ cups nonfat dry milk powder
> 1 cup SPLENDA® Granular
> ½ cup water
> 1 tablespoon + 1 teaspoon reduced-calorie margarine

> 1½ cups purchased graham cracker crumbs
> ¼ cup chopped walnuts
> ¼ cup mini chocolate chips

Preheat oven to 350 degrees. Spray 2 baking sheets with butter-flavored cooking spray. In a large glass microwaveable bowl, combine dry milk powder, SPLENDA®, and water. Cover and microwave on HIGH (100% power) for 60 seconds, stirring after every 30 seconds. Remove from microwave. Stir in margarine and graham cracker crumbs. Add walnuts and chocolate chips. Mix gently just to combine. Drop batter by tablespoonfuls onto prepared baking sheets to form 24 cookies. Lightly flatten cookies with the bottom of a glass sprayed with butter-flavored cooking spray. Bake for 8 to 10 minutes. Do not overbake. Place baking sheets on wire racks and let set for 5 minutes. Remove cookies from baking sheets and continue to cool on wire racks.

Each serving equals:

HE: 1 Bread • ½ Fat-Free Milk • ½ Fat • ¼ Slider • 16 Optional Calories

174 Calories • 6 gm Fat • 6 gm Protein • 24 gm Carbohydrate • 181 mg Sodium • 159 mg Calcium • 1 gm Fiber

DIABETIC EXCHANGES: 1 Starch • 1 Fat • ½ Fat-Free Milk

Oatmeal Coconut Cookies

Double your pleasure means double the flavor in this coconutty cookie. I'm a big fan of using extracts to convince you you're eating a lot more coconut than you actually get.

○ Serves 12 (2 each)

½ cup reduced-calorie margarine
1 cup SPLENDA® Granular
1 egg, or equivalent in egg substitute
½ teaspoon coconut extract
1 cup quick oats
1 cup cake flour
1½ teaspoon baking powder
½ teaspoon baking soda
½ cup flaked coconut

Preheat oven to 350 degrees. Spray 2 baking sheets with butter-flavored cooking spray. In a large bowl, cream margarine and SPLENDA®, using a sturdy spoon. Stir in egg and coconut extract. Add oats, flour, baking powder, and baking soda. Mix gently just to combine. Fold in coconut. Drop batter by tablespoonful onto prepared baking sheets to form 24 cookies. Lightly flatten cookies with the bottom of a glass sprayed with butter-flavored cooking spray. Bake for 10 to 12 minutes. Do not overbake. Place baking sheets on wire racks and let set for 5 minutes. Remove cookies from baking sheets and continue to cool on wire racks.

Each serving equals:

HE: 1 Fat • ¾ Bread • ¼ Slider • 8 Optional Calories

117 Calories • 5 gm Fat • 3 gm Protein • 15 gm Carbohydrate • 197 mg Sodium • 31 mg Calcium • 1 gm Fiber

DIABETIC EXCHANGES: 1 Fat • 1 Starch

Oatmeal Chip Cookies

Abbott and Costello, Ginger Rogers and Fred Astaire—great teams live forever in our memories, right? Well, here's another great team that deserves just as much adoration. Oatmeal and chocolate are a dream team that will win your heart! ◐ Serves 16 (2 each)

1 teaspoon baking soda
1 teaspoon hot water
1½ cups SPLENDA® Granular
⅔ cup reduced-calorie
    margarine
⅓ cup unsweetened applesauce
2 eggs, or equivalent in egg
    substitute

1½ teaspoons vanilla extract
1 teaspoon table salt
1½ cups all-purpose flour
2 cups quick oats
½ cup mini chocolate chips

Preheat oven to 375 degrees. Spray 3 baking sheets with butter-flavored cooking spray. In a small bowl, combine baking soda and hot water. Set aside. In a large bowl, cream SPLENDA®, margarine, and applesauce, using a sturdy spoon. Stir in eggs, vanilla extract, baking soda mixture, and salt. Add flour and oats. Mix gently just to combine. Fold in chocolate chips. Drop batter by tablespoonful onto prepared baking sheets to form 32 cookies. Lightly flatten cookies with the bottom of glass sprayed with butter-flavored cooking spray. Bake for 8 to 9 minutes. Do not overbake. Place baking sheets on wire racks and let set for 5 minutes. Remove cookies from baking sheets and continue to cool on wire racks.

Each serving equals:

HE: 1 Bread • 1 Fat • ¼ Slider • 17 Optional Calories

150 Calories • 6 gm Fat • 4 gm Protein •
20 gm Carbohydrate • 322 mg Sodium •
13 mg Calcium • 2 gm Fiber

DIABETIC EXCHANGES: 1 Starch • 1 Fat

Oatmeal-Maple Cookies

It's snowing outside, and the only cure for the shivers is a cup of hot chocolate and these old-fashioned cookies that taste the way Grandma's best always did! The oatmeal gives them an extra touch of healthy fiber. ☻ Serves 12 (2 each)

½ cup reduced-calorie margarine	1 teaspoon baking powder
1 cup SPLENDA® Granular	¼ teaspoon baking soda
1 egg, or equivalent in egg substitute	1½ teaspoons ground cinnamon
¼ cup sugar-free maple syrup	1½ cups quick oats
¾ cup reduced-fat biscuit baking mix	¼ cup chopped walnuts
	½ cup seedless raisins

Preheat oven to 375 degrees. Spray 2 baking sheets with butter-flavored cooking spray. In a large bowl, cream margarine, SPLENDA®, and egg until mixture is light and fluffy, using a sturdy spoon. Stir in maple syrup. Add baking mix, baking powder, baking soda, and cinnamon. Mix gently just to combine. Fold in oats, walnuts, and raisins. Drop batter by tablespoonful onto prepared baking sheets to form 24 cookies. Lightly flatten cookies with the bottom of a glass sprayed with butter-flavored cooking spray. Bake for 10 to 12 minutes. Do not overbake. Lightly spray tops with butter-flavored cooking spray. Place baking sheets on wire racks and let set for 5 minutes. Remove cookies from baking sheets and continue to cool on wire racks.

Each serving equals:

HE: 1 Fat • ¾ Bread • ⅓ Fruit • ¼ Slider • 12 Optional Calories

155 Calories • 7 gm Fat • 3 gm Protein • 20 gm Carbohydrate • 285 mg Sodium • 46 mg Calcium • 2 gm Fiber

DIABETIC EXCHANGES: 1 Fat • 1 Starch

Oatmeal Surprise Cookies

Ever bite into a cookie and discover it was more than you expected? That's the idea behind these yummy munchies that sparkle with fruity goodness.   ○   Serves 16 (2 each)

⅔ cup reduced-calorie margarine
½ cup unsweetened orange juice
1½ cups SPLENDA® Granular
2 eggs, beaten, or equivalent in egg substitute
½ teaspoon vanilla extract
1⅓ cups cake flour
1¼ cups quick oats
1 teaspoon baking soda
½ cup seedless raisins

Preheat oven to 375 degrees. Spray 3 baking sheets with butter-flavored cooking spray. In a large bowl, combine margarine, orange juice, SPLENDA®, eggs, and vanilla extract. Add flour, oats, baking soda, and raisins. Mix gently just to combine. Drop batter by tablespoonfuls onto prepared baking sheets to form 32 cookies. Flatten cookies with the tines of a fork, making a crisscross pattern. Bake for 10 to 12 minutes. Do not overbake. Place baking sheets on wire racks and let set for 5 minutes. Remove cookies from baking sheets and continue to cool on wire racks.

Each serving equals:

HE: 1 Fat • ¾ Bread • ¾ Fruit • ¼ Slider • 1 Optional Calorie

125 Calories • 5 gm Fat • 3 gm Protein • 17 gm Carbohydrate • 177 mg Sodium • 12 mg Calcium • 1 gm Fiber

DIABETIC EXCHANGES: 1 Fat • 1 Starch

Lemon Coconut Bars

What a pretty dessert this recipe produces, but as the old saying goes, "Pretty is as pretty does." These do "pretty" up proud! They're sweetly tart and tartly sweet, with enough luscious coconut to send your soul on a tropical fling.　　　●　　Serves 12 (2 each)

$1\frac{1}{2}$ cups + 3 tablespoons all-purpose flour ☆
$1\frac{1}{2}$ cups SPLENDA® Granular ☆
$\frac{1}{2}$ cup reduced-calorie margarine
2 eggs, or equivalent in egg substitute
$\frac{1}{2}$ teaspoon baking powder
$\frac{1}{4}$ teaspoon table salt
$\frac{1}{4}$ cup lemon juice
$\frac{1}{2}$ teaspoon coconut extract
$\frac{1}{4}$ cup chopped walnuts
$\frac{1}{4}$ cup flaked coconut

Preheat oven to 275 degrees. Spray a 9-by-13-inch cake pan with butter-flavored cooking spray. In a large bowl, combine $1\frac{1}{2}$ cups flour and $\frac{1}{2}$ cup SPLENDA®. Add margarine. Mix well using a pastry blender or 2 forks until mixture becomes crumbly. Pat mixture into prepared pan. Bake for 10 minutes. Meanwhile, in a large bowl, beat eggs with a wire whisk until fluffy. Stir in remaining 3 tablespoons flour, remaining 1 cup SPLENDA®, baking powder, and salt. Add lemon juice, coconut extract, walnuts, and coconut. Mix well to combine. Carefully spread mixture over partially baked crust. Increase oven temperature to 350 degrees. Continue baking for 10 to 12 minutes. Place pan on a wire rack and allow to cool completely. Cut into 24 bars.

HINT: Place hand in a plastic sandwich bag when patting crust into pan.

Each serving equals:

HE: 1 Fat • ¾ Bread • ¼ Protein • ¼ Slider •
3 Optional Calories

126 Calories • 6 gm Fat • 3 gm Protein •
15 gm Carbohydrate • 174 mg Sodium •
22 mg Calcium • 1 gm Fiber

DIABETIC EXCHANGES: 1 Fat • 1 Starch

Lemon-Coconut Crunch Bars

These bars are fun to make and fun to eat. Did you ever think you'd be cooking with soda pop? Take it from me, it's a fantastic and fizzy way to get exactly the right lemony flavor in this delightful dessert!

○ Serves 12 (2 each)

1 (8-ounce) can reduced-fat crescent rolls
½ cup SPLENDA® Granular
2 tablespoons cornstarch
1 cup nonfat dry milk powder
1 cup diet lemon-lime soda pop
1 (8-ounce) package fat-free cream cheese
1½ teaspoons coconut extract
6 tablespoons chopped pecans
6 tablespoons flaked coconut

Preheat oven to 425 degrees. Spray a rimmed 9-by-13-inch baking sheet with butter-flavored cooking spray. Pat rolls into pan, being sure to seal perforations. Bake for 5 to 6 minutes or until light golden brown. Place baking sheet on a wire rack and allow to cool. Meanwhile, in a large saucepan, combine SPLENDA®, cornstarch, dry milk powder, and soda pop. Cook over medium heat until mixture thickens and starts to boil, stirring constantly with a wire whisk. Remove from heat. Stir in cream cheese and coconut extract. Fold in pecans. Spread mixture evenly over cooled crust. Evenly sprinkle coconut over top. Refrigerate for at least 2 hours. Cut into 24 bars.

Each serving equals:

HE: ⅔ Bread • ½ Fat • ⅓ Protein • ¼ Fat-Free Milk • ¼ Slider

142 Calories • 6 gm Fat • 6 gm Protein • 16 gm Carbohydrate • 288 mg Sodium • 132 mg Calcium • 1 gm Fiber

DIABETIC EXCHANGES: 1 Starch • ½ Fat

Apricot Meringue Bars

Meringues take a bit more time to fix, but the result is so beautiful and tasty, they're worth the trouble. I'd serve these for a card party luncheon or when old friends come for a long-awaited visit.

○ Serves 12 (2 each)

½ cup reduced-calorie
    margarine
1½ cups SPLENDA®
    Granular ☆
2 eggs, separated
1 teaspoon vanilla extract

1 cup all-purpose flour
½ teaspoon table salt
¼ teaspoon baking powder
1 cup apricot spreadable fruit
¼ cup chopped walnuts

Preheat oven to 350 degrees. Spray a 7-by-11-inch biscuit pan with butter-flavored cooking spray. In a large bowl, cream margarine and ½ cup SPLENDA®, using a sturdy spoon. Stir in egg yolks and vanilla extract. Add flour, salt, and baking powder. Mix gently just to combine. Pat mixture evenly into prepared pan. In a small bowl, stir spreadable fruit until softened. Spread evenly over crust. In a medium bowl, beat egg whites with an electric mixer on HIGH until soft peaks form. Add remaining 1 cup SPLENDA®. Continue beating until stiff peaks form. Carefully stir in walnuts. Evenly spread meringue mixture over apricot layer, being sure to seal to edges. Bake for 18 to 22 minutes or until firm. Place pan on a wire rack and allow to cool completely. Cut into 24 bars.

HINTS: 1. Place hand in a plastic sandwich bag when patting crust into pan.
      2. Any flavor spreadable fruit can be used.

Each serving equals:

HE: 1 Fat • ⅔ Fruit • ⅓ Bread • ¼ Protein •
¼ Slider • 10 Optional Calories

---

158 Calories • 6 gm Fat • 2 gm Protein •
24 gm Carbohydrate • 208 mg Sodium •
15 mg Calcium • 1 gm Fiber

DIABETIC EXCHANGES: 1 Fat • 1 Fruit • 1 Starch

Mom's Applesauce and Raisin Bars

My friend Barbara's mom always stirred applesauce and raisins into her oatmeal when she was a little girl, and when Barbara tried these, she said that they reminded her of her mom's sweet touch with cereal! Check that your applesauce is the natural, unsweetened kind.

Serves 8 (2 each)

¼ cup reduced-calorie margarine
¾ cup SPLENDA® Granular
1 egg, or equivalent in egg substitute
1 cup unsweetened applesauce
1 cup all-purpose flour
1 teaspoon baking soda
1 teaspoon apple pie spice
½ teaspoon table salt
½ cup seedless raisins
¼ cup chopped walnuts

Preheat oven to 350 degrees. Spray a 7-by-11-inch biscuit pan with butter-flavored cooking spray. In a large bowl, cream margarine, SPLENDA®, and egg until mixture is light and fluffy, using a sturdy spoon. Stir in applesauce. Add flour, baking soda, apple pie spice, and salt. Mix gently just to combine. Fold in raisins and walnuts. Spread batter evenly into prepared pan. Bake for 24 to 26 minutes. Place pan on a wire rack and allow to cool completely. Cut into 16 bars.

Each serving equals:

HE: 1 Fat • ¾ Fruit • ⅔ Bread • ¼ Protein • 9 Optional Calories

166 Calories • 6 gm Fat • 3 gm Protein • 25 gm Carbohydrate • 380 mg Sodium • 18 mg Calcium • 2 gm Fiber

DIABETIC EXCHANGES: 1 Fat • 1 Fruit • 1 Starch

Cliff's Applesauce Bars

I've layered the apple flavor in these fragrant delights, and my husband, Cliff, thinks they are just the perfect snack along with a tall glass of milk! Make sure you choose a brand of apple juice with no added sugar—read labels!   ☻   Serves 8 (2 each)

> 1¼ cups reduced-fat biscuit baking mix
> ¼ cup quick oats
> ¼ cup + 2 tablespoons SPLENDA® Granular ☆
> 1½ teaspoons ground cinnamon ☆
> ½ cup seedless raisins
> ¼ cup chopped walnuts
> 1½ cups unsweetened applesauce
> 2 tablespoons no-fat sour cream

Preheat oven to 350 degrees. Spray a 7-by-11-inch biscuit pan with butter-flavored cooking spray. In a large bowl, combine baking mix, oats, ¼ cup SPLENDA®, and 1 teaspoon cinnamon. Stir in raisins and walnuts. In a small bowl, combine applesauce and sour cream. Add applesauce mixture to baking mix mixture. Mix gently just to combine. Spread batter evenly into prepared pan. In a small bowl, combine remaining 2 tablespoons SPLENDA® and ½ teaspoon cinnamon. Evenly sprinkle mixture over top. Bake for 20 to 25 minutes or until a toothpick inserted in center comes out clean. Place pan on a wire rack and allow to cool completely. Cut into 16 bars.

Each serving equals:

HE: 1 Bread • ¾ Fruit • ¼ Fat • 8 Optional Calories

160 Calories • 4 gm Fat • 3 gm Protein •
28 gm Carbohydrate • 225 mg Sodium •
38 mg Calcium • 2 gm Fiber

DIABETIC EXCHANGES: 1 Starch • 1 Fruit • ½ Fat

Oatmeal Peanut Butter Bars

Love the taste of peanut butter but don't always trust yourself to measure properly? Try chewing a piece of sugar-free gum while you're cooking with foods you feel may be too tempting to handle. That way, you're unlikely to pop an unmeasured blob of peanut butter into your mouth. But you can still enjoy the food you love when just the right amount is used in a recipe.

○ Serves 8 (2 each)

> ¾ cup quick oats
> 3 tablespoons reduced-fat biscuit baking mix
> 1 teaspoon baking powder
> 1 cup SPLENDA® Granular
> ½ cup + 2 tablespoons reduced-fat peanut butter ☆
> 1 egg, or equivalent in egg substitute
> ½ cup fat-free half & half
> ½ cup no-fat sour cream
> 1 tablespoon vanilla extract

Preheat oven to 350 degrees. Spray a 9-by-9-inch cake pan with butter-flavored cooking spray. In a small bowl, combine oats, baking mix, baking powder, and SPLENDA®. In a large bowl, combine ½ cup peanut butter, egg, half & half, sour cream, and vanilla extract. Add oatmeal mixture. Mix gently just to combine. Spread batter evenly into prepared pan. Bake for 18 to 22 minutes or until lightly browned. Drop remaining 2 tablespoons peanut butter by teaspoon over warm top. Using a butter knife, carefully spread peanut butter over top. Place pan on a wire rack and allow to cool completely. Cut into 16 bars.

Each serving equals:

HE: 1 Protein • 1 Fat • ½ Bread • ¾ Slider •
11 Optional Calories

---

205 Calories • 9 gm Fat • 8 gm Protein •
23 gm Carbohydrate • 293 mg Sodium •
88 mg Calcium • 2 gm Fiber

DIABETIC EXCHANGES: 1½ Starch/Carbohydrate •
1 Meat • 1 Fat

Grandma's Graham Cracker Bars

Downright delectable—these cozy, delicious homemade treats are fruity and nutty, moist and sweet. What a great choice for a holiday cookie swap!   ○   Serves 8 (2 each)

2 eggs, or equivalent in egg
   substitute
2 tablespoons + 2 teaspoons
   reduced-calorie margarine
¼ cup fat-free half & half
¼ cup unsweetened applesauce
1 tablespoon vanilla extract
¾ cup SPLENDA® Granular

1 cup + 2 tablespoons
   purchased graham
   cracker crumbs
6 tablespoons all-purpose flour
1 teaspoon baking powder
¼ teaspoon baking soda
½ cup seedless raisins
¼ cup chopped pecans

Preheat oven to 350 degrees. Spray a 7-by-11-inch biscuit pan with butter-flavored cooking spray. In a large bowl, beat eggs with a wire whisk until fluffy. Stir in margarine, half & half, applesauce, and vanilla extract. Add SPLENDA®, graham cracker crumbs, flour, baking powder, and baking soda. Mix gently just to combine. Stir in raisins and pecans. Pat mixture evenly into prepared pan. Bake for 15 to 20 minutes. Place pan on a wire rack and let set for at least 10 minutes. Cut into 16 bars.

HINT: Place hand in a plastic sandwich bag when patting mixture into pan.

Each serving equals:

HE: 1 Bread • 1 Fat • ½ Fruit • ¼ Protein •
17 Optional Calories

179 Calories • 7 gm Fat • 4 gm Protein •
25 gm Carbohydrate • 241 mg Sodium •
64 mg Calcium • 1 gm Fiber

DIABETIC EXCHANGES: 1 Starch • 1 Fat • ½ Fruit

Peanut Buster Bars

You'll "bust yer buttons" with excitement, not excess weight, when you discover just how scrumptious these brownie bars are! I tested and tested to get these just right, and I think you'll agree that they're splendidly nutty. ● Serves 8 (2 each)

> ¾ cup SPLENDA® Granular
> 1 egg, or equivalent in egg substitute
> 2 tablespoons reduced-fat peanut butter
> ⅓ cup fat-free half & half
> 2 tablespoons no-fat sour cream
> 1 cup reduced-fat biscuit baking mix
> ¼ cup chopped dry-roasted peanuts
> ¼ cup mini chocolate chips

Preheat oven to 350 degrees. Spray a 7-by-11-inch biscuit pan with butter-flavored cooking spray. In a large bowl, combine SPLENDA®, egg, peanut butter, half & half, and sour cream. Add baking mix, peanuts, and chocolate chips. Mix gently just to combine. Spread batter evenly into prepared pan. Bake for 20 to 25 minutes. Place pan on a wire rack and allow to cool completely. Cut into 16 bars.

Each serving equals:

HE: ⅔ Bread • ½ Protein • ½ Fat • ¼ Slider • 10 Optional Calories

142 Calories • 6 gm Fat • 4 gm Protein • 18 gm Carbohydrate • 228 mg Sodium • 42 mg Calcium • 1 gm Fiber

DIABETIC EXCHANGES: 1 Starch • ½ Meat • ½ Fat

Chocolate Chip Pecan Bars

Of course I'd find a way to include my favorite nuts in a fast and fun bar cookie recipe—don't I just about always? The applesauce works real wonders in keeping the bar batter moist.

Serves 12 (2 each)

> 6 tablespoons reduced-calorie margarine
> ¼ cup unsweetened applesauce
> ½ cup SPLENDA® Granular
> ¼ cup fat-free milk
> 1½ teaspoons vanilla extract
> 1 cup + 2 tablespoons all-purpose flour
> ½ teaspoon baking soda
> ¼ cup mini chocolate chips
> ¼ cup chopped pecans

Preheat oven to 350 degrees. Spray a 7-by-11-inch biscuit pan with butter-flavored cooking spray. In a large bowl, cream margarine, applesauce, and SPLENDA® using a sturdy spoon. Stir in milk and vanilla extract. Add flour and baking soda. Mix gently just to combine. Carefully spread batter into prepared pan. Evenly sprinkle chocolate chips and pecans over top. Bake for 15 to 20 minutes. Place pan on a wire rack and let set for at least 10 minutes. Cut into 24 bars.

Each serving equals:

HE: 1 Fat • ½ Bread • ¼ Slider • 3 Optional Calories

---

101 Calories • 5 gm Fat • 2 gm Protein •
12 gm Carbohydrate • 123 mg Sodium •
12 mg Calcium • 1 gm Fiber

DIABETIC EXCHANGES: 1 Fat • 1 Starch

Becky's Congo Bars

My daughter, Becky, has loved these old-timey treats since she was a little girl. Now that she's a mom and all grown-up, these are still the ones she asks for when she comes for a visit!

● Serves 8 (2 each)

> ¼ cup reduced-calorie margarine
> ¾ cup SPLENDA® Granular
> ¼ cup no-fat sour cream
> 1 egg, or equivalent in egg substitute
> ½ cup fat-free milk
> 1 tablespoon vanilla extract
> 1 cup + 2 tablespoons all-purpose flour
> 1 teaspoon baking powder
> ½ teaspoon baking soda
> ¼ cup mini chocolate chips
> ¼ cup chopped walnuts

Preheat oven to 350 degrees. Spray a 7-by-11-inch biscuit pan with butter-flavored cooking spray. In a large bowl, cream margarine and SPLENDA® using a sturdy spoon. Stir in sour cream, egg, milk, and vanilla extract. Add flour, baking powder, and baking soda. Mix gently just to combine. Fold in chocolate chips and walnuts. Spread batter evenly into prepared pan. Bake for 18 to 22 minutes. Place pan on a wire rack and allow to cool completely. Cut into 16 bars.

Each serving equals:

HE: 1 Fat • ¾ Bread • ¼ Protein • ¼ Slider • 18 Optional Calories

---

159 Calories • 7 gm Fat • 4 gm Protein •
20 gm Carbohydrate • 234 mg Sodium •
74 mg Calcium • 1 gm Fiber

DIABETIC EXCHANGES: 1 Fat • 1 Starch

Marshmallow Fudge Bars

Grand, glorious, and so dee-licious, you'll be glad you chose these for your next children's party. The marshmallows melt just enough to be velvety smooth, and the chocolate enrobes them in beauty!

● Serves 12 (2 each)

> ½ cup reduced-calorie margarine
> ¾ cup SPLENDA® Granular
> 2 eggs, or equivalent in egg substitute
> 1 teaspoon vanilla extract
> ¾ cup all-purpose flour
> ¼ teaspoon baking powder
> ½ teaspoon table salt
> 2 tablespoons unsweetened cocoa powder
> 1 cup miniature marshmallows
> ¼ cup mini chocolate chips
> ¼ cup chopped walnuts ☆

Preheat oven to 350 degrees. Spray a 7-by-11-inch biscuit pan with butter-flavored cooking spray. In a large bowl, cream margarine and SPLENDA®, using a sturdy spoon. Stir in eggs and vanilla extract. Add flour, baking powder, salt, and cocoa. Mix gently just to combine. Fold in marshmallows. Evenly spread batter into prepared pan. Sprinkle chocolate chips and walnuts evenly over top. Bake for 10 to 12 minutes. Place pan on a wire rack and allow to cool completely. Cut into 24 bars.

Each serving equals:

> HE: 1 Fat • ½ Slider • ⅓ Bread • ¼ Protein •
> 16 Optional Calories

> 177 Calories • 9 gm Fat • 4 gm Protein •
> 20 gm Carbohydrate • 316 mg Sodium •
> 25 mg Calcium • 1 gm Fiber

> DIABETIC EXCHANGES: 1½ Fat • 1 Starch/Carbohydrate

Delightfully Good Walnut Bars

Isn't it a comfort to know that walnuts are good for us, that they contain the kind of oil that helps the heart, not hurts it? Notice how I save some walnuts for the top of these bars? That's because we eat with our eyes as well as our taste buds, and they just taste better with a crunchy garnish.   ☻   Serves 12 (2 each)

> ⅓ cup reduced-calorie margarine
> 1 cup SPLENDA® Granular
> 2 eggs, or equivalent in egg substitute
> ¼ cup unsweetened applesauce
> 1½ teaspoons vanilla extract
> ¾ cup reduced-fat biscuit baking mix
> 6 tablespoons purchased graham cracker crumbs
> ½ cup chopped walnuts ☆

Preheat oven to 350 degrees. Spray a 7-by-11-inch biscuit pan with butter-flavored cooking spray. In a large bowl, cream margarine and SPLENDA®, using a sturdy spoon. Stir in eggs, applesauce, and vanilla extract. Add baking mix and graham cracker crumbs. Mix gently just to combine. Fold in 6 tablespoons walnuts. Carefully spread batter into prepared pan. Evenly sprinkle remaining 2 tablespoons of walnuts over top. Lightly spray top with butter-flavored cooking spray. Bake for 15 to 20 minutes. Place pan on a wire rack and let set for at least 10 minutes. Cut into 24 bars.

Each serving equals:

HE: 1 Fat • ½ Bread • ⅓ Protein •
10 Optional Calories

111 Calories • 7 gm fat • 2 gm Protein •
10 gm Carbohydrate • 173 mg Sodium •
18 mg Calcium • 1 gm Fiber

DIABETIC EXCHANGES: 1 Fat • 1 Starch/Carbohydrate

Josh's Candy Cake Brownies

Instead of worrying about how much candy your children are eating, why not stir up a batch of these kid pleasers named for my sweet-toothed grandson Josh? They've got the same ingredients as many favorite candy bars (nuts, chocolate), but they're much better for the kids who gobble them down.   ♥   Serves 8 (2 each)

2 tablespoons no-fat sour cream
½ cup fat-free milk
1 egg, or equivalent in egg substitute
¾ cup SPLENDA® Granular
¾ cup reduced-fat biscuit baking mix
¼ cup unsweetened cocoa powder
¼ cup chopped dry-roasted peanuts
¼ cup mini chocolate chips

Preheat oven to 350 degrees. Spray a 7-by-11-inch biscuit pan with butter-flavored cooking spray. In a large bowl, combine sour cream, milk, and egg. Stir in SPLENDA®. Add baking mix and cocoa. Mix gently just to combine. Fold in peanuts and chocolate chips. Spread batter evenly into prepared pan. Bake for 18 to 22 minutes. Place pan on a wire rack and let set for at least 10 minutes. Cut into 16 bars.

Each serving equals:

HE: ½ Bread • ½ Slider • ¼ Protein • ¼ Fat •
1 Optional Calorie

116 Calories • 4 gm Fat • 4 gm Protein •
16 gm Carbohydrate • 152 mg Sodium •
45 mg Calcium • 1 gm Fiber

DIABETIC EXCHANGES: 1½ Starch • ½ Fat

Almost "Fudge" Brownies

Don't let the name fool you—there's nothing "almost," tastewise, about these brownies. They're amazingly easy to prepare, and they can be "doctored" with little additions to personalize them for a special occasion. ☯ Serves 8 (2 each)

⅓ cup reduced-calorie margarine

2 tablespoons fat-free sour cream

1 cup SPLENDA® Granular

2 eggs, or equivalent in egg substitute

2 tablespoons unsweetened applesauce

1½ teaspoons vanilla extract

¼ cup unsweetened cocoa powder

¾ cup cake flour

Preheat oven to 350 degrees. Spray an 8-by-8-inch cake pan with butter-flavored cooking spray. In a large bowl, cream margarine, sour cream, and SPLENDA® using a sturdy spoon. Stir in eggs, applesauce, and vanilla extract. Add cocoa and flour. Mix gently just to combine. Carefully spread batter into prepared pan. Bake for 14 to 16 minutes. Place pan on a wire rack and let set for at least 10 minutes. Cut into 16 bars.

Each serving equals:

HE: 1 Fat • ½ Bread • ¼ Protein • ¼ Slider • 3 Optional Calories

---

113 Calories • 5 gm Fat • 3 gm Protein • 14 gm Carbohydrate • 111 mg Sodium • 16 mg Calcium • 1 gm Fiber

---

DIABETIC EXCHANGES: 1 Fat • 1 Starch

Super-Duper Snacks, Sauces, Smoothies, and So Much More

Whenever I put together my "miscellaneous" section in a cookbook, I have the best time choosing what sorts of recipes to include. This time around, I went a little wild, offering what I feel is a sensational selection of goodies for all kinds of occasions and even just every day. Whether you're cooking for 1 or 20, whether you're bringing lunch to your job or working out of your home, whether you're 21 or 91, these are sure to hit the spot!

Want a party beverage that will make your guests dive for the punch bowl? I can't choose between **Cranberry Orange Cocktail Smoothie** and **Sangria Sipper!** Need a little creamy something to soothe a craving at 4 p.m.? **Coffee Shop Cappuccino Mocha Shake** is just the thing! Remember the glories of old-fashioned picnic food? Make **Mom's Bread and Butter Pickles** or **Old-Time Piccalilli!** Why not bake up my **Festive Yeast Bread** and top it with **Strawberry Field Jam?** That's my idea of heaven.

Sangria Sipper

Lots of us prefer nonalcoholic beverages, and this one is lovely enough to serve at a dinner party. If you've got a crowd coming, quadruple the recipe and serve it in a punch bowl, with lots of citrus fruit slices floating on top! ☯ Serves 4 (1 cup)

1½ cups unsweetened grape juice
½ cup unsweetened orange juice
2 tablespoons SPLENDA® Granular
2 tablespoons lemon juice
2 tablespoons lime juice
2 cups diet ginger ale
4 orange slices (optional)

In a tall pitcher, combine grape juice, orange juice, and SPLENDA®. Add lemon juice and lime juice. Mix well to combine. Cover and refrigerate for at least 2 hours. Just before serving, stir in diet ginger ale. Pour into tall glasses filled with ice. If desired, garnish each glass with an orange slice.

Each serving equals:

HE: 1 Fruit • 3 Optional Calories

84 Calories • 0 gm Fat • 1 gm Protein •
20 gm Carbohydrate • 28 mg Sodium •
17 mg Calcium • 0 gm Fiber

DIABETIC EXCHANGES: 1 Fruit

Strawberry Romanoff Soda

This is my new favorite summer specialty—perfect when your strawberries are rosy-ripe and supersweet. It's a frothy, festive, and fabulous feel-good treat.   ☺   Serves 2

> 1 tablespoon lemon juice
> ½ cup unsweetened orange juice
> 2 tablespoons SPLENDA® Granular
> 1 cup sliced fresh strawberries
> ¼ cup crushed ice
> 1 cup cold club soda
> 1 cup sugar- and fat-free vanilla ice cream

In a blender container, combine lemon juice, orange juice, SPLENDA®, strawberries, and ice. Cover and process on BLEND for 15 to 20 seconds or until mixture is smooth. Pour ½ cup mixture into 2 tall glasses. Stir ½ cup club soda into each. Top each with ½ cup ice cream. Serve at once.

Each serving equals:

HE: 1 Fruit • ½ Fat-Free Milk • ½ Slider •
6 Optional Calories

140 Calories • 0 gm Fat • 5 gm Protein •
30 gm Carbohydrate • 76 mg Sodium •
143 mg Calcium • 2 gm Fiber

DIABETIC EXCHANGES: 1 Fruit • ½ Fat-Free Milk •
½ Other Carbohydrate

Coffee Shop
Cappuccino Mocha Shake

How can anyone feel deprived when sipping a tall glass of such velvety richness! I love how the cinnamon gives this sensational shake that little extra pizzazz. ● Serves 2 (1 full cup)

> 1 cup fat-free milk
> 1 teaspoon dry instant coffee crystals
> 1/4 cup SPLENDA® Granular
> 1 cup sugar- and fat-free chocolate ice cream
> 1/8 teaspoon ground cinnamon

In a blender container, combine milk, coffee crystals, and SPLENDA®. Cover and process on BLEND for 10 seconds. Add ice cream and cinnamon. Re-cover and continue processing on BLEND for 15 seconds or until mixture is smooth. Serve at once.

Each serving equals:

HE: 1 Fat-Free Milk • 1/2 Slider • 12 Optional Calories

---

140 Calories • 0 gm Fat • 8 gm Protein •
27 gm Carbohydrate • 114 mg Sodium •
273 mg Calcium • 0 gm Fiber

DIABETIC EXCHANGES: 1 Other Carbohydrate •
1/2 Fat-Free Milk

Cranberry Orange Cocktail Smoothie

What an enchanting holiday surprise—you'll adore the contrast between tart cranberry and sunshine-sweet orange juice. This is party food that promises that everyone will have a splendid time!

● Serves 8 (¾ cup)

> 3 cups reduced-calorie cranberry juice cocktail
> ½ cup unsweetened orange juice
> ¼ cup SPLENDA® Granular
> 3 cups sugar- and fat-free vanilla ice cream
> 8 thin orange slices (optional)
> 4 maraschino cherries, halved (optional)

In a blender container, combine cranberry juice cocktail, orange juice, and SPLENDA®. Cover and process on BLEND for 10 seconds. Add ice cream. Re-cover and continue processing on BLEND for 15 seconds or until mixture is smooth. Pour into 8 glasses. If desired, garnish each glass with an orange slice and maraschino cherry half.

Each serving equals:

HE: ½ Fruit • ¼ Fat-Free Milk • ½ Slider

96 Calories • 0 gm Fat • 3 gm Protein •
21 gm Carbohydrate • 40 mg Sodium •
104 mg Calcium • 0 gm Fiber

DIABETIC EXCHANGES: ½ Fruit •
½ Other Carbohydrate

Banana Orange Milk Shake

What a great, refreshing way to meet the morning! You get some healthy fruit and a calcium boost—and no one will say you can't have a milk shake for breakfast. (It's also a wonderful, kid-pleasing snack.) ☺ Serves 2 (1 cup)

> ¾ cup plain fat-free yogurt
> ½ cup cold unsweetened orange juice
> ¼ cup SPLENDA® Granular
> 1 cup (1 medium) diced banana

In a blender container, combine yogurt, orange juice, and SPLENDA®. Cover and process on BLEND for 10 seconds. Add banana. Re-cover and process on BLEND for 15 to 20 seconds or until mixture is smooth. Serve at once.

HINT: To prevent banana from turning brown, mix with 1 teaspoon lemon juice or sprinkle with Fruit Fresh.

Each serving equals:

> HE: 1½ Fruit • ½ Fat-Free Milk • 12 Optional Calories
>
> ---
>
> 156 Calories • 0 gm Fat • 6 gm Protein •
> 33 gm Carbohydrate • 72 mg Sodium •
> 192 mg Calcium • 2 gm Fiber
>
> ---
>
> DIABETIC EXCHANGES: 1½ Fruit • ½ Fat-Free Milk

Cranberry Punch

What could be easier than pouring all these ingredients into your favorite pretty pitcher and inviting your favorite people to toast a new job, a new baby, or the New Year? It's also perfect in a punch bowl, and if you want to float some ice cubes in it but not water it down, fill your ice tray with this mixture before the party.

◑ Serves 12 (¾ cup)

> 4 cups cold reduced-calorie cranberry juice cocktail
> 1 (6-ounce) can frozen lemonade concentrate, thawed
> 1 (6-ounce) can frozen limeade concentrate, thawed
> ¼ cup SPLENDA® Granular
> 4 cups cold club soda

In a large pitcher, combine cranberry juice cocktail, lemonade concentrate, limeade concentrate, and SPLENDA®. Stir in club soda. Pour into glasses filled with ice.

HINT: For a big crowd or if you want leftovers, double the recipe. Punch will keep for several days.

Each serving equals:

HE: 1½ Fruit • 12 Optional Calories

104 Calories • 0 gm Fat • 0 gm Protein •
26 gm Carbohydrate • 19 mg Sodium •
8 mg Calcium • 0 gm Fiber

DIABETIC EXCHANGES: 1½ Fruit

Creamy Hot Chocolate Mix

Why make your own hot chocolate powdered drink when you can buy the packets already mixed? I can give you a couple of terrific reasons—it's fresher, and it's cheaper. Plus, you can choose your favorite unsweetened cocoa powder. I look for Dutch-process cocoa, and if you can find it, give Ghirardelli a try. ● Serves 24

5 cups nonfat dry milk powder
1 cup fat-free nondairy creamer
1½ cups SPLENDA® Granular
½ cup unsweetened cocoa powder

In a large bowl, combine dry milk powder, nondairy creamer, SPLENDA®, and cocoa. Mix well to combine. Store in an airtight container. For each serving, combine 1 cup hot water and ¼ cup chocolate mix in a large cup.

Each serving equals:

HE: ¼ Fat-Free Milk • ¼ Slider • 14 Optional Calories

56 Calories • 0 gm Fat • 4 gm Protein •
10 gm Carbohydrate • 59 mg Sodium •
144 mg Calcium • 0 gm Fiber

DIABETIC EXCHANGES: ½ Fat-Free Milk

Homemade Chocolate Sauce

Wouldn't you love to open your fridge and see a jar of your very own chocolate sauce, ready to turn that glass of milk into a child's favorite fantasy? This is rich and sweet and oh-so-smooth.

● Makes about 2 cups

1 cup unsweetened cocoa powder
2 cups SPLENDA® Granular
¼ teaspoon table salt
2 cups water
1 tablespoon vanilla extract

In a medium saucepan, combine cocoa, SPLENDA®, and salt. Stir in water. Cook over medium-low heat for 5 minutes or until mixture is thickened and smooth, stirring constantly. Remove from heat. Add vanilla extract. Mix well to combine. Let set for 10 minutes, stirring occasionally. Pour mixture into a glass jar and cover. Refrigerate. Use for iced cocoa, chocolate milk, and shakes. Will keep for 1 week.

Each 1 tablespoon serving equals:

HE: 12 Optional Calories

12 Calories • 0 gm Fat • 0 gm Protein •
3 gm Carbohydrate • 19 mg Sodium • 3 mg Calcium •
1 gm Fiber

DIABETIC EXCHANGES: 1 Free Food

Simple Raspberry Sauce

If you keep a package of frozen raspberries on hand, in almost no time at all, you can have a delectable dessert topping to offer guests or dazzle family members. Try it over sugar-free and fat-free ice cream, angel food cake, or fresh melon.

❂ Serves 4 (full ⅓ cup)

> 1 (12-ounce) package frozen unsweetened raspberries
> ½ cup SPLENDA® Granular

Evenly arrange raspberries in an 8-cup glass measuring bowl. Microwave on HIGH (100% power) for 2 minutes. Add SPLENDA®. Mix well to combine. Continue to microwave on HIGH for 1 minute. Mix gently to combine. Cover and refrigerate for at least 15 minutes. Gently stir again just before serving.

HINTS: 1. Great on ice cream, pancakes, or French toast.
2. Frozen unsweetened strawberries, blueberries, or peaches work well also.

Each serving equals:

HE: 1 Fruit • 12 Optional Calories

68 Calories • 0 gm Fat • 1 gm Protein •
16 gm Carbohydrate • 0 mg Sodium •
25 mg Calcium • 4 gm Fiber

DIABETIC EXCHANGES: 1 Fruit

Mom's Homemade Cherry Pie Filling

The name says it all: "homemade"—not just pie filling from a can but prepared with love. Here's an easy and delicious version you can make your own. ☉ Serves 8

> 1 (15-ounce) can tart red cherries, packed in water, drained, and
>   ½ cup liquid reserved
> ½ cup water
> 3 tablespoons cornstarch
> ¾ cup SPLENDA® Granular
> 10 to 12 drops red food coloring

In a medium saucepan, combine reserved cherry liquid, water, cornstarch, and SPLENDA®. Add cherries and red food coloring. Mix gently to combine. Cook over medium heat until mixture thickens and starts to boil, stirring often and being careful not to crush cherries. Remove from heat. Place saucepan on a wire rack and let set for at least 15 minutes, stirring occasionally. Use in any recipe calling for 1 can cherry pie filling.

HINTS: 1. Excellent with 1 teaspoon almond extract stirred in after removing from heat.
2. Use 2 cups of any chopped fruit, replace ½ cup cherry liquid with water and a complementary food coloring for any flavored fruit pie filling.

Each serving equals:

HE: ½ Fruit • 16 Optional Calories

40 Calories • 0 gm Fat • 0 gm Protein •
10 gm Carbohydrate • 4 mg Sodium •
6 mg Calcium • 1 gm Fiber

DIABETIC EXCHANGES: ½ Fruit

Sweet Summer Salsa

When my garden was brimming with gorgeous ripe tomatoes, I created this tangy delight. It takes some chopping, but the end result is so much tastier than the kind you buy in a jar. (If you like your salsa a little less sweet, reduce the amount of SPLENDA®.)

4 cups peeled and chopped fresh tomatoes
½ cup finely chopped red onion
½ cup finely chopped red bell pepper
½ cup finely chopped green bell pepper
1 cup SPLENDA® Granular
2 tablespoons chopped fresh basil or 1 teaspoon dried basil leaves
⅛ teaspoon black pepper

In a medium saucepan, combine tomatoes, onion, red pepper, and green pepper. Stir in SPLENDA®, basil, and black pepper. Cook over medium heat for 15 minutes, stirring occasionally. Place saucepan on a wire rack and let set 15 minutes, stirring occasionally. Spoon mixture into a covered container. Refrigerate for at least 2 hours. Makes 3 full cups. Will keep up to 1 week.

1 tablespoon serving equals:

HE: 8 Optional Calories

8 Calories • 0 gm Fat • 0 gm Protein •
2 gm Carbohydrate • 1 mg Sodium • 1 mg Calcium •
0 gm Fiber

DIABETIC EXCHANGES: 1 Free Food

Italian Veggie Relish

Every good Italian restaurant features a colorful and aromatic antipasto display, and among the choices will usually be some tangy, crunchy vegetables. Your eyes will feast first, and then your taste buds. What a splendid start to a meal!   ◐   Serves 6 (⅓ cup)

> ½ cup fat-free Italian dressing
> 3 tablespoons SPLENDA® Granular
> 1½ cups finely chopped unpeeled zucchini
> 1 cup shredded carrots
> ¼ cup finely chopped red and/or green bell pepper
> ¼ cup finely chopped onion

In a medium bowl, combine Italian dressing and SPLENDA®. Add zucchini, carrots, bell pepper, and onion. Mix well to combine. Cover and refrigerate for at least 1 hour. Gently stir again just before serving.

Each serving equals:

HE: 1 Vegetable • 16 Optional Calories

32 Calories • 0 gm Fat • 1 gm Protein •
7 gm Carbohydrate • 294 mg Sodium •
21 mg Calcium • 1 gm Fiber

DIABETIC EXCHANGES: 1 Vegetable

Garden Patch Relish

You can never have too many crunchy fresh side salads during those long, hot summer months, right? If you're a fan of this type of recipe but you've never stocked your pantry shelf with celery seed or mustard seed, I recommend treating yourself to these special spices. Their intense flavor makes all the difference!

½ cup SPLENDA® Granular
¼ cup white distilled vinegar
¾ teaspoon table salt
½ teaspoon yellow mustard seed
¼ teaspoon celery seed
3 cups finely shredded cabbage
1½ cups unpeeled and shredded cucumber
½ cup chopped red bell pepper

In a large bowl, combine SPLENDA®, vinegar, salt, mustard seed, and celery seed. Add cabbage, cucumber, and red pepper. Mix well to combine. Spoon mixture into a covered container. Refrigerate for at least 24 hours. Makes 2 cups. Will keep for 1 week.

2 tablespoon serving equals:

HE: ¼ Slider

20 Calories • 0 gm Fat • 1 gm Protein •
4 gm Carbohydrate • 224 mg Sodium •
21 mg Calcium • 1 gm Fiber

DIABETIC EXCHANGES: 1 Free Food

Chunky Spaghetti Sauce

Here's a terrific way to make spaghetti sauce that will convince your dinner guests that it's been cooking for *hours* on your stove. Lots of family coming for supper? You can easily double or triple this recipe. ☺ Serves 4 (¾ cup)

½ cup finely chopped onion
½ cup finely chopped green bell pepper
1 cup finely chopped fresh mushrooms
1 (8-ounce) can tomato sauce
1 (15-ounce) can diced tomatoes, undrained
2 tablespoons SPLENDA® Granular
1½ teaspoons Italian seasoning

In a medium saucepan sprayed with olive oil-flavored cooking spray, sauté onion, green pepper, and mushrooms for 6 to 8 minutes. Stir in tomato sauce, undrained tomatoes, SPLENDA®, and Italian seasoning. Lower heat and simmer for 10 to 12 minutes, stirring occasionally.

Each serving equals:

HE: 2½ Vegetable • 3 Optional Calories

---

64 Calories • 0 gm Fat • 2 gm Protein •
14 gm Carbohydrate • 507 mg Sodium •
32 mg Calcium • 3 gm Fiber

DIABETIC EXCHANGES: 2 Vegetable

Sweet Salsa Dip

This dip can be just as spicy as you like—and if Cliff is mixing it up, it will be HOT HOT HOT! I prefer it milder, but you'll see that the cream cheese and sour cream lighten the impact of the salsa a bit.

○ Serves 8 (¼ cup)

> 1 (8-ounce) package fat-free cream cheese
> ½ cup no-fat sour cream
> 1 cup chunky salsa (mild, medium, or hot)
> ½ cup SPLENDA® Granular
> 2 teaspoons dried parsley flakes

In a large bowl, stir cream cheese with a sturdy spoon until soft. Add sour cream. Mix well to combine. Stir in salsa, SPLENDA®, and parsley flakes. Cover and refrigerate for at least 30 minutes. Gently stir again just before serving.

HINT: Great with veggies, tortilla chips, or crackers.

Each serving equals:

HE: ½ Protein • ¼ Vegetable • ¼ Slider • 1 Optional Calorie

---

56 Calories • 0 gm Fat • 5 gm Protein • 9 gm Carbohydrate • 380 mg Sodium • 101 mg Calcium • 1 gm Fiber

---

DIABETIC EXCHANGES: ½ Meat • ½ Other Carbohydrate

Holiday Nut Spread

This is wonderfully good any time of the year (as long as you have some cranberries stored in the freezer), but it's especially nice during the holiday season!   ☺   Serves 6 (¼ cup)

1 (8-ounce) package fat-free cream cheese
2 tablespoons orange marmalade spreadable fruit
⅓ cup SPLENDA® Granular
1 cup fresh or frozen whole cranberries, finely chopped
¼ cup chopped walnuts

In a medium bowl, stir cream cheese with a sturdy spoon until soft. Stir in spreadable fruit and SPLENDA®. Add cranberries and walnuts. Mix well to combine. Cover and refrigerate for at least 30 minutes. Gently stir again just before serving.

Each serving equals:

HE: 1 Protein • ½ Fruit • ⅓ Fat • 5 Optional Calories

91 Calories • 3 gm Fat • 6 gm Protein • 10 gm Carbohydrate • 187 mg Sodium • 112 mg Calcium • 1 gm Fiber

DIABETIC EXCHANGES: 1 Meat • ½ Fruit • ½ Fat

Cliff's Tomato Bacon Dressing

Tired of the same old vinaigrette? Eaten ranch until you're ready to roll over? Here's a dressing that got Cliff's attention, and if it's good enough for my favorite long-distance trucker, it's going to win you over too. ☻ Serves 8 (2 tablespoons)

¾ cup fat-free French dressing

2 tablespoons fat-free mayonnaise

2 tablespoons sweet pickle relish

2 tablespoons white distilled vinegar

2 tablespoons SPLENDA® Granular

¼ cup purchased real bacon bits

1 teaspoon dried onion flakes

1 teaspoon dried parsley flakes

In a medium bowl, combine French dressing, mayonnaise, sweet pickle relish, vinegar, and SPLENDA®. Add bacon bits, onion flakes, and parsley flakes. Mix well to combine. Cover and refrigerate for at least 30 minutes. Gently stir again just before using.

Each serving equals:

HE: ½ Slider • 18 Optional Calories

57 Calories • 1 gm Fat • 1 gm Protein • 11 gm Carbohydrate • 411 mg Sodium • 1 mg Calcium • 1 gm Fiber

DIABETIC EXCHANGES: ½ Other Carbohydrate

Creamy Poppy Seed Dressing

You may not believe that a few poppy seeds can flavor a simple dressing, but they're a powerful and very pleasing spice. This is best when stirred before serving, and it becomes even better if you can let it wait an hour or so. ● Serves 6 (2 tablespoons)

½ cup fat-free mayonnaise
¼ cup SPLENDA® Granular
1 tablespoon apple cider vinegar
1 teaspoon poppy seeds

In a small bowl, combine mayonnaise, SPLENDA®, and vinegar. Add poppy seeds. Mix well to combine. Cover and refrigerate for at least 30 minutes. Gently stir again just before using.

Each serving equals:

HE: 16 Optional Calories

16 Calories • 0 gm Fat • 0 gm Protein •
4 gm Carbohydrate • 160 mg Sodium •
8 mg Calcium • 0 gm Fiber

DIABETIC EXCHANGES: 1 Free Food

Italian Restaurant Salad Dressing

Sure, you can find pretty good Italian dressing in a bottle, ready-made. But just as you feel special when the waiter blends your dressing at the table during a special occasion meal, you and your family will taste the difference when you take the time to stir up your own. Enjoy! ☉ Serves 8 (2 tablespoons)

½ cup fat-free mayonnaise

⅓ cup white distilled vinegar

2 teaspoons vegetable oil

1 tablespoon lemon juice

¼ cup SPLENDA® Granular

¼ cup grated reduced-fat Parmesan cheese

¼ teaspoon dried minced garlic

1 teaspoon Italian seasoning

1 teaspoon parsley flakes

In a large bowl, combine mayonnaise, vinegar, oil, lemon juice, and SPLENDA®, using a wire whisk. Add Parmesan cheese, garlic, Italian seasoning, and parsley flakes. Mix well using a wire whisk. Cover and refrigerate for at least 30 minutes. Gently stir again just before serving.

Each serving equals:

HE: ¼ Fat • ¼ Slider • 1 Optional Calorie

30 Calories • 2 gm Fat • 0 gm Protein •
3 gm Carbohydrate • 142 mg Sodium •
16 mg Calcium • 0 gm Fiber

DIABETIC EXCHANGES: 1 Free Food

Strawberry "Ice Cream"

Did you know you could use your blender to make a kind of soft, smooth, spectacular strawberry dessert? The frozen strawberries act like ice cubes in chilling the mixture, and the fizzy lemon-lime soda gives it just a bit of sparkle.　☻　Serves 2 (1 cup)

> ⅓ cup nonfat dry milk powder
> ¼ cup SPLENDA® Granular
> ⅓ cup cold diet lemon-lime soda
> 2 cups frozen unsweetened strawberries

In a blender container, combine dry milk powder, SPLENDA®, and diet soda. Add 1 cup strawberries. Cover and process on BLEND for 30 seconds or until strawberries are chopped into small pieces. Add remaining 1 cup strawberries. Re-cover and continue processing on BLEND for 30 to 45 seconds or until mixture is smooth. Spoon into 2 dessert dishes. Serve at once.

Each serving equals:

HE: 1 Fruit • ½ Fat-Free Milk • 12 Optional Calories

---

136 Calories • 0 gm Fat • 5 gm Protein •
29 gm Carbohydrate • 71 mg Sodium •
185 mg Calcium • 4 gm Fiber

DIABETIC EXCHANGES: 1 Fruit • ½ Fat-Free Milk

Dill Party Pinwheels

This recipe always reminds me of the aproned hostesses of the 1950s serving canapés to their guests. It's savory and pretty, perfect for a festive appetizer. ○ Serves 8 (4 each)

1 (8-ounce) package fat-free cream cheese
¼ cup dill pickle relish
2 tablespoons SPLENDA® Granular
1 teaspoon dried onion flakes
1 (8-ounce) package reduced-fat crescent rolls

Preheat oven to 375 degrees. In a medium bowl, stir cream cheese with a sturdy spoon until soft. Stir in pickle relish, SPLENDA®, and onion flakes. Unroll crescent rolls and separate into 4 rectangles. Spread a full ¼ cup cream cheese mixture over each rectangle. Roll rectangles up and refrigerate for at least 10 minutes. Cut each chilled rectangle into 8 slices. Arrange slices on ungreased baking sheets. Lightly spray tops with butter-flavored cooking spray. Bake for 12 to 14 minutes or until lightly browned. Place baking sheets on wire racks and let set for 5 minutes. Serve warm or cold.

Each serving equals:

HE: 1 Bread • ½ Protein • 2 Optional Calories

120 Calories • 4 gm Fat • 6 gm Protein •
15 gm Carbohydrate • 435 mg Sodium •
81 mg Calcium • 1 gm Fiber

DIABETIC EXCHANGES: 1 Starch • ½ Meat

Hit the Trails Munch Mix

Want a reward for committing to a healthy walking regimen? This high-energy snack blend is an ideal choice for a take-along treat on your next hike. Just make sure to wear comfortable shoes, choose a familiar route, and maybe invite a buddy to join you. This recipe will feed eight, so invite the whole gang!

● Serves 8 (full ½ cup)

> 1½ cups Wheat Chex
> 2 cups Corn Chex
> ½ cup seedless raisins
> ½ cup chopped dried apricots
> ½ cup chopped dry roasted peanuts
> ½ cup SPLENDA® Granular
> ½ teaspoon ground cinnamon

In a large bowl, combine Wheat Chex, Corn Chex, raisins, apricots, and peanuts. Add SPLENDA® and cinnamon. Mix well to combine. Store in an airtight container.

Each serving equals:

HE: 1 Bread • 1 Fruit • ½ Fat • ¼ Protein •
6 Optional Calories

180 Calories • 4 gm Fat • 4 gm Protein •
32 gm Carbohydrate • 197 mg Sodium •
67 mg Calcium • 3 gm Fiber

DIABETIC EXCHANGES: 1 Starch • 1 Fruit • 1 Fat

Festive Yeast Bread

Does your bread machine sit there on your counter collecting dust because you just aren't sure what to do with it? Or perhaps you're bored making the same old, same old bread? I like the challenge of coming up with something different, and I think I succeeded with this raisin-nut loaf.   ○   Serves 12

   ¾ cup water
   ¼ cup no-fat sour cream
   1 egg, or equivalent in egg substitute
   1 teaspoon vanilla extract
   1½ teaspoons table salt
   1 tablespoon + 1 teaspoon reduced-calorie margarine
   3 cups bread flour
   ½ cup SPLENDA® Granular
   ½ teaspoon ground cinnamon
   1½ teaspoons active dry yeast
   ¾ cup seedless raisins
   ½ cup chopped walnuts

In a bread-machine container, combine water, sour cream, egg, vanilla extract, salt, and margarine. Add bread flour, SPLENDA®, and cinnamon. Make an indentation on top of dry ingredients. Pour yeast into indentation. Follow your bread machine instructions for a 1½ pound loaf. Add raisins and walnuts when "add ingredient" signal beeps. Continue following your machine's instructions. Remove loaf from machine and place on a wire rack to cool. Cut into 12 slices. Makes one (1½-pound) loaf.

Each serving equals:

HE: 1½ Bread • ½ Fruit • ½ Fat • ¼ Protein •
9 Optional Calories

---

188 Calories • 4 gm Fat • 6 gm Protein •
32 gm Carbohydrate • 319 mg Sodium •
19 mg Calcium • 2 gm Fiber

DIABETIC EXCHANGES: 1½ Starch • ½ Fruit • ½ Fat

Basic White Bread

I almost called this "better than basic" because fresh bread made at home is better than just about any loaf you can buy in a plastic bag at your store. But it's easy enough to deserve that name, and it's a bread you can serve anytime to anyone. ☯ Serves 12

1 cup water
⅓ cup nonfat dry milk powder
1 egg, or equivalent in egg substitute
1½ teaspoons table salt
1 tablespoon + 1 teaspoon reduced-calorie margarine
3 cups bread flour
¼ cup SPLENDA® Granular
1½ teaspoons active dry yeast

In a bread-machine container, combine water and dry milk powder. Stir in egg, salt, and margarine. Add bread flour and SPLENDA®. Make an indentation on top of dry ingredients. Pour yeast into indentation. Follow your bread machine instructions for a 1½ pound loaf. Remove loaf from machine and place on a wire rack to cool. Cut into 12 slices. Makes one (1½-pound) loaf.

Each serving equals:

HE: 1½ Bread • ¼ Slider • 1 Optional Calorie

125 Calories • 1 gm Fat • 5 gm Protein •
24 gm Carbohydrate • 322 mg Sodium •
28 mg Calcium • 1 gm Fiber

DIABETIC EXCHANGES: 1½ Starch

Mediterranean Yeast Bread

Have you seen loaves of gourmet bread studded with olives and wondered what they might taste like? I decided to stir up a version that provided less sodium per slice than those recipes. I think combining olives with Parmesan cheese makes this a winner!

● Serves 12

½ cup fat-free milk
½ cup water
1 egg, or equivalent in egg
    substitute
1 tablespoon olive oil
1 tablespoon Italian seasoning
1½ teaspoons table salt

3 cups bread flour
¼ cup grated reduced-fat
    Parmesan cheese
2 tablespoons SPLENDA®
    Granular
1½ teaspoons active dry yeast
½ cup chopped ripe olives

In a bread-machine container, combine milk, water, egg, olive oil, Italian seasoning, and salt. Add flour, Parmesan cheese, and SPLENDA®. Make an indentation on top of dry ingredients. Pour yeast into indentation. Follow your bread machine instructions for a 1½ pound loaf. Add olives when "add ingredient" signal beeps. Continue following your machine's instructions. Remove loaf from machine and place on a wire rack to cool. Cut into 12 slices. Makes one (1½-pound) loaf.

Each serving equals:

HE: 1½ Bread • ½ Fat • 15 Optional Calories

134 Calories • 2 gm Fat • 5 gm Protein •
24 gm Carbohydrate • 369 mg Sodium •
30 mg Calcium • 1 gm Fiber

DIABETIC EXCHANGES: 1½ Starch • ½ Fat

Strawberry Field Jam

I've been making jam since I was a little girl, but even if you never learned how from a grandmother or aunt (or your mom, of course), you can still learn to preserve your own crop of berries, using the latest in healthy jam making. (If your neighbor has the strawberry patch and you've got loads of tomatoes, arrange a trade!)

◐ Makes about 4 half pints

> 6 cups sliced ripe fresh strawberries
> 3 cups SPLENDA® Granular
> 2 tablespoons lemon juice
> ¼ cup boiling water
> 1 (¾-ounce) package fruit pectin for lower sugar recipes

In a large saucepan, mash 4 cups strawberries with a potato masher. Add remaining 2 cups strawberries, SPLENDA®, and lemon juice. Mix well to combine. Bring mixture to a boil, stirring often. Lower heat and simmer for 15 minutes, stirring often. In a small bowl, combine boiling water and dry fruit pectin, using a wire whisk to blend. Stir in strawberry mixture. Bring mixture to a boil again and continue boiling for 1 minute, stirring constantly. Carefully ladle hot mixture into hot sterilized half-pint jars, leaving a ½-inch headspace. Seal and process in a boiling-water canner for 15 minutes.

Each 1 tablespoon serving equals:

HE: 8 Optional Calories

8 Calories • 0 gm Fat • 0 gm Protein •
2 gm Carbohydrate • 0 mg Sodium • 2 mg Calcium •
0 gm Fiber

DIABETIC EXCHANGES: 1 Free Food

Blueberry Rhubarb Jam

Are you surprised to see this combination of fruit when it's almost always the strawberry that's partnered with rhubarb? I like bending culinary rules, especially when the result is as beguiling as this delectable jam.   ◐   Makes about 4 half pints

> 3 cups fresh or frozen unsweetened blueberries,
>   thawed and undrained
> 3 cups finely chopped fresh or frozen rhubarb, thawed
> 3 cups SPLENDA® Granular
> 2 tablespoons lemon juice
> 2 tablespoons cold water
> ¼ cup boiling water
> 1 (1¾-ounce) package fruit pectin for lower sugar recipes

In a large saucepan, combine blueberries, rhubarb, SPLENDA®, lemon juice, and cold water. Bring mixture to a boil, stirring often. Lower heat and simmer for 10 minutes, stirring often. In a small bowl, combine boiling water and dry fruit pectin, using a wire whisk to blend well. Stir into blueberry mixture. Bring mixture to a boil again and continue boiling for 1 minute, stirring constantly. Remove from heat and continue stirring often for 1 minute. Carefully ladle hot mixture into hot sterilized half-pint jars, leaving a ½-inch headspace. Seal and process in a boiling-water canner for 10 minutes.

Each 1 tablespoon serving equals:

HE: 8 Optional Calories

8 Calories • 0 gm Fat • 0 gm Protein •
2 gm Carbohydrate • 0 mg Sodium • 4 mg Calcium •
0 gm Fiber

DIABETIC EXCHANGES: 1 Free Food

Homemade Meatless Mincemeat

Classic mincemeat may not appeal to everyone, but this version leaves out the meat—and stirs in truly amazing flavor! What can you do with this yummy stuff? Spoon it into individual tartlets, bake a pie, even spoon it on top of your breakfast cereal.

◑ Makes about 4 pints

> 10 cups cored, unpeeled, and finely chopped cooking apples
> 2 cups seedless raisins
> 1¼ cups unsweetened apple juice
> ¾ cup apple cider vinegar
> 2½ cups SPLENDA® Granular
> 1 tablespoon apple pie spice

In a large saucepan, combine apples, raisins, apple juice, and vinegar. Add SPLENDA® and apple pie spice. Mix well to combine. Cook over low heat for 2 hours or until mixture thickens, stirring occasionally. Carefully ladle hot mixture into hot sterilized pint jars, leaving a ½-inch headspace. Seal and process in a boiling-water canner for 20 minutes.

Each ¼ cup serving equals:

HE: 1 Fruit

60 Calories • 0 gm Fat • 0 gm Protein •
15 gm Carbohydrate • 1 mg Sodium •
10 mg Calcium • 1 gm Fiber

DIABETIC EXCHANGES: 1 Fruit

Mom's Bread & Butter Pickles

Never made your own pickles, but always wondered if you could? I'm delighted to supply an easy but utterly reliable recipe! You may have to purchase a few of the special ingredients, but once you discover how good these are, you'll be making them often—and maybe even for holiday gifts. ☻ Makes about 4 pints

8 cups peeled and sliced
    cucumbers
1½ cups sliced onion
1 large clove of garlic
2½ tablespoons pickling salt
3 cups ice cubes

2 cups SPLENDA® Granular
1 teaspoon ground turmeric
1 teaspoon celery seed
1 tablespoon yellow mustard
    seeds
1½ cups apple cider vinegar

In a large glass or plastic bowl, combine cucumbers, onion, garlic, and pickling salt. Evenly arrange ice cubes over top. Cover with a clean cloth and let set at room temperature for 3 hours. Remove garlic. Place mixture in a large colander and rinse and drain well. In a large saucepan, combine SPLENDA®, turmeric, celery seed, mustard seeds, and vinegar. Add drained cucumber mixture. Mix well to combine. Cook over medium heat for 5 minutes, stirring occasionally. Carefully ladle hot mixture into hot sterilized pint jars, leaving ½-inch headspace. Seal and process in a boiling-water canner for 10 minutes.

Each 1 tablespoon serving equals:

HE: 4 Optional Calories

4 Calories • 0 gm Fat • 0 gm Protein •
1 gm Carbohydrate • 137 mg Sodium •
2 mg Calcium • 0 gm Fiber

DIABETIC EXCHANGES: 1 Free Food

Old-Time Piccalilli

This highly seasoned vegetable relish is a terrific way to use the vegetables from your summer garden, but even if you buy most of the ingredients at the supermarket or a farm stand, you'll be impressed by just how good this healthy veggie dish tastes.

⊙ Makes about 2 pints

> 3 cups peeled and chopped green tomatoes
> 3 cups peeled and chopped red tomatoes
> 2 cups finely chopped cabbage
> 1 cup finely chopped onion
> ½ cup finely chopped green bell pepper
> ½ cup finely chopped red bell pepper
> 2½ tablespoons pickling salt
> 1½ cups apple cider vinegar
> 1¼ cups SPLENDA® Granular
> 1 tablespoon mixed pickling spices

In a large glass or plastic bowl, combine green and red tomatoes, cabbage, onion, green pepper, red pepper, and pickling salt. Cover with a clean cloth and let set at room temperature for 3 hours. Drain mixture well, but do not rinse, pressing to remove as much liquid as possible. In a large saucepan, combine vinegar and SPLENDA®. Tie the pickle spices in a spice bag or a 4-inch square of cheesecloth. Add spice bag to vinegar solution. Mix gently to combine. Bring mixture to a boil, stirring occasionally. Lower heat, cover, and simmer for 15 minutes, stirring often. Stir in drained vegetables. Continue to simmer for 20 minutes, stirring occasionally. Remove spice bag. Ladle hot mixture into hot sterilized pint jars, leaving a ½-inch headspace. Seal and process in a boiling-water canner for 15 minutes.

Each 1 tablespoon serving equals:

HE: 8 Optional Calories

8 Calories • 0 gm Fat • 0 gm Protein •
2 gm Carbohydrate • 225 mg Sodium •
4 mg Calcium • 0 gm Fiber

DIABETIC EXCHANGES: 1 Free Food

Sweet

Occasion

Menus

"Ain't She Sweet?"
Mother's Day Supper

> Broccoli Cashew Salad
> Rosemary Stewed Tomatoes
> Baked Italian Chicken
> Luscious Lemon Meringue Pie

"Happy Birthday, Sweet Sixteen"
Birthday Bash

> BBQ Loose Meat Sandwiches
> Layered Party Pea Salad
> Cranberry Punch
> Mud Pie Cake

"Sweet Temptation"
Anniversary Dinner

> Wilted Green Bean & Lettuce Salad
> Corn Bread Pudding
> Chicken with Caribbean Pecan Sauce
> Hello Dolly Chocolate Cake

"Sweet Dreams" Country Picnic

> Mom's Bread & Butter Pickles
> Pam's Potato Salad
> Meat Loaf Patties with Grande Sauce
> Devil's Food Cupcakes

"Home Sweet Home"
Family Reunion Luncheon

> Best Three-Bean Salad
> Skillet au Gratin Cabbage
> Becky's Porcupine Meat Loaf
> Apple and Peanut Butter Crumb Pie

"Sweets for the Sweet" Dessert Party

> Applesauce Nut Bread
> Holiday Banana Cranberry Meringue Pie
> Baked Almond Cheesecake
> Apricot-Pecan Bread Pudding

Making Healthy Exchanges Work for You

You're ready now to begin a wonderful journey to better health. In the preceding pages, you've discovered the remarkable variety of good food available to you when you begin eating the Healthy Exchanges way. You've stocked your pantry and learned many of my food preparation "secrets" that will point you on the way to delicious success.

But before I let you go, I'd like to share a few tips that I've learned while traveling toward healthier eating habits. It took me a long time to learn how to eat *smarter*. In fact, I'm still working on it. But I am getting better. For years, I could *inhale* a five-course meal in five minutes flat—and still make room for a second helping of dessert!

Now I follow certain signposts on the road that help me stay on the right path. I hope these ideas will help point you in the right direction as well.

1. **Eat slowly** so your brain has time to catch up with your tummy. Cut and chew each bite slowly. Try putting your fork down between bites. Stop eating as soon as you feel full. Crumple your napkin and throw it on top of your plate so you don't continue to eat when you are no longer hungry.

2. **Smaller plates** may help you feel more satisfied by your food portions *and* limit the amount you can put on the plate.

3. **Watch portion size.** If you are *truly* hungry, you can always add more food to your plate once you've finished your initial serving. But remember to count the additional food accordingly.

4. **Always eat at your dining room or kitchen table.** You deserve better than nibbling from an open refrigerator or over the sink. Make an attractive place setting, even if you're eating alone. Feed your eyes as well as your stomach. By always eating at a table, you will become much more aware of your true food intake. For some reason, many of us conveniently "forget" the food we swallow while standing over the stove or munching in the car or on the run.

5. **Avoid doing anything else while you are eating.** If you read the paper or watch television while you eat, it's easy to consume too much food without realizing it, because you are concentrating on something else besides what you're eating. Then, when you look down at your plate and see that it's empty, you wonder where all the food went and why you still feel hungry.

Day by day, as you travel the path to good health, it will become easier to make the right choices, to eat *smarter.* But don't ever fool yourself into thinking that you'll be able to put your eating habits on cruise control and forget about them. Making a commitment to eat good, healthy food and sticking to it takes some effort. But with all the good-tasting recipes in this Healthy Exchanges cookbook, just think how well you're going to eat—and enjoy it—from now on!

Healthy Lean Bon Appetit!

Index

I want to hear from you . . .

Besides my family, the love of my life is creating "common folk" healthy recipes and solving everyday cooking questions in *The Healthy Exchanges Way*. Everyone who uses my recipes is considered part of the Healthy Exchanges Family, so please write to me if you have any questions, comments, or suggestions. I will do my best to answer. With your support, I'll continue to stir up even more recipes and cooking tips for the Family in the years to come.

Write to: JoAnna M. Lund
             c/o Healthy Exchanges, Inc.
             P.O. Box 80
             DeWitt, IA 52742-0080

If you prefer, you can fax me at 1-563-659-2126 or contact me via e-mail by writing to HealthyJo@aol.com. Or visit my Healthy Exchanges Internet website at: http://www.healthyexchanges.com.

Now That You've Seen
Cooking Healthy with Splenda®, Why Not
Order *The Healthy Exchanges Food Newsletter?*

If you enjoyed the recipes in this cookbook and would like to cook up even more of my "common folk" healthy dishes, you may want to subscribe to *The Healthy Exchanges Food Newsletter*.

This monthly 12-page newsletter contains 30-plus new recipes *every month,* in such columns as:

- Reader Exchange
- Reader Requests
- Recipe Makeover
- Micro Corner
- Dinner for Two

- Crock Pot Luck
- Meatless Main Dishes
- Rise & Shine
- Our Small World

- Brown Bagging It
- Snack Attack
- Side Dishes
- Main Dishes
- Desserts

In addition to all the recipes, other regular features include:

- The Editor's Motivational Corner
- Dining Out Question & Answer
- Cooking Question & Answer
- New Product Alert
- Success Profiles of Winners in the Losing Game
- Exercise Advice from a Cardiac Rehab Specialist
- Nutrition Advice from a Registered Dietitian
- Positive Thought for the Month

The cost for a one-year (12-issue) subscription is $25. To order, call our toll-free number and pay with your VISA or MasterCard.

1-800-766-8961 for customer orders
1-563-659-8234 for customer service

Thank you for your order, and for choosing to become a part of the Healthy Exchanges Family!

Have You Tried These Healthy Exchanges Books?

Healthy Exchanges Cookbook   0-399-52554-8
   $13.95/$19.95 Can.
The Diabetics Healthy Exchanges Cookbook   0-399-52235-2
   $14.00/$20.00 Can.
The Heart Smart Healthy Exchanges Cookbook   0-399-52474-6
   $14.00/$20.00 Can.
The Strong Bones Healthy Exchanges Cookbook   0-399-52337-5
   $13.95/$19.95 Can.
The Arthritis Healthy Exchanges Cookbook   0-399-52377-4
   $13.95/$19.95 Can.
Cooking Healthy with a Man in Mind   0-399-52779-6
   $16.95/$24.99 Can.
Cooking Healthy with the Kids in Mind   0-399-52605-6
   $13.95/$19.99 Can.
A Potful of Recipes   0-399-52650-1   *$15.95/$22.99 Can.*
The Open Road Cookbook   0-399-52862-8   *$17.95/$27.00
Can.*
The Healthy Exchanges Diabetic Desserts Cookbook
   0-399-52884-9   *$17.95/$27.00 Can.*
Another Potful of Recipes   0-399-52929-2   *$17.95/$27.00 Can.*
Hot Off the Grill   0-399-52914-4   *$17.95/$27.00 Can.*
Healthy Exchanges® Sensational Smoothies   0-399-52964-0
   $17.95/$27.00 Can.

AVAILABLE WHEREVER BOOKS ARE SOLD

About the Author

JoAnna M. Lund, a graduate of the University of Western Illinois, worked as a commercial insurance underwriter for eighteen years before starting her own business, Healthy Exchanges, Inc., which publishes cookbooks, a monthly newsletter, motivational booklets, and inspirational audiotapes. Healthy Exchanges Cookbooks have more than 1 million copies in print. A popular speaker with hospitals, support groups for heart patients and diabetics, and service and volunteer organizations, she has appeared on QVC, on hundreds of regional television and radio shows, and has been featured in newspapers and magazines across the country.

The recipient of numerous business awards, JoAnna was an Iowa delegate to the national White House Conference on Small Business. She is a member of the International Association of Culinary Professionals, the Society for Nutritional Education, and other professional publishing and marketing associations. She lives with her husband, Clifford, in DeWitt, Iowa.